Plum, Courgette & Green Bean Tart

Lisa Rose Wright

Plum, Courgette & Green Bean Tart
Copyright © Lisa Rose Wright 2020

The right of Lisa Rose Wright to be identified as the author of this work has been asserted by her in accordance with the Copyright Designs and Patents Act 1988

All rights reserved. No part of this publication may be reproduced, transmitted, or stored in a retrieval system in any form or by any means, without permission in writing of the author.

Any queries please contact me at
lisarosewright@msn.com

Cover design by Maayan Atias at
spacecadetstudio@yahoo.com
All photographs © Lisa Rose Wright

ISBN: 9798650916727

The second thing people usually ask about our home, after "where's that?" is "Why Galicia?" Even now locals still ask us why we chose Galicia, and even now we can only answer honestly that Galicia chose us.

I hope this book will better explain to friends, family, and everyone who would like to know more about this timeless, gentle land, its proud, friendly people, its traditions and its glorious gastronomy, just how we came to be chosen by Galicia.

§

This book is written for all the people who have helped us since we arrived here in beautiful green Galicia, especially our wonderful vecinos and all our friends named in these pages, with the greatest of thanks.

And a very special thank you to mum for having the foresight to keep all those letters home.
Without you this book would not have been possible.
Love you tons

§

I hope you enjoy this first volume of our adventures in Galicia. If you are curious about this place we call home and would like to see more, just download my free photo album which accompanies this book.
The link is at the back.

Oh and don't forget the recipes to accompany each month, also at the back, including the cover recipe itself – Plum, courgette & green bean tart.
Enjoy eating this book!

CONTENTS

PROLOGUE	1
INTRODUCTION	8
AUGUST	35
SEPTEMBER	62
OCTOBER	83
NOVEMBER	106
DECEMBER	129
JANUARY	154
FEBRUARY	176
MARCH	200
APRIL	223
MAY	246
JUNE	269
JULY	292
AUGUST	315
THE STORY CONTINUES	334
THE RECIPES	336
ACKNOWLEDGEMENTS	353
ABOUT THE AUTHOR	354

PROLOGUE
In the beginning

The rain was coming down in torrents. It cascaded from rooftops and, unhindered by such niceties as gutters, poured enthusiastically onto the head of anyone unlucky enough to be caught *sin paragua*. As it happened the only two people likely to be outdoors on such a day, without benefit of an umbrella, were currently staring out through the rain-streaked windows of a cold, slightly damp, third floor flat somewhere in central Galicia onto the massed ranks of multi-coloured nylon below.

Native *Galegos* are far too canny to go outdoors without their trusty umbrella at the ready, hooked into the back of their jacket collar. After all, Galicia *is* the wettest part of Spain, described variously in guidebooks as; like Ireland, green and wet, drizzly and windswept, or even 'of little interest to foreign homebuyers'. And to me memorably, by Chris Stewart in his Andalusian adventures, as 'dank Galicia'.

"Why Galicia?" asked the better informed of our friends to whom we told of our plans. "It always rains there, doesn't it?"

At that moment, watching the rain melting the window panes, I pondered the wisdom myself. This was our fifth and, I sincerely hoped, final house hunting trip to Galicia, and surprisingly the first time we had encountered real Galician rain.

PROLOGUE

Galicia is an autonomous community situated in the far northwest of Spain above Portugal. On a map, Iberia appears as a lady's head (with Portugal as her face) and Galicia forms the fringe of her hair – check out the atlas if you don't believe me. This quiet and largely rural part of the Spanish mainland is isolated by the river Miño to the south, the sierras of Ancares and O Courel to the east and treacherous seas to the north and west. The *Costa da Morte* is not named the coast of death for nothing, having had more than its fair share of shipwrecks over the years. Galicia was one of the few regions of Spain not to be settled by the Moors. It considers itself to be Celtic in tradition with a distinct personality, far removed from the more arid Mediterranean *costas*, and a distinct language – a little like Castilian, a little like Portuguese, a lot like *Galegos* themselves – unique.

This was also the place we had chosen to make our new home.

§

Soon after S and I met we realised that we had both long dreamed of leaving the rat race and being self-sufficient, of seeking the Good Life. Cornwall had proven too expensive, Ireland too wet and Scotland too cold. Neither of us fancied France nor the Spanish Mediterranean coasts. Then, one April, S suggested a walking holiday along the old European pilgrim route, *El Camino de Santiago*. Having never heard of The Way of St. James, I enthusiastically started to look for any information I could find. It seemed from my research that the *Ruta de la Costa* or North Coast Route would be perfect in late spring.

Galicia has many pilgrim routes criss-crossing its beautiful countryside, all converging on the ancient city of Santiago de Compostela. The best known route is the French Way which leads over the Pyrenees and through the high Spanish *meseta* or tablelands. The northern route has been in use since medieval times. At that time, increasing numbers of robberies along the main inland routes meant that pilgrims sought out alternative, safer roads to reach the shrine of St. James the Greater. We had three weeks and decided that Gijón to Santiago, at a mere 333 kilometres, was easily achievable. We even practised some long distance walking beforehand – in the English fens where I was working at the time, an area where a molehill is considered a high point. I had not considered the possibility of hills on our walk.

All my careful planning had also failed to come up with the most important truism of any long distance walk, pack lightly. Having studied the Confraternity of St. James booklet, *Pilgrim Guides to Spain B: Ruta de la Costa,* it appeared that there were few *albergues* or pilgrim hostels along the coastal route and long stretches without food or water. Consequently, we packed tent, sleeping bags, roll mats, gas stove, kitchen sink. Well, no, not the last one but it felt like it. The packs were too heavy. It was far hotter than I had been led to believe (see early entries about Galician weather). It was way hillier than I expected (see entry about walking practice). And we had blisters. So we did what any sensible people might do under those circumstances, we turned inland and went house hunting!

As good fortune would have it, during my planning I had come across an estate agency selling old houses in Galicia for renovations. A number of the properties on their website looked interesting and the prices seemed unbelievably low. I had had the foresight to bring their telephone number with us and we were soon whisked away on a whistle-stop adventure visiting ancient ruins half-built houses in backyards, houses encrusted in vines and ivy, and houses hanging over precipitous cliffs.

Galicia had, and still has, many beautiful, tumbledown stone houses crying out for TLC. Unfortunately a great many of these houses are owned by multiple, disparate, and even on occasions feuding, family members. At least one of these members will, at any given time, refuse to sell. Or (as we found to our cost later) the property will be owned by a number of people, at least one of whom has disappeared without trace in a Latin American country.

The estate agent was a jolly, friendly chap who drove, with no consideration for other road users or the sensitivities of his passengers, in the exact centre of any highway, whilst carrying on a conversation in *Galego*. Ninety percent of his monologue we did not understand, the remaining ten percent was flung aside by sheer terror. Antonio showed us a great many properties, overcoming any objections or problems in his inimitable, and we later came to realise, very Galician style...

No space for a septic tank? – at a property literally overhanging the river Sil with spectacular views. No problem, just let it empty into the river.

No land? – at a beautiful stone property with no space to expand. No problem, have that piece there. But who does it belong to? Not important, have it as a gift.

No room for a staircase? – in a modern but incredibly poorly-designed renovation. No problem, use a ladder.

Towards the end of our stay, we fell in love with a stone farmhouse high in the hills of Ourense province and with distant views, on a clear day, to the great river Miño. Despite our best efforts – and the sometime hindrance of our friend Antonio – the owner, last known whereabouts Venezuela, could neither be traced nor proven to have died. The latter despite the fact that he would have been a hearty 110 years old if still living.

After eighteen months of frustration, dozens of emails, two return trips to cajole and bully and plenty of hoping, we gave up. But we had been bitten by the Galician bug. Back in the fens I spent hours scouring the internet for Galician houses and Galician estate agents.

§

The following year we were back in Galicia with a new enthusiastic estate agent and far too many jumpers for the 22°c March temperatures of that 'cold wet' area.

Our new best friend Mark took us on a whirlwind tour covering hundreds of kilometres and introducing us to beautiful houses and the gastronomy of Galicia.

We started our tour with lunch. Being surrounded on two sides by the wild Atlantic and Cantabrian seas, Galicia is rightly proud of its seafood. Mark was keen for us to try the local *salpicón de marisco*, a slightly vinegared, fish and seafood platter, at a glorious seafood restaurant which sadly we have never managed to find again. A man after my own heart when it comes to food, Mark was so enthusiastic and the food so delicious that it seemed rude to say we had eaten our cheese butties on the plane.

Our long weekend turned into a marathon of viewings, thirteen in all, including one dropped in on the way back to the airport. All were interesting but none were quite right.

An old watermill perched half-way up the side of the second highest waterfall in Galicia was spectacular, incredibly noisy due to the water cascading within an arm's reach of the window and with an ingenious indoor shower courtesy of the hole in the roof just below the mill race, but not terribly practical.

A huge, stately building, to the north of Lugo which loomed out of the mist as we approached along a tiny track walled in by giant standing stones, had a mummified cat in the kitchen and seemed far too much to tackle for a first project.

A run-down farmhouse in the flatlands, with its own stone gatehouse and moat, was worryingly close to the slowly rising river.

An interesting business proposition right on the *camino* came with one totally derelict house and one half-decent one full to the eaves with old clothes. It also had a listed, wooden, painted *hórreo* or grain store, and a close-up view of the new motorway fifty metres from the first floor bedroom window.

An attractive stone house, near to a picturesque village with a stream running through it, had a piece of land, totally within its boundaries like a Venn diagram, which belonged to someone else: someone who would need to drive a large tractor straight through our new garden to reach his twenty metre square bit of land.

An unusual house, with huge standing stones forming some of the internal walls, would have been perfect if we were in Australia as it faced north, so receiving no sunlight at all to the garden here in Galicia.

A good opportunity also in the flat tablelands to the north of Lugo, had a *Tyrannosaurus rex* sized hole in the wall and fish in the well.

Our first choice house had lots of land for our self-sufficiency project, beautifully restored outbuildings and a woodland with bags of potential: until the owners doubled the price and decided to keep the wood for themselves.

PLUM, COURGETTE & GREEN BEAN TART

Far from being daunted by these alarming setbacks, we were energised and found ourselves falling more and more under the spell of this stunningly beautiful part of Spain.

As work in the 'newting' line (we both worked as field ecologists trapping and releasing reptiles and the European-protected great crested newts) tends to dry up in winter when our subjects are mainly asleep, we left Mark with a long list of requirements and on the plane home took the decision to relocate to Galicia in November for a three month sojourn of serious house hunting and, it would turn out, serious rain.

INTRODUCTION
Winter in Galicia

The first week of November saw us on a ferry bound for France, confident that we had a flat to rent and more wonderful properties to view. I was in equal measure both excited and apprehensive. I also had a bad back and a rotten cold!

The journey through France from Cherbourg was slow due to my being totally unable to sit for more than a couple of hours at a time and our long standing refusal to use toll roads if we can possibly help it. We stayed in a couple of *chambre de hôtes* and enjoyed the passing scenery. Crossing into Spain we discovered cheaper petrol and nicer accommodations (*pensiones*) for lower prices, once more reinforcing our decision to choose Spain over our closer neighbour. We left the beautiful port town of Ribadeo, the gateway to Galicia on the north coast, on a beautiful sunny November morning and arrived at our first stop, the Roman city of Lugo two hours later.

Within two days, we had found our forever home.

We both fell in love with *A Casa do Campo* on our first viewing, a rainswept November morning. Mists were rising, water dripped onto the kitchen range from gaping holes in the roof and there were bare, dead looking trees in the garden, which the Spanish estate agent, Mark's colleague Maribel, enthusiastically promised us would be laden with fruit come August.

Mark, true to his word, had found us two houses which matched our criteria almost perfectly. Both were the same price. *A Casa do Campo* had a large, separate allotment where I could imagine growing my future vegetables, a beautiful ancient chestnut wood carpeted with crisp, golden leaves and vigorous brambles, lovely views south across the valley and peaceful walks along an old track just beyond the house. The second property, on the far side of Lugo, also had good views, 1.6 hectares of land with water rights, a useful outbuilding and a functioning toilet. We revisited both places two, three times. We measured everywhere and everything. We drew up plans for both properties, looking at how much each might cost to renovate. I wrote long lists of pros and cons but our hearts - and the fact that *A Casa do Campo* was only a short uphill jaunt into a small market town and therefore, and much more importantly, a short downhill jaunt back home - sold it to us.

Once decided, all we had to do was sign on the dotted line.

Unfortunately wanting something which is on the market in Galicia and managing to buy it, as we had already found, are not the same thing. We transferred monies and withdrew cash in case we needed to pay the illegal but very Spanish 'black money' on the day. We were told the paperwork was going through. Then that it wasn't. We were told someone had died. Then that someone wanted more money. We were told the house was off the market and finally that the family had handed the property over to another estate agent to sell.

Sunday 3rd December. Wet!!
Dear Mum
Thank you all for my birthday cards. Had

INTRODUCTION

a lovely birthday dinner at the Chinese restaurant in Lugo. We invited the estate agent and his family. The whole meal for 7 of us was less than a take away for 2 at home so your birthday money will go a long way haha. Mark and family bought me a lovely poinsettia and a bottle of Galician cream liqueur. Had a free bottle of Chinese wine from the restaurant too so we can celebrate for a while!!

Mark thinks the house will go through okay. He knows the new estate agent a little and rang him for us. There is some story of a lady who died having two daughters so there needs to be paperwork sorted. I don't really understand what is going on, just wish it would hurry up as I wanted to dig over the allotment and put some of the manure that is piled up in the barns to good use... it's certainly well-rotted after 12 years or more. S tells me I need to be patient but that is a virtue which has yet to arrive at the grand old age of 42!

There was a big market (feira) in town on the 1st. Held each month, it takes up most of the streets. There is livestock for sale just out of town as well as local cheeses, hams, and honey (will buy you a jar next time, very tasty). The local produce is housed in a huge round building. It is full of delicious smells, dozens of stalls and lots of shouting. I got tricked into buying two cheeses by a tiny and very canny lady in a pinny. She

PLUM, COURGETTE & GREEN BEAN TART

put the cheeses into my hands to feel how heavy they were, then when both hands were full, dropped them in a bag. Hands dusted, done deal and me standing wondering how I'd got caught! Still, we love cheese and they are very tasty.

Everyone is extremely friendly. I think being English is still a novelty here and thankfully no lager louts to spoil our collective reputation. On the day of the fair we saw the post lady, who S had let into the flats on one occasion, and she says 'You are the English, Happy Birthday, I have a card for you from England.' She told me her birthday was also the next day. I can't help wondering if our postie at home would know me or my address if we met in the street. I think not.

Tell Aunty Jean it is pig killing time. We missed the Spanish estate agent killing hers or we would've asked to help. Yes, she has sheep too and makes lovely cheese. Everyone here seems to keep animals. We walked along the main street in town yesterday and through an open garage door we spotted a pig carcass just hanging there! Self-sufficiency seems the norm and everyone is more than willing to show us how to grow things and kill things...we just need a house first!

The house (A Casa do Campo... or the country house) is very large with 3 big barns downstairs and another huge barn at the

INTRODUCTION

side. It has a kitchen and 4 bedrooms (one of which will be a bathroom) and a big extension which has marvellous views down to the river and the water mill and will be our upstairs lounge/sunroom. There are only six houses in the village and we are number 6. It will be the shortest address we have ever had... no road names. The people behind seem youngish and are very friendly and the houses all seem in good condition (except number 6). It is only half an hour walk into the town and we can recommend both eateries we have tried there!

There are some lovely bits of old furniture in the house. I am thinking of renovating them. I could even sell some on to people who want old stuff... potentially a good market, especially Brits buying B&Bs. Just need to manage to buy the house first!

Found out in the paper that there is a new road being built between Ourense and Ponferrada and one option goes very near to the other house we tried to buy 2 years ago up in the hills so good job they couldn't sell it eh?

Hoping you can get flights in January so we can introduce you to the delights of pulpo...a regional delicacy and very tasty. Think you will like this area. We certainly do. It is very green (and a tad damp at the moment though it was 15° the other day and not less than 8° overnight so far), quite hilly and very friendly.

PLUM, COURGETTE & GREEN BEAN TART

The flat is a bit noisy at times... the problem of concrete buildings with no insulation and a butcher's on the ground floor to which we have finally tracked the 'thud thud thud' which wakes us up at 10am every morning ha!
Love you tons
Xxx

We had rented a flat in Monterroso, a small town just ten kilometres from the house, through our Spanish estate agent, Maribel. When we viewed the flats we had agreed on a second floor south-facing one-bed flat. Unfortunately when we arrived that particular flat was, for some incomprehensible reason, being used to store apples, walnuts and other produce so we were given a third floor north-facing one instead. It was freezing! The kitchen had two air bricks in there for health and safety reasons with holes as big as – well, bricks actually. The draught blew around our feet in a most cooling manner while we ate dinner. The heating was via electric storage radiators, which cooled down just in time for us to relax in the afternoons. And the sun never penetrated the rooms at all.

Worse, it was not fully furnished as we had expected. The sofa was so old and saggy that, to save my already dodgy back and make the sofa vaguely functional, S used some hardboard that had been left next to a skip downstairs as a base to support the cushions. The bed was so soft we rolled together and stayed there all night. We got into the habit of having a hot bath each evening before jumping into the icy bed whilst we were still feeling the warmth.

Maribel was wonderful though. She lent us blankets, sheets, crockery and cutlery, pots and

INTRODUCTION

pans, and miscellaneous kitchen wares. Below the flat we found a fabulous 'pound' shop which stocked all sorts of useful stuff and we augmented our borrowed equipment with sharp knives, mugs, tea towels and other goodies.

We loved the town and met many neighbours. Time passed...

Monday 11th Dec and the sun is shining!!
Dear Mum

What do I do with a poinsettia? At the moment it is dropping leaves like it's autumn. It will be bald soon! Don't think it likes the cold flat much... can't blame it!

We were pulled over by the traffic police at a check point today. A friendly young chap was checking my licence and documents when an older one came sauntering across looking a bit bemused and asked S, who was sitting in the car still, for his documents. 'No, she was driving' he said. The officer peered into the car... oops the steering wheel is on the wrong side! Poor chap couldn't get over it, must've told us three times that the wheel is on the left in Spain... in case we thought he was daft... as if!

At least the incident cheered me up. Apparently the family selling the house went to the notary yesterday and almost came to blows as one thinks the house is worth more money so does not want to sell... The saga goes on! Think I'll just set up a tent in a field somewhere and squat.

PLUM, COURGETTE & GREEN BEAN TART

Friday - Still sunny and really quite warm. We have been looking around the area sightseeing as nothing is happening with the house. Do hope we can sort it out as we've not seen anything else we prefer despite visiting properties with everyone we can and even tagging along on viewings with other Brits, just for something to do.

Visited a couple of properties the other day. At the first one the lady had a fantastic fire going in the kitchen (wood-burning range like most of the houses here). It was only a small room and she had had to open all the windows as it was stiflingly hot. At the second one the lady showing us round sent her husband off to light the range whilst we were viewing the upstairs. As she proudly opened the door to the kitchen there was a huge billow of smoke before hubby appeared looking like a sweep, but more embarrassed. It seems the range lighting had not gone to plan. We did try very hard to keep straight faces!

Mark says a Madrid based daughter thinks 'our' house is undervalued although the others are happy with the price. I guess Madrid prices are like London. Better not let her see the info about that derelict tin barn you sent me out of the Telegraph, (400k! Boy what a bargain!). It all seems so complicated… you would think things like this would be sorted before they put the house on the market.

INTRODUCTION

Jen and her dad popped in this morning, we met them at Mark's if you remember. They also bought through him and live in another village quite near the flat. They moved in just before we arrived and have been really friendly. They are off back to the UK for Christmas and nearly caught us in bed! It <u>was</u> 10am. They had brought their own mugs for tea though so all's well.

Mark has invited us over for New Year which is really kind. We may see if the Chinese is open for Christmas day lunch as it would be warmer than the flat and we enjoyed it on my birthday!

We revisited a house we had seen before and quite liked in the flatlands beyond Lugo on Weds. It has a gatehouse and a moat at the front. The river was half way across the garden and the gatehouse flooded. Glad we didn't buy that one then! Also revisited our second choice house yesterday. Very friendly neighbour asked if we were buying it. Lots of land but more work to do I think (although it does have a flushing loo) and farther from town. An hours walk uphill! Me legs ache today!

We will keep looking as we have nothing else to do but I really hope to be able to sort A Casa do Campo.

I am sitting outside on a wall in the sunshine writing this. We are by the 'beach'. The council have put a swimming pool down by the river. There are picnic benches

PLUM, COURGETTE & GREEN BEAN TART

under the trees and BBQ pits to use and a riverside walk. There are also tennis courts and changing rooms and a campsite. It's very picturesque and probably very busy in summer though there's only the odd dog walker around now.

We are getting quite well acquainted with the area. Mark says we know the surrounds better than the local estate agents because we have walked most of them. Nothing much else to do in the absence of a house! Certainly our local bars seem to recognise us now and some of them even speak slowly for us! Not sure if the Spanish is improving or not. Some days are better than others and some people clearer than others. Our landlady Pilar is very clear, as is her husband, though he drops in the odd French word to 'help' us which of course it doesn't!! The osteopath speaks far too quickly. Last time we had a 10min conversation to establish it was the 'time of the month' so I could not therefore use the infrared machine!! Still, we get along okay and I am teaching him some English words. He seems very good. Not sure what he is doing but my back doesn't hurt so much.

We are continuing our wildlife spotting, just watching a treecreeper nearby hopping down a tree trunk. We have seen several salamanders, toads (including a squashed, sadly, fire toad) and newts and a tiny froglet. There are some great tracks down

INTRODUCTION

here by the river. The water has dropped a bit so there is lots of smooth silt down the bank. Perfect for spoor.

Anyway, we are looking at yet more houses this pm so fingers crossed. We promise that one way or another we will have somewhere for you to visit next year...by hook or by crook haha
Love you tons
Xxxxxxx

Unsure what was happening with *A Casa do Campo,* we visited more houses with Mark, with Maribel, and even with a Dutch estate agent Mark knew. We travelled many kilometres and traipsed through numerous wrecks but nothing matched up to *A Casa do Campo.*

Mark kindly agreed to talk to the new estate agent, Suso, for us and act as our negotiator. At first he was told other people were interested but Mark persisted. He knew the 'other' people were us! Eventually they came to an agreement. The price had gone up by 12,000 euros and Suso, wanted 10,000 euros deposit, to 'hold' the property. Once he had his money we could have a key. Suso wrote out a bizarre invoice for the 10,000 euros. Mark amended it. More time passed...

Christmas Eve. Very sunny and warm!!
Dear mum
It has been lovely weather this week, cold at night but up to 18° during the day. Christmas seems very peaceful here. None of that mad rush for pressie and food shopping. Queues at the supermarket

PLUM, COURGETTE & GREEN BEAN TART

remain static at around 3 people and we had quite a job finding greetings cards to send. The newsagent just had a few on the counter as a sort of afterthought! We do however have piped music in the street to get us into the mood and the flats are rather noisy as all the families get together for Christmas Eve.

Traditional grub seems to be capons. Huge, fat, white, castrated cockerels sold with their heads on and presented with their bums in the air. There was even a fair in Vilalba dedicated to them last weekend. There also seems to be a lot of empanadas (big, flat, meat pies) for tonight.

10.30pm Decided to go out later tonight as it was noisy until the early hours yesterday and was becoming very lively in town just as we were heading home. Have just got in after being ejected from the last bar open and left on the streets with our vinos in hand because they were all off to have their Christmas dinner with the family. We had only just sat down when the bar owner came out in her coat and said 'vamos!' ...let's go! We will learn the rules one day haha.

Christmas Day evening. Just back from Lugo. Lovely and sunny again but frosty. Had a smashing Chinese meal... still full and have brought a doggy bag back too. I assume you are all full too by now. I don't miss the turkey but a bit of Christmas pud wouldn't go amiss for supper!

INTRODUCTION

Really looking forward to you visiting. We have been planning trips so bring your walking boots (and a brolly, just in case the weather breaks) and tell Belle flip-flops are not brilliant in winter in Galicia!! We are hoping to have the house key by then so we can show you around (you will have to use your imagination inside but I'm sure you'll love it!)

S is trying to send a text, the phone is playing up and he is getting a little frustrated. Odd isn't it that an inanimate object can do something that nothing else can... get my patient other half annoyed!! We had to get a Spanish SIM card as the UK company didn't activate roaming for us. Unfortunately all the info is in Spanish. Mind you we have a fool-proof way to stop those annoying sales calls... answer in English and they tend to go away!!!

Boxing Day - Not a holiday here so everything is back to the normal hectically slow pace. Have booked you into the hotel and at the same time visited a house for sale that the hotel owners, Augusta and Pepe, knew of (not really for us). They are very friendly and speak English as they lived in London for a number of years. Your room has a nice view of the twin hills beyond the town and is only a 10min walk to our flat.

The 'new' estate agent Suso says we can have a key once he gets the deposit in his account (all seems very cloak and dagger).

PLUM, COURGETTE & GREEN BEAN TART

His invoice said for cleaning services!! At least we will be able to show you round.

Just had sausage, egg and chips for dinner. The fattest sausage you ever did see and hardly any fat, it didn't shrink at all. S says all the food here is tasty. Not mass produced and mainly local. May try a rabbit for New Year though don't tell Belle!

Our social calendar is busy once again. We are invited to Jen's on Friday (she is bringing us some marmite back from UK as we are almost out), then to Mark's for New Year's Eve dinner which I know will be huge and very tasty.

Oh yes, if you get chance could you cut out and bring the Michael Wright columns from the Telegraph (La Folie) as we don't know if he's married his American girlfriend yet!!
Love you
xxxxxxxxxx

Diary Wednesday 27th December
A Casa do Campo property description for the Derbyshire Life equivalent in Spain. (Future!!)
A fantastic opportunity to acquire this stunning, unique and characterful stone property which retains many original features and yet has been renovated to an exacting standard. Comprising 4 beds and 2 bathrooms.
A gated entrance opens onto south-facing landscaped gardens, including a large useful barn, outdoor stone oven, spring-fed well and chicken coop.
The main entrance leads off a delightful east-facing breakfast terrace. A second door from the

INTRODUCTION

terrace leads to a large utility/cloakroom. From the tile-floored entrance hall is the large family kitchen with hand-made units, marble worktops and original range cooker and stone sink.

Also off the entrance hall is a 16m^2 pantry. (There is a second cool room, the 'cheese store' behind the kitchen.) The pantry leads through to the 'barn', an impressive double height living/dining space featuring exposed stone walls and roof beams, and with French doors opening onto a second terrace and westerly views over chestnut woods.

There is a mezzanine space within the barn with a 'snug' area heated by a wood-burning stove below. Stone stairs and a doorway lead to the first floor comprising 2 double beds and a large family bathroom. The beautiful internal hallway featuring more exposed stonework leads to a further bedroom with adjoining dressing room and to a magnificently appointed sunroom featuring original chestnut ceiling and wide ranging views to the east and south over rolling countryside to a river below.

Below the sunroom, with its own entrance, is the guest accommodation comprising a lobby /entrance hall, a large shower room and 25m^2 guest room looking south over the garden to the river and water mill below.

Also included are a further barn which could be used for storage, animal quarters or equally developed as a playroom or further bedroom; a separate 1500m^2 allotment and an orchard area with many mature fruit and sweet chestnut trees.

The property is situated on the outskirts of a small hamlet of only 6 houses with countryside beyond and many country walks from the doorstep, yet is only 5 minutes from a market town with banks, shops, school and health centre. Well I can dream haha!!

PLUM, COURGETTE & GREEN BEAN TART

Friday 29th December Drizzly but mild
Dear Mum,

We have a key!!!!!!! Very exciting. It is a huge antique thing which weighs a ton and reminds me of the ones we had to carry on our belts at Friern Hospital. We spent an enjoyable morning measuring up all the rooms and drawing it all out properly. Don't worry about bringing your gardening stuff as it seems we can supply rakes, hoes, hammers and spades from the house. We even have some old clothes and boots... though you may not fancy those haha.

After getting decidedly filthy ferreting around the cobwebs in the house we went over to Jen's... we did have a wash before entering the house. She had invited our local estate agent Maribel and her son Pablo over. We had a delightful 'Spanglish' evening but the funniest was when Jen gave us the marmite. 'What is it, is it like marmalade (jam)?' Well no, it's savoury. Pablo wanted to try it first - hated it, couldn't get the taste out of his mouth quickly enough. His mum tried it 'mmm this is lovely'. Could've videoed the encounter for the Marmite ad campaign. Love it or hate it!!

Sat pm. Back at A Casa do Campo. Raining so at least we can see where the roof is leaking (that is most of it!). We are going to buy a couple of those nice blue boiler suits to stop me having to wash our clothes so often!!

INTRODUCTION

Have measured all the rooms and started to empty some of the rubbish left behind. No one seems to empty houses before they sell them here. Have found correspondence going back decades. Probably fascinating if we could read any of it. Oh, and can you think of a good use for a cupboard full of goat hair? At least we hope that's what it is!

Jan 1st Happy Noo 'ear you one eyed…

Spent yesterday morning drawing up all our measurements for the house then had a huge supper at Mark's with big langoustines, capon, lashing of vino and our uvas de suerte or lucky grapes. You have to eat one grape on each of the twelve strokes of midnight for luck throughout the year – much more difficult than it sounds, especially as we were talking and missed the first bong!

Straight to the market this morning for our shiny new boiler suits. Picked up more cheese from the tiny but very scary lady (I was ready this time and got away with only one!).

Dinner out yet again. Maribel, the local estate agent invited us over together with Jen and her dad for lots more food including a very tasty brawn made with pigs face. We somehow ended up having a strange Spanglish argument about the UK royal family (oddly the Spanish were all royalists and adored 'Lady Di', the Brits not).

PLUM, COURGETTE & GREEN BEAN TART

Had a strange incident at the house today .A chap turned up trying to break into the barn (we had propped the doors closed from inside as they were broken). Turns out he had been promised the chariots (old bullock carts) and had come to collect. This information we got from Mark who we quickly rang to translate as we didn't understand a word the chap was saying. Mark negotiated down to one cart and an old woodwormy table which had apparently been made by said chap's grandfather and he toddled off with the cart following, hooked to the back of his tractor!

We have been clearing yet more junk (and haven't even started on the ornaments and dollies yet) including a very tasteful stuffed red squirrel posed on a tree stump! No charity shops to give things to here but we will give you first preference!!

Have invited Jen to see the house now we have the key and to buy them lunch in town for being so helpful and kind. Saturday is another holiday, Reyes Santos or epiphany, when the children traditionally get their presents, the same as Jesus did. Although as at home Santa Claus or 'Papa Noel' seems to have got himself in on the act too.

Send us a text as you board so we can set off in good time. It's only about an hour to the airport. So if everything is on time we will see you about 1pm Saturday.

Xxxxxxxxx

INTRODUCTION

Diary Friday 5th January
Sitting in the flat this evening, wrapped up like polar bears as usual, when I heard music and shouting. Not liking to miss anything going on, and anything for an excuse to leave the flat, we raced downstairs and followed the crowd. In the round building (which we call the rotunda but I think everyone else calls the cupola) we found a Galego/biblical scene. On stage were Mary, Joseph and a (real) baby Jesus. The floor area had been turned into a landscape of grass and trees with shepherds tending their flocks (a half dozen sheep and lambs). There were chairs laid out and quite an audience gathered. The three kings arrived (no camels) then all the children were given sweets up on stage. One of the 'shepherds' was a young lad with Down's syndrome. He had obviously been told he shouldn't leave the flock but he was hopping up and down, desperate for his sweets. Luckily one of the cleaners took pity on him and took over sheep watching while he galloped up to the stage! All great fun though it was a good job we knew the story as we didn't understand a word!
We tried to light the stove at the house this morning but ended up with a kitchen full of smoke... don't think I've got the hang of it yet. The well water is still brown and disgusting but our new neighbour Carmen says we can use her well for as long as necessary which is amazingly kind.

Diary Tuesday 9th January
More problems with the house. Now arguing over the chestnut wood. Mark says it is one parcel of land contiguous with the bit on the west side. The new agent Suso says that plot was split years ago (but doesn't show on the 'sixpac', the online land registry map) and isn't for sale. Don't want someone to own the land right outside the barn as

that was where we were going to put our French doors! Am totally fed up…again!

The new agent was right. We checked with the notary and the land was legally split many years previously but the changes never registered (it was not compulsory in those days and of course cost money). I was ridiculously upset again so we went off to think it over. All our difficulties; new estate agents, more money, then less land and all the issues in between had nearly broken me.

The problem was we still hadn't found a house we preferred despite all our viewings. After much agonising (on my part. S, as always, was merely and annoyingly realistic) we decided to be circumspect. Even with the inflated price and without the chestnut wood it would be far cheaper than any equivalent property we could buy in the UK. The notary had confirmed the piece of land right outside our door was still included in the 'plot', together with four chestnut trees and the 'orchard' piece. We bit the bullet and agreed, with a proviso that the estate agent would register all the separate areas and amalgamate them into one before we bought, and that all the remaining items of furniture etc. were to be sold with the house. We didn't want any more chariot incidents.

For the next few days we had some time off from worrying about the house as we had important visitors arriving and needed to clean up the flat and the car and to try and present our wonderful ruin as something mum could see her daughter living in!

Sunday 21st Jan Sunny and mild
Dear mum,
Sorry your journey back was rough but glad you got to see our ruin. I think you

liked it??? I'm sure it will look more homely in summer when the rain isn't puddling on the floor in the kitchen or the walls running with water. Of course there is lots to do but you know how handy the lad is and I'm not totally useless in the DIY department! By next year we may even have a bedroom for you - honest!

Of course here it has been quite pleasant and warm since you left... even flip-flop weather! We have had a trip to the seaside at Ortigueira in the NW corner of Galicia. Very pretty place although it was a bit blowy on the harbour. They have a cemetery on a hill overlooking the sea in probably the best position in town. S says when their time is up in the stone tombs the bones can be swept straight into the water!

We went to see some houses with the Dutch estate agent, John. It was arranged ages ago as insurance in case ours didn't come off so we thought it would be a trip out. Some nice holiday-sized properties on the coast (a lot more expensive than inland) and a whole village for sale at 150,000 euros! We did see one place we liked. Nearer to Santiago in a small village surrounded by pine trees, from the front it looked lovely, good straight stone walls. Then we went round the back and... well, there wasn't any back! In fact the façade was all there was. The rest of the house was a large pile of rubble with a demolished staircase in the

PLUM, COURGETTE & GREEN BEAN TART

middle! Hilarious. Good job the paperwork seems to be going ahead now.

Tuesday. Woke to snow though it soon cleared and the sun came back out for our trip to Lugo. Unfortunately as it was sunny we didn't think to take a brolly and by the time we arrived it was sleeting and cold so we had to go for hot chocolates at the Café Central. So thick you can stand a spoon up, it is really a melted chocolate bar and with a big wodge of lemony cake to go with it, a meal in itself - oh and did I mention it is yummy!! We somehow managed lunch too, at our favourite café Recatelo (from our camino days) for only 5.50€ for 3 courses plus coffee (they were quite disturbed one day when we declined coffee as it is 'incluido'). We called at Carrefour on the way back to get some wine to thank our friends for looking after the house in the UK. Got a mix of cheaper and more expensive wines as they are wine buffs and we want to see what they think. At less than 18€ for 9 bottles (the cheapest was 69 cents) I hope it's okay!!

Love you tons XXXXXXXX

We booked our ferry home for early February. The estate agent had said the changes we wanted on the *catastral* or land tax register would take two months so there was little point in hanging around any longer. We kept busy in the meantime clearing the house and moving things we wanted to keep to Jen's for storage. I suppose in hindsight it was a

INTRODUCTION

stupid thing to do but we thought the paperwork was going through imminently so carried on as if we already owned the place. We took blankets to wash at the flat. I hung them on the lines in the central tunnel from where they promptly blew away and onto our neighbour's balcony below: an omen for later. We moved a couple of wonderful sweet chestnut *pries-dieu* or prayer stools to keep safe and dry until we could restore them, and took Jen the squirrel. It was hers if the house fell through – a joke, I thought!

On January 25th, just two weeks before we had to catch the ferry home, we turned up at the house with a big tub of woodworm killer to paint onto the pine floors in the newer part of the house. Our key wouldn't turn. S tried. Still no luck. The lock had been changed. We were locked out of our own house!

We drove straight to the estate agent's and demanded to know what was going on. Had they sold from under us? Suso's secretary assured us that there was no problem, the family had just decided that they didn't want anyone going into the house until it was signed for. I couldn't understand this. We had had the key a month and now they decided we couldn't go inside when all we had done was clear the house of junk? I was so angry I promptly burst into tears and threw the key onto the desk. An act I still regret as it was a very nice key.

I couldn't bear to tell mum about this latest disaster so glossed over it in my last few letters home. Of course, I realised, much much later, that someone in the village must've seen us loading the kneelers and blankets and maybe even the squirrel, into the car and told the family we were stealing things from the house. As I say, stupid, but in my defence I really did think things were going ahead at that point.

PLUM, COURGETTE & GREEN BEAN TART

Sunday 28th Jan. Lovely sunny day but frosty
Dear Mum
  Apologies for the paper – didn't seem worth buying more now as our pile of items to leave with poor Jen is steadily turning into a mountain. How on earth have we managed to accumulate so much in 3 months!
  It's been a glorious day. After toiling in the allotment for almost 2 hours we lay in the orchard watching the buzzards high above and listening to the robin singing in the chestnut trees. S said 'can you imagine yourself living here?' Oh yes most definitely!
  We popped into the café for a hot chocolate on the way back and bumped into the family who are actually selling the house. Pepe, the son, said 'can I ask you a personal question?' 'Si?' thinking the usual: do you have kids? Are they coming too? No, he wanted to know how much we are paying for the house! I wrote it down on a napkin as I'm still not good with large numbers. He wrote down how much they were getting for it. There was a difference of 18,000€ which is Suso's fee. (Nice job if you can get it as he didn't even find the buyers, Mark had already done that.) Turns out they were told they could get more money for the house with this agent but they are basically getting the same and the agent the rest of the inflated price we are paying. Pepe kept saying 'tres milliones, tres milliones' (three

INTRODUCTION

million pesetas) which they still work in for large amounts despite having the euro for 6 years... bit like someone I know with shillings haha.

I tried to suggest that they could sell direct to us missing out the agent's fees and we could meet in the middle over price. Everyone happy. At least that's what I wanted to say but my Spanish is just not good enough for such a convoluted conversation so we will see. They bought our hot chocolates anyway so that's okay.

We have finally done something we promised ourselves ages ago. Climbed those two rocky hills you could see from your hotel window. They are called Castelos Ambarros and we found there is actually a road most of the way so it was only about half an hours climb. Great views from the top. Of course S had to climb right onto the rocky bit at the very top and wave his arms about. Good job he didn't blow away!

We have taken most of our acquired stuff to Jen's. She has offered to put us up when we come back to sign - whenever that turns out to be! Which is really nice of her as we would rather be here for the occasion even though Mark has power of attorney for us.

We land at Portsmouth at 9am Thursday so should see you by mid-afternoon. Hopefully this should beat us, just!
See you very soon
Xxxxxx

PLUM, COURGETTE & GREEN BEAN TART

There was absolutely nothing we could do in the short time we had left, even if I could have spoken enough Spanish to have a further discussion with the family or with the estate agent. But no-one could stop me digging the allotment over, so on sunny days we dug what I sincerely hoped was going to be my cabbage patch come the next year.

We walked more and more, so much so that we were stopped and (politely) questioned by the local police – who were we, did we live here, why were we walking? We also had to visit the bank as we had opened a Spanish account but had still to receive our bank card. No problem, they would send it to the UK if we gave them the address. This proved difficult as the computer wouldn't accept our UK postcode. We were taking so long that a couple of customers came over to 'help'. In inimitable *Galego* style, they peered over our shoulders and suggested changes to the teller. No one mentioned the line behind which customers are supposed to stand, nor the fact that this was a supposedly private transaction. We left with the promise of our card within a week whilst pondering on the wonderful people we had met here.

On our last night we had invited our Spanish estate agent Maribel for a farewell drink as she had always been incredibly helpful even after the change of agent debacle. When we arrived at the designated bar we found a dozen others there, from the girl at the bread shop, Monserrat, who had persistently tried to improve our Spanish every time we visited, to Maribel's helpful and efficient secretary Cruz, and even people we had only met in passing. Although I still couldn't follow the entire conversation, everyone seemed sad we were leaving and we had to promise to hurry back. After all the trials we had had with the house I assured everyone I wasn't about to give up now. But all the good wishes were enough to have me in tears, again!

We left Galicia on a sunny morning in February and arrived two days later to a snowy, cold England. I couldn't wait to get back to *A Casa do Campo* but first we had a job to finish and newts to catch.

AUGUST
Plums galore

Diary Thursday 9th August Casa do Campo Day 1
HOT!
Wish I'd brought all those old jam jars with us now. I've never seen so many plums. In fact I can't believe that this is the same garden we viewed on that rainy day in November. Those unprepossessing twigs in winter are now huge, green, living beings laden, and I mean laden, with fruit.
So far I've counted 6 different types of plum... a red one with sweet yellow flesh, a tart purple one with green flesh, a tiny, yellow Mirabella type, a greengage, a dark purple damson type and an incredibly scented pink blush one. All ripe and all over the ground!

I don't think we would have had space for those jam jars even if I had known we needed them. Our 15 year old Escort was loaded to bursting point and almost waddled down the road, scraping her undercarriage, as we set off four days earlier for our new *vida dulce* in Galicia.

Being a born organiser I had measured to an inch the available space. At the bottom were two large plastic boxes, one each. Mine contained cooking utensils, pots and pans, and some seeds to get our kitchen garden started. S took tools to get

AUGUST

the house started. Our trusty stereo stacking system and cassettes were in a third box. Above were two large rucksacks of clothes, a box of cleaning stuff, and another huge tin of woodworm killer tucked into a large pan (luckily no one at customs inspected too carefully... 'Any inflammables madam?'). On the top was bedding, a blow up mattress, two deckchairs and a camping stove.

The journey to Portsmouth from the north of England was surprisingly uneventful despite the wallowing nature of the over-burdened car. On board the ferry we watched Portsmouth disappear as we toasted our new life with two bottles of Black Sheep Bitter. Having forgotten the bottle opener (no one's perfect!) I decided to prise mine open with my penknife. The neck cracked but the contents were rescued and I filtered the glass through my teeth whilst pondering on the sure omen of this incident. Though of what I have no idea.

§

The ongoing problems with *A Casa do Campo* had continued from the time we left Galicia in February to the final, sweet end in May.

We had returned to the UK and our spring work as newt-catchers as planned. I kept up an insane amount of correspondence with Mark, who was still kindly liaising with the new agent, with the new agent Suso's secretary, and with anyone else who would listen. Paperwork was missing. People had died (again?). Inheritors were arguing over the price (still?). Weeks dragged by and I despaired. Trying to ignore the whole thing was my best bet. So I worked and translocated amphibians and reptiles, and generally enjoyed my wonderful job. And I worried and worried. Finally we got word that we could sign the first week in May.

We immediately gave notice that we were off again, though only for a long weekend. Our employer was much more sanguine than we expected, I think our excitement was infectious. As we were working on the airport at Stansted at the time, distance was not a problem. We even got a lift from a colleague to departures. We told Jen our news and were promised not only a bed but a lift from the airport.

We were ready to roll!

Tuesday 8th May dawned bright and sunny. Our appointment at the notary's was for 10.30am. We were there early, nervous and excited. The notary's office was on the second floor. There was no lift and I couldn't help wondering how many elderly people had heart attacks climbing the stairs. They obviously managed, as when we entered the whole gang were there. Our friend Pepe, from our meeting in the bar, with his parents aged 88 and 90; his mother's sister, the other inheritor of the property, aged 92 with her daughter; a colleague of Suso, come for his money; and Mark, still helping out and there to translate for us. An argument seemed to be in progress and everyone was looking daggers at one particular lady. Mark explained that before we arrived the lady, who lived in Madrid, had asked the notary if the black money they would receive was taxable.

Now, an explanation may be necessary for those of you who have not been party to this very Spanish method of payment and tax avoidance, which thankfully has all but been eliminated in modern day transactions. In Spain, the notary is a government agent responsible for overseeing the legal aspects of various transactions including wills and house sales. They note the selling price and calculate taxes due on the sale, including – and this is important – the taxes due on any profit made due to a difference between the purchase and sale

AUGUST

price. (Or, if the property has not been registered previously, the sale price and its original worth as determined by the state.) Spaniards, like all good citizens, do not like to pay unnecessary taxes and have found an ingenious way around it: sell the property for a lower declared amount and have the buyer pay the remainder in cash (the 'black'). Of course if the buyer then sells later they have to do the same or their profit, and therefore taxes, will be greater yet. And so on – a self-perpetuating problem.

We, of course, wanted no part of this strange custom but it appeared to be the done thing so we had brought along the cash in case we couldn't avoid it on the day.

Asking a government official whether black money is taxable, or even mentioning it at all, does not at first glance appear terribly sensible. Again, in Spain even this peculiarity had been 'legitimised'. The notary would leave the room after the sale was concluded for the declared amount and whilst the black money was counted out. He was therefore not involved in any illegality but the vendors and buyers had a safe and secure place to count the monies. Odd but true!

Our notary had, we were told, ignored this lady for as long as humanly possible. She persisted, asking over and over whether the black money they were receiving would be taxed. The notary had finally turned and allegedly said, "Madam, I have ignored you but I cannot do so any longer. There will not now be any black money on this transaction. It will all be declared as it should." End of story, and the reason the others were looking so angry. Oops!

Surprisingly, the actual sale went fairly smoothly. One piece of land had been missed from the deeds or *escritura* which both I and Pepe simultaneously picked up on. I was proud of following the conversation well enough for that! S had mistakenly been written in as divorced rather than single so that had to be rectified. Once the *escritura* had been agreed we produced the two bank drafts. One in each of the sisters' names.

The 'Madrid' woman again butted in. "How do we know they are both for the same amount?" Cheques were swapped and closely examined. We had given the wrong one to the wrong sister! But luckily the amounts tallied. Still unsatisfied, the 'Madrid' woman complained the cheque was in her mother's name not hers.

The notary, who must have had the patience of a saint, explained that the house belonged to her mother not her. "She needs to bank the cheque and then, if you are very lucky, she may give you some of it."

Then came the counting of all that cash we had brought with us and which now had to be checked in the presence of the notary and duly added to the purchase price. The older folk wanted to count their money themselves. It took months, years! "One hundred, two hundred, three hundred… erm where was I? One hundred, two hundred…" Eventually everyone was declared satisfied and we received the (new and not at all interesting) key. *A Casa do Campo* was finally ours.

Although we completed on the house in May, work kept us in England for another frustrating three months. But the day arrived and at last we were on our way to our new life in Galicia.

§

We arrived at the house at 10am on Thursday 9th August, raring to go. We couldn't get in! The metal gates leading to the side garden were firmly closed. A little too firmly. They wouldn't budge. After some pushing and pulling and some peering over the top on tip-toes, we realised the bar was on and the gates jammed shut. S ploughed his way through the undergrowth around the back of the house to approach from another angle. In no time he was on the other side of the gate, bar in hand. The gates slowly opened, sticking on the vegetation which seemed to have gone rampant since we last saw our 'estate'. The grass, which had been green, lush and tall when we signed in May, now resembled a thatched roof – golden, stiff and matted. The heat was stifling, even at ten in the morning. On his way round to rescue me and the car, S had obviously found a large patch of greater celandine, a pernicious weed which has a delightful habit of staining any material permanently and irretrievably yellow. His jeans never did come clean.

We drove the car into the garden and looked around. To our left was the 'long barn', a long (obviously), low stone building with a wooden slated front to allow air circulation. From our earlier delvings we knew it was well-built but mainly full of junk. Immediately next to us was a semi-circular stone structure which was the old bread oven or *horno.* The *horno* had no chimney and the roof around and above it was black with soot. Inside it was fully five feet in diameter. The traditional accoutrements for bread baking, a long wooden *pala* or bread paddle and the *rastrillo de horno,* a wooden rake for clearing the ash, were hanging nearby. I looked forward to firing it up one day. Next to the oven was an area around three metres square, full of weeds and moss. I had ideas for this area but they would have to wait.

At the end of the garden in front of us, was a magnificent stone and wood building set high above the ground and a good ten feet above the sunken lane beyond our boundary. This was our *hórreo* or grain store. It would have been used to store maize, the wide stone overhang above the steps deterring the most persistent of rodents. Now it looked like the rest of our new home, old, tattered and in need of plenty of work. The *hórreo* would be a project far into the future.

The way to the house, off to our right, was shaded by huge grape vines, with trunks as thick as my leg, growing up and over rickety looking wooden posts. From the supports hung fat bunches of white grapes. The 'path' sloped downwards gently to the east-facing terrace area where we planned to set up our camping table and washing area. The morning sun was bathing the terrace in a mottled light, filtering through the fruit trees just beyond.

Wielding our new key, I unlocked the heavy wooden door and pushed it open. The damp coldness hit me. It had been cold of course all last winter but now, with the sun outside so hot, I was shocked. I remembered one mild day during our winter in Galicia (before our old key was taken away) when we decided to 'air' the house by opening all the doors and windows. Within twenty minutes all the internal walls and the stone steps were running with water as the warm damp air outside hit the icy cold stonework inside forming condensation on every surface. We panicked, immediately closing up the house once again. We had learnt a valuable lesson when it comes to airing out old buildings, *poco y poco* as our neighbours would say, bit by bit.

Still, this was our first day at *A Casa do Campo* and we had lots to do. I had made a long list of jobs in order of importance. First was to clean the floors upstairs so we could lay out our 'furniture'. I organised that whilst S went off to procure a butane bottle so I could cook dinner.

His task, it seemed, was not to be a simple one. First, he tried the *ferreteria* (hardware store) in town. They had gas bottles but he couldn't have one without bringing in an empty bottle to swap. Next he asked at the agricultural shop. Same story there. S offered to buy an empty bottle but that was not possible. He was finally directed to a place near the cemetery. "I spotted gas bottles in a cage and dogs and chickens running around. An old man with no teeth appeared and I tried to explain what we wanted." The old chap brought S back to the house to collect the empty bottle we didn't have, then they disappeared again. "He took me to the next village. It's the chap who pinched our chariot and is a relative I think. The gas man made him give us a spare bottle."

By the time S had finished journeying around the neighbourhood I had the floors treated for woodworm or *carcoma* in Spanish - a word we would hear a lot in the next few months - and the deckchairs set up. S inflated the mattress and plugged in the stereo. We had dinner, a vegetable paella cooked outside on the two-ring gas hob we had found in one of the barns, and an early night.

Diary Friday 10th August Casa do Campo Day 2 HOT! 30°c
Didn't sleep a wink! Sooo noisy! Crickets, unidentified snufflings in the garden, something trying to get in the window and bats in the hall. I guess the sounds normally covered by the 'usual' urban noise become magnified when there is nothing else (and no window panes). Plus this morning the blow up mattress was flat!
An early mist cleared to bright sunshine before lunch but by then we were in Cousas (the cheap shop near our old flat) buying up the place. Bought a post box and wheelbarrow and a load of kilner jars for preserving the plums - all the essentials! After a busy morning we treated ourselves to lunch in Taboada, upstairs at

PLUM, COURGETTE & GREEN BEAN TART

Parillada Mencia (named after the owner's daughter). Good food and great value. The lady thinks our trip is taking a while. Tried (mainly unsuccessfully, it has to be said) to explain we are now living here. S had fish and chips for a starter. I opted for a lighter snack of Russian salad with almost a full jar of mayo on the side. We had a mixed grill (churrasco) for mains. The waitress returned after we had finished and gabbled something at high speed. I must've looked blank as eventually she went off and wrote it down! Basically she had asked if we wanted dessert now, or if we wanted more dinner first then dessert afterwards! Gosh! This is my sort of place!

Had a productive afternoon (despite lunch) tidying the attic room for our boxes when they arrive. The floorboards in there are amazing, 30cm wide, thick, old chestnut boards. They are almost black with age and polished by generations of feet walking over them. Bet they could tell a story or two. I also reorganised the kitchen so I can find stuff, while S explored the grounds thinking about the sewerage. This would be a good idea. I'm not keen on the woods already... bitten by mosquitos this morning whilst squatting. Cruel when one's knickers are round one's ankles and one can't run away!!

Diary Sunday 12th August Day 4 Hot.
Blow-up mattress flat again... think we have a problem!
S drawing-pinned plastic sheeting over the broken window panes to stop some of the insects sneaking in at night then started digging his trench for our sewer pipes. The first step to a loo. Yippee!! We have decided that, as the bathroom-to-be needs so much work just to get the floor safe, the first WC will be the utility one. This means a longer initial pipework (all along the

back of the house to where the septic tank will be) and a WC in our current living room for a while – and why not? – but should be quicker in the end, I hope. Cleaned as much of the kitchen as I can. At least it's dry now, no puddles on the floor, though it still smells a bit musty everywhere. The marble tops were rather stained but cleaned up well with some Vim I found and a lot of elbow grease. Have put the gas hob on the side next to the sink (and near to the nice airy – that is, holey – window). Pots and pans lined up neatly on the worktop. I measured up for the new windows for the kitchen, upstairs bedrooms and bathroom-to-be, cleaned as many cobwebs as I could from the other rooms and shifted some more junk. The middle bedroom will be our 'tool room' for the time being.

Fiesta on in town so wandered in later to have a look. Just leaving about midnight as everyone else was coming in!

We had decided to set up home in the newest part of the house, a brick built extension that would originally have been a large terrace area on the first floor. It had decent floors (that is without any human-sized holes), a good ceiling (also *sin* holes) and the least sieve-like roof in the house. It also had wide-ranging views, down the valley beyond our fruit trees to the east and across the river to woodland in the south. There were two rooms. One was our bedroom, designated the 'sunroom' for reasons which may become clear, with the leaky mattress and nothing much else. The second was our living room, eventually to be a utility.

The rest of the upstairs rooms, which were to be a bathroom and two bedrooms at some time in the distant future, were dilapidated bordering on dangerous. The floors were more hole than wood, the ceilings soggy and hanging down where water had penetrated. Everywhere smelt damp and we had mouldy photos of the Virgin Mary on every wall. We had silently agreed not to use the tiny old bathroom, stuck as it was in the upstairs hall, with its sewer pipe emptying onto the garden but do as bears do until S could plumb in a toilet.

The kitchen was useable though we had to be careful to cover food due to bits dropping off the woodwormy wooden ceiling and field mice sneaking in under the ancient wooden door to help themselves to crumbs. Cutlery and crockery were kept clean and dust free in one of the plastic boxes we had brought along. Food in another. The rest of the downstairs rooms: the 'storeroom' which was to be my walk-in pantry and the 'barn' (our future huge living/dining room), were still animal pens.

Once we had the basics sorted out – bed, food, and erm... toileting facilities, it was time to start on my second list. This one was for stuff such as electric, gas and water. And the paperwork to register us, the house and the car. Easy!

Diary Monday 13th August Day 5 Hot
Into town for supplies and to start the paperwork trail but everything closed for the fiesta! Luckily Chantada, our next town along southwards, was open. Getting a gas bottle to replace our neighbour's and a contract was not so easy. Repsol, the gas company said they couldn't give us a contract without visiting for a safety check. In inimitable Galician style they did give us a spare bottle though (not charged for until we get the contract!). We eventually found the Fenosa office to swap names on the electric bill. Met a new friend whilst asking directions, he speaks English and kindly helped us in the Fenosa office. The lady there seemed more interested in looking at a photo album a friend had brought in than dealing with the huge snaking line of customers

but eventually changed the details. We explained the actual meter number didn't seem to tally with that on the bill we had found in the house but she didn't think that was a problem. Also found the window place (asked a lady in town who has nice windows where she bought them) but it is closed until 3rd September. Oh well!

We soon found that the window factory was not the only place to be closed until September. We needed to see the town architect to obtain permissions to renovate our roof but he was also away until September. The notary had our deeds which we needed to register the house and…yes, he was on holiday too. My plans were already going awry!

Luckily the health centre was open. They told us that to register with a GP we needed a residency certificate (*empadronamiento*) from the town hall. We hopped straight to the *ayuntamiento* to get the certificate but inadvertently discussed registering the house instead, due to my not altogether perfect Spanish. We were sent to Chantada. When we finally found the place we realised it was the land registry. Oops! They took our *copia simple* (simple copy of the deeds) and said registration would take two months. I counted that as a success, of sorts.

Wednesday 15th August Hot and humid
Dear mum,
I'm writing this in the living room sitting in a (not entirely comfortable) deckchair listening to a CD and the crickets outside as darkness falls. It's warm and so far dry - inside anyway. Two rain showers earlier but only a couple of leaks, sorted with the aid of buckets. 23-29°C in the day 15° overnight.

PLUM, COURGETTE & GREEN BEAN TART

One week has gone already, four fiestas, 100s of plums consumed and lots of adventures...

Arrived in Galicia last Wednesday after a good run from Bilbao to Jen's. The ferry trip was excellent with lots of whale watching thanks to Clive, the wildlife chap on P&O. We stopped for lunch at Cadavedo from our walking days and were amazed that our painful (nay, agonising) 2 week walk whizzed past in just 2 hours driving! We had only time to drop our bags at Jen's and grab a bite before she whisked us away to an international dance festival in Monterroso compered by our Spanish estate agent's son Pablo. Very professional Cossack dancers, a wonderful local dance school and a rather elderly troop from Ponferrada who promenaded genteelly but had much more stamina than us at 12.30a.m. All for free! The Cossack dancers alone would have been good enough for a west end show. It was also very loud. The Spanish don't do quiet appreciation so there was much shouting, whistling and clapping. It all conspired to keep us awake anyhow!

Despite the late night we had a productive day on Thursday and now have a bedroom and a living area with deckchairs and a functioning stereo system... perched on top of one of our newly restored 'potty' cupboards (found in the bedroom. Sweet

AUGUST

chestnut polishes up beautifully but boy was the cloth mucky afterwards).

The kitchen is clean and with the old gas hob functioning we are looking quite homely. Outside is our daytime eating, working and washing area. S even put me a washing line up.

Carmen is still supplying our water but the well seems to be clearing... at least it doesn't look like I'm pulling a pint of ale out of the tap (brown and frothy!!) Will get it tested next week at the pharmacy. Carmen tells us the water is from a spring and very pure.

The garden is looking incredibly productive despite, or maybe because of, 12 years of neglect. We have plums galore. All delicious. The figs (green, annual ones) are nearly ripe; there are grapes, pears and apples (including an absolutely laden cooking apple on the allotment) together with peaches and nectarines for later. The walnuts are loaded too as are the chestnuts. We will do well as fruitarians... or fruit and nut cases haha.

I have planted herbs near the terrace and am digging out a patch near the hórreo (grain store) for the blackcurrant cuttings we brought with us... they seem to have survived their journey!

S has started digging out our sewerage trench along the back of the house, laboriously hacking through the granite bedrock by hand... I'm sure he's having fun!! The joys of not being on mains water! We have managed to get out and about into town to sample the local vino but still have a number of bars to try (around 10 or so!!).

Jen has been wonderful, letting us use her shower and providing produce (in exchange for plums). We went over to collect all our stored boxes yesterday as there wasn't room in the car when we arrived! Sadly we couldn't have squirrel back as he had disappeared! Apparently Jen wasn't very keen on having a stuffed squirrel (can't think why!) so had put him in a tree outside where he would feel more at home. Then he vanished! As their house is very secure (even if someone desperately wanted to steal a stuffed squirrel) we assume a fox or buzzard took it. I can imagine the scene... 'Here, kids, a nice squirrel for tea.' 'Tastes like sawdust mum.' 'Mmm fast food's not what it was kids.' Actually I'm quite sad about poor squirrel!!

Jen also kindly gave us a spare mattress she didn't need. Had fun trying to get it home. We had to strap it to the car roof. First S opened all the doors and tied the rope around the roof but then the doors wouldn't close. So he untied all the rope, closed the doors and opened the windows. We retied the rope around the door frames then had to climb in the windows to drive home. Lucky no Guardia Civiles were

AUGUST

around as we were probably not terribly legal. Worth it for a comfortable bed though!

Augusta at the hotel in Monterroso has helped us with translations and her daughter, Silvia is contacting some electricians so we can have a bit more power. Furniture expected at the end of the week (fiestas not withstanding). Today was national day but back to normal (whatever that is) tomorrow.
Love you tons
Xxx

Thurs am. Another beautiful sunny morning. Will have to get up earlier, the sun is already on the terrace. S has shaved and I've been watching the different birds in the dead tree. Lots of butterflies too and rather noisy crickets. Beautiful!

Diary Friday 17th August Day 9 Hot
Just had a refreshing shower in our own Eden! Old hosepipe found in the barn warms up lovely when attached to the water tap on the well and left in the sun for a bit, although you only get a hose length of hot water so have to be a bit quick with the final rinse! Nevertheless my hair feels silkier than it has for ages (and dust free). Think the water is quite drinkable now despite the odd lingering bit of rust! Must remember to get it tested.
Bottled my first lot of plums (from the self-sufficiency book). Poured hot syrup over washed plums in the kilner jars then brought them to the boil slowly until the liquid in the jars was boiling. Could've squashed more into some of the jars...

PLUM, COURGETTE & GREEN BEAN TART

still, will see how they last. Did one each of yellow, purple, green and red. Very pretty.

Diary Wednesday 22nd August Day 14 Cloudy/drizzle. Sunshine eve
What excitement! We have furniture! A real bed tonight and best of all sitting on a comfy sofa instead of a deckchair. After a bit of wrangling yesterday, the shipping company agreed to deliver today but refused to send any help. The driver apparently is just that and we had 2 hours to unload once he arrived!
At 9.50am we had a phone call from the driver. I eventually elicited that he was up on the main road but that there was a problem. As we drove up to meet him, finding pieces of tree branches every few yards, we guessed what had happened: he had tried to come down the lane but, being a rather tall and rather wide container lorry, had started clipping the trees and panicked. He was reluctantly persuaded to try again and, with me sitting shotgun (and reassuring him that no one would sue him for damage), we reached the village.
"Nada mas arboles pero es un poco narrow" I muttered in my best Spanglish.
He looked askance but we continued, only slightly clipping Carmen's telephone line. The sight of her hanging out of the bedroom window in dressing gown holding up the line so he could pass below was a wonderful example of Galician neighbourliness that will stay with me.
"Mi corazon, my heart" says the driver, holding his chest in, I hoped, an exaggerated manner.
Anyway, he had a nice rest while we unloaded the excellently packed stuff from Davenports with me supervising from inside the van giving useful directions such as 'Attico, Terraza, Kitchen' for each item.

The only casualties were the washing machine which somersaulted over S' back due to overenthusiasm by our two electrician helpers and S' back being pulled by gallantly breaking the fall of said washing machine.
We will evaluate the damage to either tomorrow.

Thursday 23rd August. Sun, hot later. Lovely evening
Dear mum,
  Sitting writing this on a (very) comfy sofa! The furniture arrived yesterday. All went very smoothly with the help of two new English friends, Cris and Steve, who are buying near the coast but renting nearby at the moment, and Silvia's electricians who offered to help for an hour. Had fun getting the van here and even more fun getting the poor driver back out. The village is a tad narrow for his rather large container lorry. He managed to turn round okay at ours but with Carmen's wobbly hórreo, the turn past the barns was too much of an angle. Took an hour with S and I giving instructions... forward, stop. Back a bit, stop. Forward etc. Told him he was a very good driver which pleased him but he kept saying 'madre mía, my heart'. Don't think he will volunteer for that run again poor chap.
  Seem to have had a successful week so far! Ordered the septic tank, loo, bidet, and piping - to be delivered in two weeks or quince días as they all seem to say (after I have gone off to Santiago and the architect

PLUM, COURGETTE & GREEN BEAN TART

and the notary come back from holiday, and the window place reopens and…). We have registered ourselves with the council (empadronamiento) and the health centre (I got a 'perfecto' for my paperwork there!). The lady at the council offices, Pilar, is a vecina (neighbour). Very friendly but we had a bit of confusion over a question about our level of education… not a question I was expecting, so we needed some imaginative mime to understand! Took our well water sample to the pharmacy for testing. The lady there speaks perfect English and we don't have to pay until we collect it in a week. The electricians are coming Friday (Silvia from the hotel brought them over on Tuesday when they also volunteered to help with the furniture yesterday).

On Sunday we had an archaeological dig in the storeroom-to-be next to the kitchen. I barrowed 10 or more loads of dust and old goat or rabbit droppings to the allotment. The muck was a lot deeper than we thought. By the time we got to rock (bedrock) there was quite a step into the room. We will start filling it with rubble as we go along and eventually concrete the floor.

Have made 2 jars of fig jam, bit hit and miss without scales - they will be in a box somewhere. Not tried it yet but I'm sure we will manage to eat it as it will be sweet and fruity! Bottled some too. Gave a bag full to Augusta at the hotel and a fairy left us

AUGUST

some strawberries outside the gate in return while we were boozing in town (Good bar, big café on the corner, La Scala, nice tapas and lively card games!).

Hope you get this before your hols. If so have a good time, otherwise, hope you had a good time and the weather was kind. We seem to be doing better than anywhere - Mallorca, the Canaries and south Spain have floods as does Asturias and the Basque region. Here is generally light drizzle/mist am then fine and cool or sunny and hot pm and usually clear at night with loads of stars, and crickets, and owls hooting, and the bats of course chasing the moths around the light. Oh and we have red squirrels like our poor stuffed one (well, they are black really but they are red squirrels if you get me). I chased one down the road in front of the car. Honey buzzards still overhead and a noisy spotted woodpecker on the dead tree right next to our bedroom window!
Love you tons and tons
XXXXXXXXxx
PS Our postcode actually ends 5 not 0. My fault & my mobile number isn't needed at the bottom of the envelope! XXx

Diary Friday 24th August Day 16 Sun and cloud 27°c
Our new sewerage trench has almost reached the far garden wall. Acting nicely as a bucket trap. Caught a skink this am, like a small slowworm but with tiny legs too far apart which it tucks in

PLUM, COURGETTE & GREEN BEAN TART

when slithering through grass. Very quick! S made some T-shaped, wooden 'sighting posts' to check his levels. Says he knows the theory! That's okay then.
Tried lighting the old kitchen stove again. S had cleaned it all out first. Much billowing of smoke from every orifice including places smoke really shouldn't be coming from! But, we did manage to boil the kettle – the tea was only marginally smoky – and I've put some apples and spuds in overnight. The oven seemed reasonably warmish so we shall see.
S is confident that the washer has survived its precipitated dive from the wagon on Wednesday... it looks like an accident victim, covered in sticky tape and a big dent on both sides. A good illustration of why restraining bolts should always be used when moving a washing machine! Pity we don't have electric to try it. Electricians didn't turn up.

Electricians apart, we were making progress on the paperwork front – I thought. We had collected our *empadronamiento* from the town hall so arranged to visit the police station in Lugo to get our *residencia,* or ID card. At the same time we would register the car with the traffic department so we could get Spanish insurance. Jen had given us the details of a bar in Monterroso where they ordered their firewood so we could do that on the way. Maribel our Spanish estate agent, was looking into car insurance through her son Robín, whilst Carmen, our neighbour had even contacted the telephone company for us who were going to ring with a date to visit. This was going too well.

Tuesday 28th August. At home. V hot
Dear mum
 After the excitement of the dance festival

AUGUST

we thought life would be a bit quieter but it turns out August is fiesta month here in Galicia. Our local town fiesta was first. 3 nights of loud bands called orchestras which arrive in their own huge trucks that convert into a stage. It's like having Sunday night at the London Palladium just down the road. Amazing! The last 2 weekends have been really noisy until early in the morning (all the more so as we only have plastic sheeting across the windows where there used to be glass once upon a time). I was starting to get quite wound up as I had seen a nightclub up the road and thought the noise must be coming from that. I was even ready to go to the council and complain... we didn't buy a house in a peaceful, rural location for a disco to open on our doorstep! Good job I didn't. Turns out the noise was just from all the fiestas everywhere - at least one every weekend in summer. And a 'Club' in Spanish is actually a whorehouse!

I hope you are enjoying the sun as much as we are, but maybe not quite so much (30° in the shade currently) or you won't be able to move! It is really humid and we have had 2 nights of heavy thunder and lightning - very spectacular as it bounces around the valley, echoing off the hills! Kindly, it seems to stop in time for us to get up. Even better, the house seems to be standing up to the weather. Only a couple of drips in the

PLUM, COURGETTE & GREEN BEAN TART

kitchen sorted by strategically placed buckets in the loft space. Elsewhere seems ok at present. Phew!

The electricians finally arrived this a.m. They have fitted a new fuse box and sockets in the kitchen so I can have fridge, freezer and microwave going and even my breadmaker and a light. They also made the sockets in our living quarters safe and put one on the terrace so we can try the washing machine next. The smaller of the two guys did rather like his huge (seriously huge) hammer to fit everything, even the tiny clip at the back of the electric box (very Freudian) and the sockets are all a bit wonky, but S no longer needs a torch to make our evening cuppa so we are happy. Loving our hosepipe shower but have found a flaw in the system. A bit like your hot water from the coal fire, it gets too flipping hot! And no cold tap. Think how quickly we could get a tankful of hot water with our solar system... now there's a project!

S has started digging a huge hole for the septic tank having done the basics on the trench (it will need re-levelling once he has the tank in place). So far he has found a slowworm, 2 lizards, a skink and an adder plus a stag beetle and a few praying mantises (or is it mantisii?). Good job no one does ecological surveys over here or we would have to suspend work. Mind you he has carefully translocated them all.

AUGUST

I have been busy making jam to preserve some of the plums. Going to try fig ice cream now we have a working freezer.

Wednesday: Planned to go to Lugo today to get us and the car registered here but got to the petrol station and found none of the car keys would work... much to the disgust of a large wagon whose way we had totally blocked. After half an hour we managed to get one key to turn. Set off home to get the master key. Another hour of searching (I'd not listed master key for Escort anywhere on my inventory, Dad would be disappointed at me. Haha!) then Silvia kindly accompanied us to the garage. He soon had it all fixed up but we still need to get to Lugo. Mind you we did find lots of other non-inventoried things whilst going through the boxes looking for the key, so a useful exercise!

Thursday: Still not posted this! Got to Lugo today, though as usual our attempts at conquering Spanish paperwork were not entirely successful. We had the right paperwork for our ID card but they said we could only have a bit of paper not a card. Don't understand why as Jen has a card. The traffic office wanted to send my driving licence to Madrid! No thank you, I just wanted to register our address! It's very exhausting at times trying to communicate in Spanish as I love to talk (who me? haha). Did have a very nice chat to our neighbour

PLUM, COURGETTE & GREEN BEAN TART

Carmen and her cousin Araceli (who speaks some English) this evening whilst Carmen plied us with butter biscuits... yummy. Wish I had a working cooker to try these things. Jen brought us a huge marrow over, would be perfect stuffed!

Also trying to sort out the telephone. Telefonica, the Spanish BT, seem very expensive so I am looking at alternatives, meanwhile I'll ring you Saturday.

I hope the weather kept fine for you. Very variable here this week. Apparently Lugo was flooded yesterday so good job we didn't make it! I'm looking forward to college but feel rather guilty at leaving S to sort out the paperwork alone, poor lad! Will try to write to you from Santiago but I expect to be busy for a while!!

Love you lots and lots, see you in Oct. Hopefully loo will be in!

P.S Thank you for your letter. Only arrived today so a bit longer than last time.

P.P.S The long number at the end is my mobile number not the postcode! (Though it doesn't matter as it still arrives and they could always ring if they couldn't find us!)

Love you

Xxx

I said it was going too well! I have decided that paperwork, for a non-Spanish speaker, is probably one of the biggest hurdles to living happily in rural Galicia. English is rarely spoken at any large government institution although even native speakers have problems. Our Spanish friend tried to register her English car only to be sent away four times for different paperwork until she lost her temper. At least she could get angry in Spanish. I could only fume quietly.

We had been promised that the house would be registered as one plot of land before we bought it. An oversight we didn't pick up on at the notary's. The *registro* or land registry in Chantada rang to say there were problems with the *catastral* or land tax so we had to go to the *catastro* (land tax office) in Lugo which deals with this. Once there we were told the *registro* had to change ownership details first. This state of affairs went on and on through many visits and for many months. It seemed like a never ending cycle of toing and froing.

In contrast, trying to register the car here so we could get insurance for it until we could sort out the paperwork to change it into a Spanish vehicle, was just plain impossible.

Leaving behind our paperwork problems for a while, and deciding to wait until more people returned from the long summer holidays (who would choose to relocate to Spain in summer? - another of my mounting oversights) we continued making progress on the house.

We have neither mains water nor sewerage. The water from our well was being tested and we fully expected it to be potable. The sewerage was trickier. We wanted to get it sorted out as soon as possible as the existing facilities were a little primitive for our English sensibilities - we preferred the WC to empty into a tank rather than directly onto an old, and very healthy looking, apple tree.

Actually looking back there is a lot of sense to the old arrangement. With humanure being one of the big new things in recent years it would seem that, as is often the case, the *Galegos* were just ahead of their time rather than behind it. The apple tree was living proof that the fertiliser worked!

Anyway, softies that we were, we decided that new drainage and a spanking new septic tank was in order. The tank had to be below ground but therein lay a minor difficulty – solid bedrock approximately nine inches below ground level. This house didn't need any foundations. It was built straight onto the granite rock. Excellent for a stable house, not excellent to dig into with a chisel!

It was at this point that I very deliberately managed to start a CELTA course off in Santiago, staying in a flat in the centre of the city with, most importantly, a bathroom.

SEPTEMBER
Santiago and sewerage

Back before we had even managed to buy *A Casa do Campo* I had an idea that with some qualifications I could maybe teach English to earn some money in our new life. With this is mind I applied for, and won, a place to study for a CELTA (Certificate in English Language Teaching to Adults) in Santiago de Compostela starting in September.

This coincided nicely with our arrival, giving me a month to settle in. Unfortunately it left S to sort out the errant paperwork for registering the house and the car, ordering the windows, obtaining architect approval for the new roof and even writing our daily diary.

On the 2nd September, S drove me to the city where the university had arranged a flat share for the four week long course. I had originally intended to commute daily but this would have left S without transport and cost a fortune in petrol. Plus I was told that the course was very intensive, though I expected that that was an exaggeration. I was looking forward to a fun-filled month, learning new things and living in one of the most beautiful cities in Galicia. I felt only slightly guilty leaving S to sort everything out back at home.

PLUM, COURGETTE & GREEN BEAN TART

(S) Diary Monday 3rd September Sunny
Do an hour's digging for septic tank. Visit notary (very busy) for a copy of the escritura (deeds) for the register office. He says I don't need them then says wait and comes back with a copy (free). Go to architect at town hall. Manage to make myself understood. Go upstairs to fill in form. All OK until I have to guess how much the roof work will cost. He reckons 2000€ so at 2% tax that will be 40€ (that's the only reason we need permissions I think). Post some letters then visit window place (Toldao) with Lisa's drawings. Chap called Angel writes all the info down and asks lots of questions. Exchange 'phone numbers and he says he will visit when his boss is back. Confirm directions to the house. Back to house for lunch (leek and potato broth, very tasty). Explore roof space and knock down half the wall between Bed 1 (end bedroom) and bathroom to be. Shower. Wash undies, socks and overalls. Hang up washing. Tea. Fill water at Carmen's well, water currant bushes, relax.

Meanwhile in Santiago, my first day suggested this was not going to be quite the relaxing fun-filled month I had hoped for. There were six of us on the course, an eclectic mix of Southerners, Northerners, Irish and Scots. We started straight in with grammar, managing classes and teaching practice. It was hard work but the course directors seemed friendly and helpful.

I also managed to get me and my new flatmate hopelessly lost the first morning. As the 'local', and believing I knew Santiago, I led the way for our twenty minute walk to the college. Except that without my trusty compass, S, I somehow led us into a courtyard to one of the many religious buildings. Worse, as I turned to leave, the gate, which we hadn't noticed before as it was open, started to slide closed. We ran through terrified of being stuck in there until another car entered, and also of being late on our first morning.

Luckily Viv and I had hit it off straight away. I had arrived at the flat about five minutes before she did and so nabbed the larger bedroom. She was laid back about this and, thankfully, about our little diversion. By the time we arrived at the university I was already hot and exhausted. Someone else had better lead next time.

(S) Diary Tuesday 4th September Sunny
Couple of hours down hole digging for septic tank. Rivet panel back on gate (had come loose and spiky). Lunch (rest of broth from yesterday). Measure stud work for bathroom and utility room. Can't make it add up, takes me ages. Chuck some rubble in the store room ready for eventual concreting. Wash and change and into town in time to buy bread. Into La Scala. 2 vinos and tapas (1. jamón, 2. fillet pork with chorizo on top). Read paper and watch weather. Walk back to water plants. Bed

(S) Diary Wednesday 5th September Sunny
All morning rock bashing. Good progress, looking the right shape, needs tidying up and depth checking. Lunch (omelette with potatoes, leek, tomatoes and side order of Jen's leafy thing). Wash up. Wash me. Change. Check what I need at builder's merchant in town (Xesteira). Drive in. Get prices for corrugated roofing sheets (Uralitas, like the mountains), red pine for stud wall, and insulation. They don't do chestnut wood for roof beams but give me directions to wood yard nearby. Into other construction place (San Pedro) to ask about septic tank. Due in on 11th. Price up

insulation there too. Seems much too expensive. Pick up water test results from pharmacy. Fit for human consumption. Back home. Cheese butty and chocolate mousse. Pick nectarines and water plants.

(S) Diary Friday 7th September Sunny
Two and a half hours down hole. Still hard bit in corner. Blanch and freeze some nectarines. Decide to go for broke and make 2 jars of jam. Drive to window place. Closed already at 1310. Supermarket for carrots, tomatoes, chocolate mousse. Lunch (tuna stirfry). Wash up. Wash clothes, pick apples. Wash and shave, make butties, drive to Santiago to pick up Lisa.

My first week sped by in a flurry of teaching and learning. My head was overflowing with pluperfects, gerunds and past participles. We never did this lot in 'O' level English. I learnt things 'bout me own language I never knew (or knew that I needed to know). Our 'students' were a lively bunch. They all worked at the university and, by and large, had many more degrees than any of us. We had biologists, doctors, economists and psychologists. Many of them had taken the course before and knew a great deal more than us about the syllabus if not about English. They enjoyed it so much that some like Arturo, the unofficial leader of the group, had enrolled four times.

"But have you learnt anything?" I asked.

"Of course," he replied in reasonably fluent English. "But I like it so much, I come back again. It is, how is it called? *Divertido.*"

"Fun." Well, I was glad he thought so. Me? I wasn't so sure

By Friday I looked forward to seeing S and my home in equal measure.

SEPTEMBER

§

The weekend went by far too quickly. Although I enjoyed being back home, I had so much 'homework' to do that I seemed to spend most of the time working on that, other than a brief and unproductive trip to chase Angel, the window man, who had still not visited.

I was impressed with the amount of physical work S had managed to get done whilst I had been lazing about doing 'brain' work. The trench along the rear of the house was fully twenty metres in length and the septic tank hole two metres deep.

The south garden, behind the house is a triangular piece of ground with three walnut trees, two apricots and that old, healthy apple tree. It slopes gently away from the house before stopping at a haha or sunken lane which is our boundary with the neighbour. His field beyond stretches down to the water mill on the little river at the bottom of our valley.

The septic tank hole was beyond the garden wall to the west in an area of old gnarled sweet chestnuts and cherry trees we pretentiously called the 'orchard'. And it was in solid bedrock. How the trees managed to grow so tall I have no idea.

S had had an impressive week bureaucracy wise too and, not to be outdone, I had had three calls from Telefonica regarding a visit. As we had decided to price up other options I had put them off. It was only later that I was told how incredible it was to have the Spanish national telephone company actually offer an appointment. If I had only known!

We managed a night on the town with vino and tapas, most of which were bought by neighbours, or friends or relations of neighbours who we didn't know but somehow knew us. And I rang mum, as I had been too busy even to write my usual weekly letter.

PLUM, COURGETTE & GREEN BEAN TART

S drove me back to Santiago on Sunday after a nice lie in and our usual boiled eggs for Sunday breakfast. We had a chat with my flatmate. She was happy for S to stay with us the following weekend. He would come to Santiago on the Saturday and stay over until Sunday. This meant I could get my homework done on the Friday and Sunday nights, S would have only one journey there and back, and he could use our showering and washing facilities! Sorted.

(S) Diary Monday 10th September Sunny
Fiesta drumming until 0300. Not up early. Drive to Lugo. Park and walk to land tax office (catastro) with our deeds. Queue ¾ hour. Hand in all paperwork. Chap asks me lots of questions, very fast and complicated. Then tries to get me to fill in a form we have already completed. Finally puts our number into the computer and it comes up with my name. He gives me a receipt and tells me to come back in 10 days. Very frustrating! To police station for resident's certificate. Queue. Chica says I can have mine but Lisa needs to be here to collect hers. Say she is in Santiago for 3 weeks. Not a problem she can collect it when she is back. Bill for 6.70€. To bank to pay. Queue. Cashier takes 3 goes at my name. Finally gets something almost correct (at least I'm not Mr British Citizen this time). Back to police. Queue. Get certificate at last. Now 1300 so decide to have Menú del Dia nearby. Back to hotel to ask Augusta to ring insurance company to check if any word on car insurance. Agent has lost the piece of paper with car details on so insurance not done. Robin (insurance agent) promises it's not a problem. Takes details again plus he wants a photocopy of log book, insurance docs and MOT. Go home, knock down rest of dividing wall Bed 1/bathroom. Text Lisa.

SEPTEMBER

(S) Diary Thursday 13th September Sunny
Make hole for septic tank a bit longer to be on safe side. Notice my huge ex-water board chisel (that I found in the bottom of the canal once upon a time) has shrunk to half its length with all the banging! Septic tank arrives 12oo. Much heavier than I thought. Will need help to lift it in the hole. Put everything in position and realise tank will have to go deeper. Oh well. Also trench not quite level. Put everything away and have lunch (tuna, carrots, spuds). Bash a bigger hole in the barn wall underneath where the loo will go to get pipe to sit flat. (There was a crack in the wall before I started, not me!). Unwrap loo and bidet and check everything is there. Think how to fit it without pipes being in the middle of our temporary living room. Back to plumbers for extra bits. Ask for factura (receipt/invoice?) which causes some confusion. Has to be stamped? Not sure I need it anyway. Call in supermarket for cheese, bread, luncheon meat, chocolate mousse. Have tea. Water plants.

(S) Diary Saturday 15th September Sunny
Spend morning in trench, levelling and making centre line deeper to cradle the pipes to septic tank. Make good start. Wash, change, collect fruit. Lunch (spud and onion omelette). Wash up. Pack cool box. Drive to Santiago 1400ish. Meet Lisa outside bar Pola Norte where she is staying. Time for a shower, washing in and a relax before vino and tapas in the evening. Very hot and stuffy in old town so go up the hill to veggie restaurant and more vino. Sleep well.

It seemed a much better arrangement, S coming to me. I could concentrate on passing my exams and get some sightseeing in at the weekends.

Santiago old town is stunningly attractive with

narrow streets, old stone buildings and a church or chapel around virtually every corner. It has also been an UNESCO World Heritage Site since 1985.

The pilgrim route to Santiago, the *Camino de Santiago* or the Way of St. James has become increasingly popular in recent years, thanks in part to a number of books, films and documentaries including Brian Sewell's car hopping documentary and Emilio Estevez's acclaimed film, *The Way*. Santiago's beginnings as a religious pilgrimage site are a fascinating story and an interesting mix of history, politics and myth.

Alfonso II (760-842) of Asturias was, in the 9th century, busy expanding his kingdom along the Bay of Biscay and westwards into what is now called Galicia. The problem with expansion is that it begets more land and more borders to defend against enemies, of which there were many. Most notable were the Moors who had previously held the region (although they used the area mainly to collect taxes, not bothering to settle this cold northern outpost) before the King of Asturias had reconquered it. Alfonso needed help. In order to receive support from his neighbours against invasions the area required recognition and respect. It needed something Christians would want to defend. In fact the area needed a miracle.

By serendipity, and a hermit called Pelayo, a miracle was found. One July evening the hermit was meditating and praying in the forests of Libredón near to the hermitage of San Fiz when he saw 'a brilliant light from the stars falling from heaven' to a hill nearby. He hurried to give the news to the bishopric at Iria Flavia (Padrón). Bishop Teodomiro investigated and discovered the tomb of the apostle James the Greater at *Campus Stellae*, the very spot where the stars had fallen.

Legend has it that St. James (*Santiago* in Spanish) was charged with the task of evangelising

SEPTEMBER

Hispania. Some accounts say he was beheaded on his return to the holy lands, others that he was executed by Agrippa I before he could leave for his mission. His followers are said to have managed to get his body to Jaffa where they found a miraculous stone barge in which they transported his remains to Galicia. Here, either an angel received his body and transported it to *Campus Stellae* or, more bizarrely still, his followers approached a pagan queen, Loba (meaning she-wolf) asking for help transporting the body. Loba tried to deceive the disciples by sending them to the cave of a dragon. However the dragon, on sight of the cross, exploded and the disciples returned with two wild oxen which, again at the sight of the cross, had knelt to be yoked and to receive their burden.

As legends go, this leaves far more questions than answers. But, the relics found at *Campus Stellae* (or the field of stars) have been confirmed by the holy Roman Catholic Church as genuine. More importantly, they gave Alfonso II the credibility he needed for the defence of his kingdom. It is said that one of the very first pilgrims to make the journey to the site of the relics of St. James the Greater was Alfonso himself, using old Roman roads from Oviedo via Lugo along what is now called the Primitive Route or V*ia Primitiva.* The pilgrim route to St. James of the Field of Stars, or Santiago de Compostela as the new city became, is still one of the most important of Christian pilgrimages.

That September the *plaza de obradoiro* around the cathedral was heaving with limping exhausted souls, burdened with backpacks and staves, and hung about with shells and ornamentation, staring in awe at the majesty of the Cathedral of Santiago.

Following the discovery of the relics of St. James, a small hermitage was erected. This was expanded as more pilgrims poured into the area, eventually becoming a cathedral when the bishopric at Flavia Iria was moved to Santiago de Compostela in the 11th century. The cathedral itself has changed and grown over the years. One of the oldest and most beautiful facades is the *Puerta de las Platerías* or silversmith's door – a double, Romanesque doorway originally facing numerous silversmith workshops, which was opened in 1103.

Nowadays, the main trade appears to be the selling of *Camino* souvenirs; shells, figurines, t-shirts, badges, mugs and fridge magnets. Even the cathedral has a shop attached for those all-important religious souvenirs. The second most popular shop is the *pasteleria* selling the local speciality cake, *Tarta de Santiago*. Most of the cake shops have a young lady outside with a tray of Santiago cake for passers-by to try. We spent some time trying each and every offered morsel that weekend, ensuring no favouritism. I can honestly say that they were some of the worst examples of the famous almond sponge I have ever tried. Now, call me misguided, but surely the aim of offering tourists a taste of your wares is to encourage them indoors to buy a full sized cake rather than to generously sate their hunger. If this is the case then, again maybe naively, surely one should offer the very best example of your produce – not a stale, sawdust dry lump of nutty cardboard which lodges in one's throat necessitating the urgent need for water or a *Heimlich's* manoeuvre from a kind Samaritan. So poor were these offerings that I actually refused to try *Tarta de Santiago* for a long time afterwards. That is a shame, as well made these moist almondy cakes, with the cross of St. James emblazoned in icing sugar on top, are a delight.

SEPTEMBER

§

My flatmate and I were lodged a stone's throw from St. Martin's church above a family owned café-bar overlooking a cobbled plaza. We had settled into a routine of getting back from college in the evening and sitting outside the bar with a beer, enjoying the lingering sun in the square and reflecting on our day's teaching practices before getting down to more college work. It had, up until that point, been hot and sultry in the evenings. The third week of September brought a sudden change to much cooler overnight temperatures despite the continuing hot days. We had to start wearing a jumper to drink our beer!

Whilst our teaching practice continued apace, with us all gaining more confidence as time went on, confusions still arose with hilarious regularity.

One of my fellow pupil-teachers came to me one day in great excitement.

"José tells me he works with bears."

José was one of our students, a biologist doing his PhD, but I didn't think it was on bears. "Are you sure?"

"Yes, of course. He's been to Norway, Canada, all over, ask him."

"José, I understand you work with bears."

"Si, that is correct."

"Oh!" My mistake. "What types of bears? Brown bears, grizzly bears?"

"No, no, bears of prey."

The Spanish just will not pronounce those final consonants.

(S) Diary Monday 17th September
Overnight rain. Clean loft space where the soil stack has to go through. (Can't believe how they nailed the backboard for the wall clock on, nails everywhere!) Wash and change. Meet Augusta's

PLUM, COURGETTE & GREEN BEAN TART

daughter Silvia in the café before we visit the architect. As he is also in there with all the council workers I tell her there is no point rushing (he only seems to work 4 hours and has an hour's break included). Finally at his office Silvia gets to quiz him in Spanish. The form I completed was an application for a licence to work on the roof. Licence has now come through but the chica who stamps it is on holiday until October so I have to wait until then. Architect advises me if I want to put skylights in to do it at same time as I do the roof. He doesn't want to inspect the work before or after or see receipts. Says government won't pay him to go around checking works. Basically, so long as the tax is paid he doesn't care.

Thank Silvia then go on to window place. Wait ½ hour for Angel. A different Angel but at least he visits and measures up. Should get price by Wednesday. Spend 3 hours making septic tank hole deeper and chisel shorter.

(S) Diary Tuesday 18th September Cloud
Tank hole all nice and neat. Move into trench and continue levelling. Getting deeper and deeper to make sure the waste runs the right way so tank will have to go deeper too. TV programme (can't remember which one) said sewer pipes need a 1 in 40 drop. Some programme about Roman plumbing. All very fiddly as have to keep lifting pipe out and taking off a smidge more rock then rechecking level. Pine for stud wall doesn't turn up. But firewood does at 1900. Manages to back trailer through gate but tractor wheels won't fit so dumps wood where car ought to be. Move some of it. Wash, change. Walk into town. Have to have vino to get change for 'phone. Tell Les to book flight for October, to help with roof. Back to La Scala. Owner speaks some English. Quizzes me a bit.

SEPTEMBER

(S) Diary Wednesday 19th September
Finish trench in nice soil rather than rock. When I get to the end, the spirit level comes up again so tank is at the right level. Yippee! Go to window place to collect quote. Not in, can I come back in ½ hour? Go to builder's merchant. The pine doesn't come in the sizes I wanted so do quick recalculation and reorder. Back to Toldao. Angel still not in, can I ring at 1500? To supermarket. Drop chocolate mousse. Splits, so have to eat it. Too hot to stack wood so make swingometer to check circumference of tank hole. Needs corners knocking off still. Ring window place at 1500. Can I come in? Angel not there but guy gives me envelope with quote in. Red pine for stud wall arrives 1900. Stack it in barn. Stack more firewood (leña). Early night as knackered. Wake in middle of night. Realize I've ordered too much red pine. Can't get back to sleep.

(S) Diary Thursday 20th September Sunny
Off to Lugo in good time for catastro now the 10 days are up. No queue! Same guy as last time. He has a word with guy 2, then says come back in 3 months! Not happy. Wave my arms around a lot. They try to find an interpreter, unsuccessfully. I refuse to leave. Guy 2 goes to have a word with the boss (jefe). Gets on computer and does things. I explain about the parcela being split and give him the new numbers. They think this is even more of a problem. Eventually take me to see the Jefe who speaks a little English. I start again from beginning. Jefe goes on computer and finds our names and reference numbers. Puts numbers into about 20 different pages until it recognises us when the plot number is entered. Says he has changed the names but amalgamating the plots can't be done. 'What you want would be very difficult for a Spanish person, for you it is

impossible.' Doesn't explain why. Say I thought the parcelas had been changed at cartographer's ages ago. 'But not on the computer' says he! He doesn't know if the house can be registered at all! Back to hotel to ask Augusta to ring Robin to check car insurance going through. He says he needs copy of my resident's certificate. Get photocopy done and fax. (Original won't fax as folded too many times). Robin doesn't call back. Back home to cut holes in floor and ceiling for soil stack and eat chicken casserole.

(S) Diary Friday 21st September Sunny
Up nice and early to finish putting soft earth in bottom of the septic tank hole and tamp down. Make sure there are no sharp edges to catch on tank or exit pipe. C&S arrive to help manoeuvre it. Bit of trouble as I'm not tall enough to lift it very high off the ground but done and with a bit of adjustment it sits perfectly. Tea and chat then I sift soil and pack around tank so it's secure. To registry office (registro propiedad) in Chantada. Tells me catastro haven't given me what she needs to register property. I try to explain that I have been back and forward numerous times and it is 60 kilometres each way and why can't they just talk to each other. She gets secretary to write a note and says that if catastro have a problem they should ring her. Catastro are 'un desastre' she says. Try but fail to find woodyard for roofing beams. Call in and order windows from Toldao.

By the third weekend we were well into our teaching programme and I was feeling the strain due to the intensity of the brain work. I had gone from ecstasy to despair to something in between with the sheer amount of work needed to achieve a pass grade. All the pupil-teachers were feeling the stress and there had been tears and arguments with the staff, and each other on occasions, as nerves frayed.

We had also managed some laughs with our students. The English language is a wonderful thing and amazingly confusing to foreigners (and after the last few weeks, I came to realise to English speakers too.) It didn't help our poor students that between us we had such a wide range of accents and the associated mannerisms and speech intonations. Sometimes I wondered how they managed to understand us at all. Or maybe they didn't.

One of our number was trying to get the Spanish students to repeat a phrase.

"I will be late to work today, I have to go to the doctors."

There was silence. Again in her sing-song Edinburgh accent she repeated the phrase, gabbling a little this time in panic. Again there was silence. We were all willing the students to say something as we could see she was near to tears.

At last Arturo piped up. "Di dum di dum di dum, di dum di dum di dum dum."

The silent watchers all looked at each other in confusion. What? The course director was busy and appeared not to have noticed. Neither had our fellow pupil-teacher.

"Very good. Repeat."

Maybe she was just happy for some response, and the intonation was perfect. We all shrugged. Twice more the phrase, 'I will be late to work today, I have to go to the doctors' and the repeat 'di dum di dum di dum, di dum di dum di dum dum'. Smiling she dismissed the class.

Afterwards I asked Arturo what was going on.

"Well," he replied. "We had no idea what she was saying and we felt sorry for her. That's what it sounded like to us."

There were, of course, always confusions even

amongst 'old timers' like Arturo. I was asking the class for examples of firsts; first job, first car etc.

Arturo shouted, "First bet".

Bet? "Bet?" I queried.

"Yes, bet."

"Okay." I wrote B E T on the board.

"No, no! Con p!"

Ah… first pet.

False friends, words that sound similar in both languages but have totally different meanings, were always a favourite topic for confusion and for amusement at the expense of whichever person had committed the error. My flatmate was teaching 'feelings' and asked if anyone knew the word embarrassed.

A hand shot up. Felix shouted, "It is when a lady has a baby." Laughter from us clever clogs who understood Spanish. Confusion from the rest.

"*Embarazo* means pregnant in Spanish," explained Ana. "Embarrassed is to look like Felix does now," she continued to hoots of laughter and a glowing Felix.

Amusing incidents apart, the third week was another exhausting one, so our second weekend in Santiago together was a lovely boost to morale. I was impressed with the amount S had managed to achieve over the past few weeks and especially his negotiating skills.

The sun shone endlessly. We watched acrobats in the park, *La Alameda,* and walked along the river. We had *menús del dia* and tapas and ate vast amounts of ice-cream from the many alleyway shops selling a plethora of flavours. I wanted to try each one, as I had once done with my father on holiday as a child in Eastbourne (27 flavours between us over the course of a week). I took delivery of walnuts and nectarines from home for myself and my flatmate over the coming week. This was to be the last week of the course and our final

SEPTEMBER

chance to prove ourselves worthy of our certificates. The pressure was on.

(S) Diary Monday 24th September Sunny
Stack rest of firewood and clean driveway. Lay out sewer pipes in trench, measure and cut to size. Lunch. Assemble pipes and run water through them to check levels. Raise and pack sections with sieved soil. Measure for soil stack. Go to builder's merchant to buy yet more pipes, bidet tap, cement, and sand.

(S) Diary Tuesday 25th September Sunny
Cold morning. Dig out exit trench for sewer pipes. Put some of the 'orrible hair (about ½ box) down end of tank as packing. Think I'll bin the rest. Take pipes apart, clean and leave to dry. Glue pipes. Struggle as they don't seem to slide together when full of glue. Lunch (pasta). After measuring 10 times, cut hole in living room floor for loo. Got it right phew! Glue 90° joint. Can't get it back together. Have to drag whole lot outside and hit it with a lump hammer. Knock glue over. Messy.

(S) Diary Wednesday 26th September Sunny, N wind
Pop in to see if CJ, our English neighbour, knows where woodyard is. He doesn't recognise me minus the beard I had when we met at Mark's last winter! Eventually he lets me in ha! He only knows the woodyard near us. Call there. Don't do sweet chestnut but draw map to the woodyard in Chantada which does. Glue soil stack pipes and loo bendy bit. Cut and fit bit through the barn wall to trench at back. Glue. Assemble last bits, cut to size and fit to tank. Ring hotel. Still no word from Robin re. car insurance. Lunch (rice, stirfry veg and 2 fried eggs). Think I have to do

PLUM, COURGETTE & GREEN BEAN TART

something with the sloes, end up making a jar of jam. Into town to ring Les. Have 2 vinos and tapas. Home. Clean kitchen up. Bat in bedroom at 0430, flapping around causing a draught. Have to get up and show it the door.

(S) Diary Thursday 27th September
Off to find woodyard. Very helpful. They make sure they know exactly what I want, show me the wood and even find a teenage girl to help translate. Order Castaño (chestnut) for roof beams. Good price. Back to hotel to ask about car insurance again. Augusta rings Robin and he asks if we have started the process of re-registering the car. No! He says we would have to sign an oath with a lawyer to say we intended to do so!! This could drag on and on. Back to screw down loo and assemble flush. Clean dust off everything.

Our course ended on Friday 28th September and S arrived that evening for a final night in Santiago, and to help us tidy the flat.

The previous evening our students had organised a farewell meal for us at one of Santiago's best traditional *Galego* restaurants. *Dezaseis* (16) on Rua San Pedro.

From the front the restaurant blends in with the other bars and cafes on the small street. The entrance at street level is a tiny lobby with a hall table and a huge relief map of Galicia on the wall. Shallow stone steps, complete with a central slope for running barrels down, lead to a granite-walled restaurant with a long bar on the left. Beyond this traditionally furnished dining area is a surprising addition. An internal courtyard roofed in grape vines with, in summer, the light filtering through the green leaves. Beyond that are the kitchens, which are semi-open with great

SEPTEMBER

views of the chefs slaving to produce the delicious, *Galego* with a twist, dishes.

Our students had pre-ordered the meal as they wanted us to taste as much of their local cuisine as possible. I was happy to let them lead. Only three of the pupil-teachers ended up going to the dinner. Poverty or final cramming prevented the others from attending.

One of those who did go was Tom, our resident vegetarian. As Galicia is not generally renowned for its traditional vegetarian dishes, I had reminded Arturo of the need for a special *menú*. He assured me it was all in hand. Tom's starter was stuffed courgettes, which he pronounced delicious. But he hoped there was more food to come as he was still hungry. Meanwhile we were tucking into *Polbo da feira*, octopus in the style of the market (that is with potatoes). This is probably one of those Galician staples that most divides foreigners into love it or hate it camps. I know few people who say it is 'okay'. We are firmly in the love camp, though the price at the *feira* nowadays prevents us from eating it so often. Well done, octopus is meaty yet tender without a particularly fishy taste and should be smothered in salt, paprika and good olive oil to dip up with thick crusty bread.

The best *polbo* (or *pulpo* in Castilian) is generally to be found on market day. The stalls set out their gas rings and their huge stainless steel pots full of boiling water to cook the *polbo*. The wooden eating platters are rinsed in the boiling water before the *polbo* is cut up with kitchen scissors – one leg per platter – then lavishly salted and covered in virgin olive oil and sweet paprika. Many Brits have a squeamish reaction to *polbo* and a 'the tentacles stick to the roof of your mouth' feeling, but well done, like I say, I love it.

Our mains were either *bacalao* (cod) done Galician style with paprika (*Galegos* love paprika

PLUM, COURGETTE & GREEN BEAN TART

although they are not keen on hot spices in general or even spices in general) or *terneira* (veal cooked on the *plancha* or grill). Tom waited and waited. I looked at my companions, Arturo on one side and Rosa on the other.

"It comes," said Arturo as a large tureen appeared in front of Tom.

The smell was delicious, though not, I felt, entirely vegetable based. Tom dived in and between hurried mouthfuls declared it the best thing he had had since being in Spain.

Rosa passed me a spoonful. "Taste," she said.

It was delicious, and had a quite definite hammy flavour.

I raised my eyebrows at Arturo and hissed in Spanish: "there is meat in this!" knowing Tom wouldn't understand us.

Arturo grinned and Rosa said, "*si*, it is the ham bone, for flavour."

"Good isn't it?" added Arturo wickedly.

I agreed it was good and that, should either of them let on, there would be very serious repercussions.

We finished our meals with a traditional *Galego* dessert of chestnuts in milk and of course *orujo* or *augardente* (a sort of local moonshine or poteen type distilled brew made from grapes) flavoured with coffee or herbs. A lovely end to an exhausting, but yes fun, four weeks.

We said goodbye to my flatmate and to our lovely landlady Pilar on the Saturday and had a last *menú del día* at Manolo's the busiest restaurant in Santiago – with good reason. Manolo's lunches are legendary in size and proportionally tiny in price. For eight euros each we had platters of fried *chipirones* (baby squid) or huge tureens of stew for a starter, a full rack of pork ribs or half a chicken and chips for a main, bread, dessert and water.

SEPTEMBER

By Saturday evening I was home, had rung mum, who had booked to arrive on October 12th, and christened the brand new loo.

That weekend, S finished concreting in and backfilling the sewer pipes whilst I attacked the bedroom wall, knocking off the old, worn and crumbly plaster and exposing the stone wall underneath. I gloried in making a mess after my weeks of enforced idleness. I also managed to make a couple or three jars of apple puree, picked kilos of walnuts and nectarines, and enjoyed being back in the quiet of our little village.

Santiago had been interesting but it was good to be home.

OCTOBER
Language barriers

My month away teaching English to Spanish students had been an experience. It had also made me realise how woefully inadequate our Spanish still was. Yes, I could generally get my point across so long as it didn't involve too many tenses. I could understand most(ish) of what people said to me, with some hilarious misunderstandings, if they spoke slowly and carefully. But I was still unable to have a real conversation about things other than the weather. Luckily *Galegos* are as obsessed by the weather as the English.

As an émigré, I understand more than most the importance of learning the language of one's adopted country. Not just to be able to order a beer or reserve a hotel room but to be able to genuinely communicate, which is essential to get into the psyche of a community and begin to integrate and truly understand the place you have chosen to live. Unfortunately, we English, as a race, are particularly poor at learning languages. Instead we expect Johnny Foreigner to understand English as the *lingua franca* of the civilised world. Be warned, in rural Galicia this is not the case. The second language of most of our neighbours is Castilian. *Galego* being their first and most important language. Our nearest neighbour Carmen was wonderful in those early days, always speaking in clear Castilian for my benefit and helping with my frequent manglings of her language. But our other neighbours spoke only *Galego* and we struggled to understand no matter how desperately we tried.

One neighbour had a very English way of trying to make the stupid foreigners understand. She would come to within one inch of my left ear and shout in that wonderfully carrying, piercing cry she used to summon the cows from across the valley. Sadly, this method of knocking the language into me had the entirely opposite effect, literally blowing the vestiges of any Spanish out of my right ear and away across the fields, leaving me open mouthed, deaf, and temporarily incapacitated. And reinforcing her belief that these *extranjeros* are *tonto* and unable to understand simple questions.

This belief in our stupidity was, in any case, planted firmly in the collective consciousness of the village one day early in our three month winter sojourn to Galicia and shortly after we had found *A Casa do Campo.*

We had been visiting the house, clearing the myriad of ancient bills (mainly unpaid), blister packs of pills (for conditions both human and animal) and old x-rays (of every conceivable part of the body...probably human) when an outrider in the form of an elderly lady on two crutches arrived to measure our worth as new neighbours.

Whether our visitor was chosen as elder of the village, or as an acceptable sacrifice should we prove hostile (after all we were the first *extranjeros* to be seen in the village – foreigners not being widespread in these parts) and what words of welcome she intended to convey we shall never know as I had chosen the precise moment of her arrival to commune with some bees in the lower field thus missing the entire exchange.

The following, therefore, is carefully transcribed from the notes Ambassador S made at the time

PLUM, COURGETTE & GREEN BEAN TART

whilst holding the banner for Britannica on this solemn and important occasion.

Visitor: (marching forward with remarkable speed on two crutches) gabble gabble gabble.

S: (at a loss) Erm

Visitor: gabble gabble

S: *No entiendo*

Visitor: gabble gabble

S: (shouting in the direction of the woods) Lisa!

Visitor: gabble gabble?

S: (increasingly frantic) Lisa! Er, *mi mujer*, (pointing to the woods).

Visitor: (comprehending) *Non entendes o Galego*? No problem I'll switch to Castilian.

S: (mumbling) Great, I still don't understand a word.

This 'conversation' apparently continued for a brief while longer in the same vein until our visitor wandered away to muse on the eccentricities of the odd but probably harmless *Ingleses* who wave their arms around, shout into thin air and make no sense at all.

I would like to say that our language skills had come on in leaps and bounds since that early exchange but cannot, in all honesty do so. I blame my school for not offering Spanish as an option. Instead we were forced to take French, which I have never got on with and German, which I enjoyed but could not get to grips with grammatically no matter how I tried, finally failing my 'O' level dismally. I did pass French but find their pronunciation bizarre. When there are ten letters in a word why would you pronounce only five of them? Spanish I love.

Before we even knew of the existence of *A Casa do Campo* we signed up for a ten week Spanish course run by our local adult education centre. Robin, our tutor, was a great chap with a marked Lancashire accent and a positive attitude, which meant he rarely corrected anyone, even on repeated mistakes. One of our number insisted, week after week, on pronouncing *aqui* (here) as akwe rather than akey. We all repeated the correct pronunciation loudly each time we had to read out a passage but Robin never once pulled him up. I often wonder how Keith fared if he ever moved to Spain. We listened to BBC videos and worked through the course book and I began to ask complicated questions which Robin related to his Spanish friend. He would return the following week with answers for me. At the end of the course Robin gave me an old and well-written book, *An Essential Course in Modern Spanish* by H. Ramsden (who I assume did not later go on to open a chip shop, though you never know) which I still have and use to this day. The course had given us a grounding but we still had a lot of work to do before we were fluent.

We also still had a lot of work to do on our *casa* and I was keen to get back into helping create our dream house from the wreck we had bought. October though was going to be a busy month for a different reason. We had our first ever visitors arriving.

Mum and my niece were coming on the 12th but first, S' best friend and D.I.Y builder extraordinaire Les was arriving on 6th October to give him a hand with the roof and a much needed boost of male technical interaction.

Monday 1st October. Cool am but sunshine later.
Dear mum,
A day of mixed fortunes today. Went into Lugo and got my 'residencia' so I'm legally here! Don't know why they couldn't give it to S as it's just a grotty piece of green paper.

PLUM, COURGETTE & GREEN BEAN TART

Think they just wanted to see us queue up for hours! The bank made a mistake with my change on paying for the certificate so 1€ up! Went to Carrefour (hypermarket) to look for an electric cooker and chest freezer. Only one cooker and it was rubbish! The electric grill element was a single piece around the very edges of the grill. Wouldn't have cooked cheese on toast! We had lunch at Carrefour... not bad surprisingly. Battered fish and chips from the self-service counter. Feels odd to have to queue for food now that we are used to being served in our seats and paying afterwards. I tried to get a new mobile as mine is on the way out but most are locked so I wouldn't be able to use my SIM card. No unlocking service here. Not often I miss the UK but can you ask Belle how much an unlocked basic mobile would be there. Maybe you could bring one over for me. Called at the catastro (land tax registry place) but they were no more help than before. Then when we arrived home there was a letter from them to say the names had been successfully changed on the computers (or whatever it is they actually do, I've no idea haha). I think that is good news!

On to meet up with the 'Brits' at the hotel. Jen has started an expat (groan) club to meet there once a month and swap books and stuff. It was nice to see people and there were some Spanish anglophiles came along too but 'expat'!!! Whilst we were there we spoke with Robin about the car insurance (well, Augusta did on our behalf!) He is coming over on Friday so that is hopeful too. Oh and I found out that the Spanish no longer issue ID cards to foreigners only this silly green paper. At least that wasn't me anyway.

S was wandering down the street this afternoon when he spotted a 50€ note, no sign of the owner of said piece of paper so 51€ up now! He has ordered his roof beams and stuff. Les is over for a fortnight from this Saturday so you will see him. They hope to get the roof started before the rains. I'm looking forward to cooking for everyone - if I can source a cooker! (The cocina stills smokes too much to be useable sadly.)

Items to bring if you can: a large refill box of peppercorns, only have the glass grinder jars here and I already have a grinder (as big as you can please); any Telegraph crosswords and a Saturday Telegraph if you can (don't mind if it's old and you have read it first); Oh and a bay cutting, mine have died, don't know why. Thank you xx

Just had a lovely tea/supper. Found 3 perfect parasol mushrooms on the way home. Fried them in butter with frizzled cheese. Delicious.

Have lots of jobs for you both. I hope you will be in charge of produce preserving. I spent 2 hours cooking and freezing and

PLUM, COURGETTE & GREEN BEAN TART

bottling apples yesterday. Have to have a go at some peaches/apricots tomorrow, they are jumping off the tree for fun. As for the walnuts, we can't peel and dry them quickly enough. My fingers are permanently stained black from the juice. Taste wonderful though. I cracked loads yesterday and did a Waldorf pasta with our apples and some blue cheese. Delicious.

Chestnuts are not quite ready but should have some for this Christmas. Do you remember the difficulty you had trying to get some in the UK for me year before last? We shouldn't have that problem here! Will need some more net bags for the walnuts, and the chestnuts if you have any old onion bags…

There will certainly be plenty of produce left for you to eat. The grapes (both white and black ones) are lovely now and we had a lettuce of our own on our butties yesterday!

I am so pleased to be home. Santiago was nice but not to live. It was too busy and noisy for me! I am too used to the quiet of the cicadas and the dark of the stars now. S has done a great job of getting the toilet in whilst I was away. It looks quite regal, sitting there behind the sofa in the living room! We have to flush it using a bucket of water as we don't have any water to it yet but it's far far better than the woods!! I should get my course results at the end of the week then I will have to see about getting some customers although I really don't have time at the moment...too busy preserving!!

Really looking forward to seeing you both. Let us know your arrival time. Thought I had a letter today but it was the one you sent last week! Hope you get this one quicker.
Love you tons and tons
Xxxxxxxxx
PS Lady at the hotel in town was very nice. I told her it was my mum and niece coming. Everyone wants to know all about us so they will try and get info out of you xx

Renovating the old and wobbly roof was to be the biggest single project we had. All 250m^2 of it! The existing roof was bowed and leaked pretty much all over. To have it reroofed professionally would have cost in the region of thirty thousand euros and taken a small army of workmen maybe a month. We expected it to take much much longer than that at a fraction of the cost. It was a daunting task.

Galician roofs come in two main types. The ones with huge grey slates are sturdy, heavy and generally less prone to leaks but a very devil to work with. Our roof is the simpler terracotta pantile type. Long, thin curved tiles are laid overlapping, the bottom layer curve down, the top one curve upwards. Traditionally they are not held together in any way and have a habit of slipping over time. They are also more brittle than slate and not suitable for walking on.

Our roof is almost square in a plan view, with a wide overhang all the way around. This overhang means that the south-facing bedrooms upstairs get

PLUM, COURGETTE & GREEN BEAN TART

the daytime sun in winter but in summer, when the sun is much higher in the sky, they remain cool. The four quarters of the roof slope upwards, the ridges almost but not quite meeting at the midline.

Diary Tuesday 2nd October Sunny
Spent the morning cleaning the terrace and shelling walnuts... should've done that the other way round, walnut shells everywhere! Planted Jasmine cutting (grown on from UK) while S constructed more of his wall to the fosa septica and backfilled the sewerage trench. S also went into town to try and get the roof permissions out of them as Les is arriving on Saturday. No one there!
Made a batch of peach puree to bottle then cleaned and reorganised the kitchen a bit. At least I did that the right way round haha. Had hosepipe shower and hairwash. Have found a bucket of clean cold water is best for wetting my hair without using up all the precious hot, and for the final rinse. Got it down to a military precision now. Dunk hair, shampoo, wet body, gel, rinse, dunk hair and pour last of cold water over head! S continued with his wall until the insulation and corrugated sheets (uralitas... little mountains) arrived.

Diary Wednesday 3rd October Cooler
Bought a cooker in Eroski at Lalín. It's a bit tinny and small but will do the job I hope. Light enough to bring back in the car. Called to see the architect again on way back. Still not had permissions signed – how long can this take really? Tried to explain our friend was visiting soon but he wasn't at all interested.
Picked walnuts endlessly until rescued by Jen and family calling to visit. Phew.

OCTOBER

Diary Friday 5th October Warm during day.
Both into town to chase roof permissions as 'L' day tomorrow. Went upstairs to the general office this time. The chica told me the permissions were in the post. I explained that we had a friend coming to help and she said we could start anyway. We need to pay the tax at the bank once we have the form then take the paid slip back to the town hall. 'Pero, se puede empezar?' I repeated back in my best mangled Castilian. 'Si, empeza,' she replied. Okay, we will.
Wood man arrived with the chestnut roof beams. Very very bent pieces. S not happy at all. The man helpfully explained that they were straight on two sides! S more worried that it will slow down the job and make fitting the polystyrene insulation (which we chose over the rockwool) between these nice wobbly beams far more difficult. Maribel called about the car insurance. Only needed our identity numbers, as Robín had lost the previous copies!
S has got some kind of lurgy. Hope it's not the hundreds of walnuts we have been eating. And I still have a cold from Santiago so we is all set for Les tomorrow then!!

Diary Saturday 6th October Sun and cloud
Got lurgy too! Great. To airport to collect Les. A bit late arriving as we had to have a couple of emergency stops on the way plus call in a pharmacy for some pills. Couldn't remember the Spanish for diarrhoea so S had to mime...
Showed Les his cave room for the duration. Just space for his sleeping bag. He hasn't run away yet so there's hope. He arrived with a carry on rucksack most of which was filled with his squeezebox! Looking forward to that!

PLUM, COURGETTE & GREEN BEAN TART

S and Les have been friends since their schooldays. They are similar in many ways. Both are quiet and self-contained, and exceedingly practical. They also work well together.

The plan was to do the roof in sections, *poco y poco,* working anti-clockwise around the house. Les was to help make a start on the north side of the roof, above the kitchen and storeroom which were most in need of waterproofing before the winter. It was also the sensible place to get on and off the roof anyway as it is only five feet high (as opposed to the rear of the house where it is a frightening thirty feet high). The joys of living in a house built into a slope.

They started by removing all the old tiles from the first section of the roof. The old pantiles are nothing like the modern orange coloured tiles that you see. These tiles were all handmade. They vary in shape from wide, shallow tiles to narrow half-moon curves. If these tiles were shaped on the legs of the workers it conjures up some interesting mental pictures. In colour, the old tiles can be anything from dark mud to pale rose and they are full of imperfections. One of the tiles has a small white stone in the centre of it, like a tiny treasure. Others have names carved into them or even verses of poetry. It is fascinating and I could look at them all day. Luckily I wasn't the one doing the roofing.

By the time they had stacked all the tiles on the ground in front of the house we were in danger of commandeering the roadway.

Next was to clean all the accumulated flotsam from the uncovered roof and cut the nice new, and exceptionally wobbly, beams to make a level framework for the *uralitas* to sit on and the polystyrene insulation to fit into. The corrugated sheets were then nailed on and bingo! One piece of roof was waterproof. It is a tad more complicated than that but the two men worked as a tight team with almost no communication seemingly needed and got on with the job.

I was general gopher. I went back and forward into town for a sharp knife and for essential doughnuts. Back into town for nails and for sandpaper. The sandpaper was for me. I was keeping busy sanding down one of the sweet chestnut doors from the house. These were all filthy but sanded to a beautiful shine. I also had fun making a rustic bookcase from an old trunk we had found in the open loft space above our living room. It had some odd square cut-outs along one long edge and it took me a while to work out why. In the same space was a pile of old currants such as those produced by rabbits. The trunk had been used as a rabbit hutch! If it seemed an odd place to keep rabbits I was beginning to learn that nothing was beyond possibility. It did have the benefit of keeping predators away I guess! Cleaned up with some homemade shelves the trunk made a fine bookcase.

§

Les was staying with us, despite our lack of facilities, to be on the doorstep so to speak. We had had to find him a space. The only relatively waterproof and draught proof area left was the small attic room which was, at that time, piled with boxes and virtually inaccessible.

With some effort we had managed to stack the containers into a teetering three box high wall of cardboard all around a small, sleeping bag sized hole which would be Les' home for the following two weeks. It was hot and claustrophobic and of course our facilities were somewhat lacking in home comforts. Worse yet, just before Les left us, the two men put the corrugated sheets right across the single, tiny piece of glass which had, up until that point, been the only source of light in the room. Les would be sleeping in complete darkness. In return, he did play his squeeze box from the early hours. The same notes, over and over.

By the following Friday, when mum and Belle were due to arrive, the men had stripped off and replaced the first three sections of the roof. To celebrate we decided to have the day off. The men from roofing and me from endlessly picking walnuts which, if I didn't collect them every evening had nice little mouse holes in them by the next day.

Diary Friday 12th October Hot
Day off for all! To airport to collect mum and Belle. Flight ½ hour late. Drove into Santiago for lunch at Manolo's and to introduce mum to my ex-landlady. Pilar was very pleased to see me and to meet mum. Wouldn't let us pay for our teas. We went for a walk along the river and around the park. Very enjoyable day. And we brought 4 pieces of chicken home from lunch.
Dropped mum and Belle at hotel Santa Lucia in town after first checking everything was okay. Clean rooms and nicely decorated. Lady speaks no English. Very friendly though, quizzing mum endlessly! Left the ladies to shower and change then returned to collect them for a tour of the property. Mum says it looks quite homely now and admitted when she first saw it she thought we would never be able to live here (not that she had said anything at the time of course!). Back into town for drinks and tapas in Scala bar.

Mum and my niece arrived to the excitement of the town. More English were moving in! First a fisherman, then a chap on his own. An older lady, then two women buying up the town. Actually, they were all us. Les wore a fisherman's style shirt and

OCTOBER

had popped into town a couple of times, mum and Belle loved looking round the shops.

There seemed to be no language barriers for mum who continued to speak English (as her only language) to everyone she met and, amazingly, found people to speak back to her in the same language. Maybe rusty, but perfectly understandable, English.

As I'd hoped, mum got stuck into preserving our crops. Between the three of us we picked four huge tubs of cooking apples from the ancient tree on the allotment. The best ones were put into boxes, separated by paper collars and stored in the barn below the house. This is an ideal storeroom as the temperature remains constant all year round, cool, dry and dark. The rest, mum cut and froze either raw or pureed. We would have apples for a good long time.

Belle meanwhile wanted to get stuck into some demolition work. First she knocked some of the plaster off the terrace wall but I felt that wasn't sufficiently exciting for her.

Diary Monday 15th October Hot
Mum and Belle stayed in town for some shopping and a look round. Much to the locals delight. Think that between us all we have doubled the income of certain bars and shops this last couple of months. I dug a bit of the allotment and collected and shelled walnuts whilst S and L... yes, continued on the roof!
All walked into town to meet the ladies for lunch. Excellent menú at Anduriña. Probably the best paella I've tasted followed by medallions of pork fillet and some excellent homemade puddings. Good wine too!
All walked back to the house after lunch. Got Belle to knock down the old bathroom in the upstairs hallway. Can't believe how much lighter and

bigger the hall looks without it. The tiny narrow bathroom was obviously an afterthought, stuck in a corner as it was. Its presence made the hall seem so dark and claustrophobic and dare I say, spooky! Now it's an actual room (5m x 2.5m so not small at all). Waited 'til Belle had knocked most of the walls down then said we didn't want it done after all!! Luckily she didn't believe me. We both cleared out the rubble. Such a pointless bathroom really with no piped water. A concrete shower tray without a plughole. A sink that emptied into the toilet to flush it, (clever idea but without any water how would you use it?) And a toilet which emptied onto the back garden. Glad to be rid of it. Kept the rather evil looking multi-coloured dolly head toothbrush holder as a souvenir. Suggested to S we could use the WC as a planter but he wasn't impressed, no sense of style! Mum cut apricots to dry in the sunshine then created a small garden for the Buddleia and Ceanothus cuttings near to the hórreo. Looks good.
Into town in the evening for showers (courtesy of the hotel) and vinos.

I drove mum and Belle back to Santiago on the Thursday evening whilst the men continued on the roof. Driving to and from the airport was fine until I got to the automatic ticket machine to exit the car park. I hadn't realised our left hand drive car meant I was on the wrong side. I had to get out and run around the car to insert the ticket then dash back before the barrier closed again!

It had been a lovely long weekend with many laughs and plenty of good food and drink. I had managed a full Sunday lunch on the new electric cooker: locally sourced pork with our own apples, roasted, and some chestnuts mum and Belle had picked. Dessert was apple, blackberry and apricot crumble, all hand-picked by my willing helpers. We had shared our custom around the local bars and the local eateries. Most often we brought leftovers home from our meals for use another day. The sun had kindly shone every day whilst our visitors were here. Les left on the Saturday after a final evening of farewell drinks with our star worker – even if I did send him down the track to practice with his squeezebox (to the bemusement of the neighbours). The first part of the roofing project was complete and the kitchen was waterproof. S felt confident to continue alone. *Poco y poco.*

They had done well.

Diary Sunday 21st October Sunny
Up late! No visitors. Fried eggs on toast for lazy relaxed breakfast. Aired bedding. Continued to dig allotment and broke hoe again! Ground is a bit solid. It should be easier after we have some rain. Bought paint and rollers for the kitchen walls. May as well brighten it up in there.
Lunch: Left over Manolo's chicken and dried apricot stew. Very tasty!
Had a visit from a Spanish/Israeli couple from the village over the hill. Said they wanted to introduce themselves then asked if we knew where the new road was going. Have no idea what they were talking about but remembered J&R mentioning something near to them so maybe that was it. Seemed a nice couple. Don't live here permanently.
Cool in the evening. Needed a blanket over our knees in living room.

The following week we decided to attempt to sort out registering the house at the land registry in Chantada once more. They seemed oddly content with the paperwork S had finally wangled out of the *catastro*. We were told that they were actually speaking with the *catastro* office (a miracle in itself) and to be patient as everything would be okay.

We went straight to a café for hot chocolates as a celebration of almost sorting something out relating to paperwork! Buoyed by our success we visited the woodyard to order some 'straight' chestnut beams for the next bit of the roof. We also tried to visit Toldao, the window place, to see what was happening with our order but it was closed. Still, we figured two out of three ain't bad.

Thursday 25th October. Warm and sunny am. Bit of cloud and breeze now.
Dear Mum,
Definitely more autumnal. The leaves are changing colour (looks beautiful across the valley) and we had a frost this morning but it is warm during the day and we are still sitting out on the terrace to eat so we are happy!
Just received your parcel. The postie was shouting for ages before we realised he actually wanted us. Thank you for all the goodies. You could've flown back with the peppercorns nearly as cheaply though - and then you could've helped finish off dinner!
We have had beef stew with the leftovers from the grill place we visited in San Martiño with you all and some tiny new potatoes which I dug up this morning on the allotment. S reckons they will be a whole new variety of spud after 12 years of growing undisturbed over there... certainly tasty enough; followed by apple sponge (as a

change from baked apples and apple crumble) with caramel sauce. Plenty left, wish you could fly from East Mids still, you could come back and help with the produce. I'm missing my sous chef.

I have made the apple and apricot 'cheese' we found in that recipe book and made some into muesli bars. They are drying in the sun together with the last of the apricots you cut up (those are delicious in a chicken casserole). I'm going to try and get some vinegar for an apple and walnut chutney… since we have plenty of both! Tell Belle, the cooking apples are still on the tree. Doesn't look like we actually picked any!

We had 30min of drizzle yesterday and it is noticeably cooler in the house in the evening but the ground is still really dry on the allotment. S is back playing on the roof. I have started clearing that brambly patch at the side of the terrace next to where my chickens will go. Lots of black grapes growing down there so we are going to put a low trellis up for them and I've cut all the rubbish (brambles and ivy) off the pear tree. We also decided to give the kitchen a coat of paint (special offer at the ironmongers) as we will be living with it as it is for a while yet. And who knows, it may encourage the cocina to work!!

Later: Just had a lukewarm shower. Must remember to have one earlier now the sun is lower as my hosepipe was in the shade before

PLUM, COURGETTE & GREEN BEAN TART

I got to it. Just having a cup of tea on the terrace and tasting our muesli bars (pronounced delicious by us both).

It must be roofing time of year as Carmen is having her barn roof done now. One of the chaps asked if he could take some photos of our house to show his wife!! Said yes as he didn't <u>look</u> like he was snooping for the town hall. Anyway they did tell us to start on the roof. Not our fault if the post is so slow haha.

We have also had fun with the electricity people... again. Our friend (who pinched our chariot and lent us the gas bottle) turned up on Tuesday clutching another electricity bill with his address on it. I explained that we had tried to change the details and we agreed to meet at the bank on Wednesday to sort it out. The chap at the bank seemed very unconcerned that the bank account paying the bill was in the name of a dead person (Pegarto has been gone for 12 years I think) but when we checked the bill against the first one we realised they were two different meter numbers. The first bill wasn't for this house at all but another one he looks after. The second one meanwhile had our correct meter number on it. (We had tried to point out to the lady at the electric office that the meter numbers were different the first time we went but she dismissed it.) He only noticed because the second bill was for 21€

(for two months) rather than the standing charge only on an empty property. We ended up all going to the electricity office to swap all the names around. That was fun in itself because the computer had apparently somehow altered all the details for a number of houses he looks after when we changed the first bill. His name is Sergio, he is 73 and very sprightly and knows all about cholesterol and cows, and claims Galegos live long lives because of the healthy lifestyle and lack of pollution. We hope we managed to get everything sorted this time. We paid him the 21€ and he bought the coffees so that's ok!
Love you tons
Xxxxxx
PS Got another bill Friday!!
Addendum October 30th.

Took me so long to get some stamps (our post office only opens 11 'til 1 and I keep missing it) I thought you may as well get a bit extra so I reopened the envelope!

It has been another lovely day though the valley is altering daily now as the leaves change colour. The chestnut trees are still green but many of the fruit trees have lovely red and yellow leaves and of course the pines stand out now above the bare trunks. It's really beautiful. Wish I could paint! (Artistically that is, the kitchen is coming on nicely with my new white rollered walls.)

S is still roofing. He's doing the bit over the

PLUM, COURGETTE & GREEN BEAN TART

bathroom to be and the guest bedroom on the west side. I've been clearing around the chicken shed (for my future hens) after we fixed up those vines with a trellis. I filled a big bucket with glass jars (buried) and medication bottles (animal I think) and 3 packets of unopened tablets which I guess Pegarto didn't want, unless they were for animals too!

Also decided to light the stove again. We've cemented up as much as we can but it still smokes like Billy O. On the up side the kitchen is toasty warm and just about breathable if you stay seated. And it has made a lovely pea, jamón and mint soup on the top. We have put some porridge in the oven to cook overnight. Just a shame we smell like we have been to a bonfire party!

Still lots of apples on, getting through my recipes. Yesterday I made some grape jelly and a spiced apple cake (using bicarb and no egg, very tasty). Had baked apples with pork on Sunday and an apple charlotte. Still enjoying the red apples and the chestnuts, and the walnuts!

Made 3 jars of apple, walnut and apricot (in lieu of dates) chutney. Looks good. We have dug quite a bit of the allotment now. Must decide what seeds I need. Still digging up spuds as I go. Best view of any allotment when I stop for a breather. So amazingly beautiful. Think I could just stare at the changing scenery every day! I keep digging up praying mantis(es). They must hibernate underground. They don't look happy anyway!

Our clocks went back too on Sun so we are still an hour ahead. Dark just before 7pm now so we are getting up earlier to catch the daylight. Thinking about a stove in the sitting room to take off the chill.
Love you tons and tons
Xxxx

Diary Wednesday 31ˢᵗ October Warm
Continued with painting the kitchen walls. Looking so much cleaner and brighter. Like it. Made another apple cake for the freezer and re-boiled the grape jelly (hadn't set). Added some lemon juice for acidity and a bit of apple puree for pectin. Seems okay now.
S found dead rat (very dead and very old) to put into the septic tank as a starter culture... nice! After enjoying himself with dead beasties he carried on roofing over the bathroom. Had lukewarm shower again. Must think up something better for winter or we'll freeze!!
Vinos in Bar Mencia this evening. Chatted to Luisa and her husband. They keep pigs and sheep and goats and she has lots of recipes to share with me. Explained about our problems with the Repsol gas people who won't give us a contract unless we knock a huge hole in the kitchen wall... as if we need any more holes in there!! She said she would send the Galp man round who would 'sort it out'. Such wonderfully kind people here in Galicia. Luisa loves to get me to practice my Castillano then, when I think I've got it, she says something very quickly in Galego and shouts 'entendes?' and falls about laughing!

PLUM, COURGETTE & GREEN BEAN TART

I don't mind being the butt of her jokes if she keeps talking to me and letting me practice. I just wait on the day I can really answer her question with a 'yes! Of course I understand!!'

NOVEMBER
Walking over chestnuts

November is sweet chestnut month in central Galicia. No sooner have the walnuts started to fade than the blue chestnut buckets appear.

It started innocently enough that first year. Pepe, who owns the chestnut grove next to our small patch of four trees, asked if we had enough chestnuts. We honestly replied that we hadn't picked any yet (although from inertia rather than a lack of chestnuts to pick). He then kindly urged us to pick his chestnuts as he didn't live nearby.

We did think we were buying that chestnut grove with the house of course and had even worked out our possible income from it. Mark, the estate agent, had said we could get five thousand euros a year. Chestnuts fetch around one euro a kilo or twenty euros a sack full. We would have to pick around 250 sacks of *castañas* over the four week picking season to reach Mark's estimation. That's ten sacks a day. I didn't feel that was possible somehow. Concha carried two at a time, four or six a day, but what hard work.

If I close my eyes I can see my neighbour now, marching up the track, one sack slung over her right shoulder, another held in her left hand almost dragging on the ground, shouting to someone out of frame. The shouting becomes stationary. Concha is standing near to our other neighbour, Carmen, chatting about this and that with the sack still on her shoulder. I really don't know how she manages it. She is smaller than me – and I'm only 5'2" in stockinged feet – but has a strength that is quite frightening. I have a job to get myself up that hill never mind lugging two sacks of chestnuts. It must be all that *Galego* fresh air and hearty *Galego* fare.

Concha called me over one day whilst I was in the allotment. I meekly complied and after a bit of confusion – the volume does something to my translation abilities, puts them into meltdown I think – Concha eventually showed me what she meant. She was telling us to pick the chestnuts from a small grove below my allotment belonging to Marina (a friend/ neighbour/ cousin/ who knows?) from the next village who had told her to 'tell the English'.

We, of course, didn't pick those chestnuts either. We had a roof to fit and a thousand other jobs and chestnuts just didn't seem that important.

Diary Thursday 1ˢᵗ November Heavy frost. Sunny during day
Went to the market in Monterroso. Special one for All Saints Day (Todos Santos), the Feira do Ganadeiros (farmer's market). We just missed it last year when we had the flat there. It is the biggest market of the year with horses, cows, pigs, sheep, rabbits, chickens and all sorts of exotic birds; stalls along every single street as far as the eye can see and people everywhere!! There are as many pulpo stalls as clothes stalls. Most of them have set up outside a derelict shop front and put tables and benches inside for customers. A few have a menú and price board up but most don't. Lovely cow and calf at the animal bit but S said no. They <u>were</u> cute. Bought a lemon tree, honey, and a car foot pump, as tyre has a very slow puncture. Had pulpo and churrasco at one of the

pop up stalls for 20€. There were coaches coming and disgorging customers all over. One lady told me (over a rather closer than I would have liked coffee) that they had come from A Coruña, a hundred kilometres away, on a coach trip. Spent another 50€ at the 'pound' shop... on what I've no idea. Luckily shops were shut back here so couldn't spend any more. Phew!

Sunday November 4th Warm and sunny afternoons. Misty & frosty mornings. Clear and cold overnight.
Last of apples picked, walnuts in 7-8 bags hanging in the barn. Chestnuts to come - orders for Christmas welcome!
Dear mum,
 I think the population here is obsessed with chestnuts. First Pepe then Sergio exhort us to pick their chestnuts. Carmen and Concha collect bucketfuls and sackfuls a day, then last night we were happily supping vino in Scala when one of the regulars burst in declaring 'free chestnuts in the market square'. 'Free!' He repeated as we carried on supping. After a couple of false starts (the main act, the sweet chestnuts, didn't arrive until after 10pm) We were finally dragged outside, still gamely trying to finish our wine as the bar emptied and we all trooped the 30 yards to the square where a feast had been laid out. Hot roasted chestnuts, a cask of really rather good vino and virtually the entire population of the town were waiting! After the chestnuts someone arrived with a

PLUM, COURGETTE & GREEN BEAN TART

van full of lemony sponge cake! The dancing only really got going at 11 as we were thinking of leaving but we managed a quick something step before retiring gracefully to watch the light footed 80 year olds gliding around the concrete floor to the beats of salsa far into the evening. Isn't it wonderful that so many people can get together and make a party out of chestnuts and wine? Of course after our friend from the bar had initially seen us settled with food and drink, every time we stopped eating or drinking someone else plied us with 'eat, drink, dance!' So we did, to the pleasure of all concerned!

I can't believe it's November already. It's still so warm in the sun and the crickets are still chirping. The wasps and hornets are getting dopey on the grape juice. The hornets fight like old drunks, rolling around on the ground trying to sting each other. Belle would need to beware of her bare feet at the moment. One of the hornets got me yesterday. My fault, it must've been on my sleeve and I squashed him as I bent my arm! A bit sore but no side effects thankfully. Sadly can't say the same for the hornet.

I have been labelling all my produce jars. I have 4 plum, 2 greengage, 2 fig, 1 sloe and 1 nectarine jam (S did those last two); 3 chutneys; 2 grape jelly (very good with lamb); 5 bottled plums and a bottled fig.

NOVEMBER

My little cubbyhole in the kitchen is filling up nicely!

I made a chicken casserole with walnuts and grapes for dinner and a bread and butter pudding with apples and raisiny grapes for afters. Very tasty. The apple and walnut cake worked well and I've made a walnut loaf for a change of bread.

Forgot to say the vino situation is becoming critical. Since your goodbye kiss from José we hadn't seen much of him and thought we had sorted out who owed what to whom! He was in Scala last weekend but luckily we were just leaving so declined a wine. Friday we pub crawled from Mencia to the Jema where Sergio was playing dominos. Before we had sat down the barman said Sergio 'invitados' (had invited us and paid for the wine). We had just got a second one when José walked in. Sergio chatted to us a bit then left. The barman said José wanted to buy us a wine. We said no thanks as this was two and we had to work tomorrow. When we went up to pay for the second round we were told Sergio had paid for both lots. Now they are fighting over paying for our drinks... when they are not free in the square anyway! Still, who's complaining? Not us!

I'm writing this sitting outside but it's a bit cool as the sun has disappeared over the hill. Thinking of buying a wood burner for the living room as it's getting a bit nippy in there of an evening now. We will pop into the ferreteria tomorrow. We have nicknamed it Arkwright's as the owner is the spitting image of Ronnie Barker in 'Open all Hours'. Pepe (his real name) wears a blue overall and constantly rubs his hands together in anticipation of a sale. He will never willingly let a customer escape without buying something, even if it isn't what you actually went in for!! CJ says he went in last week for something and Pepe was trying to sell him some of those medical type, thin gloves. CJ said no thank you but Pepe insisted he try them. As you know, CJ has large, blacksmith's hands. He said the glove sat on one finger looking ridiculous. Pepe's comment? 'Perfect'!!

Love you

Xxxxxx

P.S Thank you for your package. Postie obviously couldn't get in the gate or make us hear so had walked all the way round and left it on the table on the terrace. That's service! I've planted the house leeks and campanula in that little triangle near the terrace.

The chestnut party was fabulous fun but I did feel we had somehow failed the chestnut appreciation test. It seemed that everyone else was out picking *castañas.*

Locals picked from dawn till dusk. Granny came with her sticks and her blue bucket. The buckets have to be blue. I tried using a green bucket one year and was almost run out of town! Kids joined in after school. Sacks were slung over shoulders or onto creaking tractors. Outsiders even came for day trips to collect windfalls from the track and take back to their city apartments, to roast over a gas hob and show their city friends how rural they were. Our beautiful red squirrels appeared after everyone had gone home for the day to take the leftovers to bury for the winter. The quiet of the ancient chestnut groves was broken by the bellowing of tractors, the shouting of the pickers and the tramping of many feet.

We meanwhile, were roofing and painting.

A van arrived to collect the bulging sacks lined up proudly outside the neighbours' doorways. I heard a beep of a horn and went outside to investigate.

"*Castañas!*" the van driver shouted, looking for our sacks.

"*Ah, no tenemos,*" I replied.

He glared rather alarmingly so I refrained from explaining why we didn't have any. I felt he wouldn't be interested.

The chestnuts go off to the local co-op to be made into puree, *marrons glacé* and brandied chestnuts and exported to France, Britain and Spain (yes, Spain is considered an export - we are Galician, not Spanish). I vowed to make more of an effort – soon.

Diary Monday 5th November Mist 'til noon then warm.
Late up...like a second Sunday! Into town to sort out the sections for the chimney if we decide to order the wood burning stove from Arkwright. Not possible to do what we want with the bits he has (we only want to put a chimney through the ceiling and the roof... doesn't everyone?). Had a tea and a bun in a café whilst S thought through his alternatives. When we returned CJ and Gala

were in there too. Gala kindly helped translate what we wanted. S reckons he can put the chimney through the wall instead.
Did a rather hot chilli for lunch. S was very brave and ate it all!
Washed bedding and had a 'bath' outside in the big plastic tub whilst S carried on roofing. Luisa had sent the Galp man as promised to 'inspect' the gas. He arrived at around 6pm. Angel is a lovely, chain-smoking, quietly spoken man who waved his cigarette around and tested the gas by holding his lighter underneath the tube... yup, that would find a leak alright. Luckily there weren't any (at least we didn't find ourselves in a puddle of broken glass on the lawn) so he said we could have a contract for him to supply the butane bottles from now on and told us he would visit every 15 days to see if we needed a new bottle. Sold us a second bottle so we have a spare when we return Sergio's to him. Will bring contract in a couple of weeks. That was easy then!!

Diary Wednesday 7th November Hot pm
Picked walnuts and some chestnuts... to the pleasure of the villagers. 'I do believe she's got it!!' Went into town for more strimmer wire and nails for the roof. The old lady at Arkwright's doesn't like to sell me a whole box of nails... 'That's a kilo,' she says, 'a lot of nails.' I know, we are using a lot of nails. 'How many do you want? I can count them.' Nope, don't think so, I've watched her do just that, it's as exciting as watching a snail cross the road, and more painful. We nearly had a tussle over the box before I managed to wrestle it from her grasp and hand over the cash. Think she misses the excitement of wrapping the individual nails in those pieces of newspaper kept on the counter for the sole purpose.

NOVEMBER

Our new straight roof beams arrived at 7pm. Lovely and straight and three times the price of the wobbly ones! Still, S is happy.

Diary Saturday 10th November Mist and sun.
One year since we arrived for our winter in Galicia. Had boiled eggs for breakfast a day early to celebrate! S cemented his box at the top of the leach field... no I don't know what for, I try not to ask! Pruned apricot and apple trees.
Into town for vinos, walking over chestnuts as we went. They squish alarmingly in the dark.

Monday 12th November. Sunny and warm during the day, Up to 18°. T shirt weather! Cold and clear overnight. Lots of stars and frosty sprinklings in the mornings. No rain but we don't mind 'til the roof is watertight!
Dear Mum,
 This is when we realise how high up we are, relatively, at 500m. Very frosty overnight now, we have to drain the hosepipe as it froze the other day... but during the day, temperatures soar to 18°C easily. Still warm enough for our Sunday boiled eggs to be served on the terrace! It is quite strange but very pleasant. The weathermen say we probably won't have any rain until December now. That would be fine by us as in another 2 weeks the 'bathroom' and the end 'bedroom' should be waterproof. I've even been promoted to roof tiler! I've done the North side as far as I can (we still need a walkway over to the south side) and it looks pretty good! Eusebio gave us a thumbs

up and Carmen was amazed. 'You know how to do this?' she asked. It's a big jigsaw really!

We would have been further along had we not had so many visitors this week. Cris & Steve, who are going to help us find out about transferring the car over to Spanish plates, visited just as I was about to have a hosepipe shower. The next day Jen and her dad came bearing scones just as I was having a shower! S was on the roof so managed to divert them and keep them chatting until I had made myself decent haha. CJ also came over with a new couple who are buying in the next village and have kids. Luckily I was dressed by then! It's good to have so many people visit. Though I suppose a real bathroom would occasionally have its advantages!

We have bought our wood burner for the living room. It looks very nice sitting in the corner of the room... will look even nicer when it is functioning! S is busy trying to make a hole in the (what we thought was a flimsy brick) wall. The bricks are flimsy but the concrete render is solid, his hammer drill won't touch it so he is having to hack away with his rather overused chisel!

The builder's merchant José (a rather overused name here I feel) has promised to send someone to look at the cocina for us too so we live in hope. He also gave us 2 big umbrellas so maybe he knows something

NOVEMBER

about the weather that we don't!

Bought a lovely piece of marble for the stove to sit on. It's a really pretty green with darker flecks and was cut and polished for us while we waited. They had a lovely black fleck granite for a worktop. I could've stayed all day in there looking round. An amazing red piece, huge it was and would look great on the bathroom wall (S says what would we stick it up with? Spoilsport) Anyway you get the idea. Will take you to visit next time you are over. Pity you can't take a piece back on the plane for a pastry board.

Wednesday 8pm Toasty warm in the living room with the new fire roaring. Sitting watching the flames.

S spent all yesterday fitting the stove and hanging off ladders to fit the shiny new chimney. He cemented the hole through the wall this morning and we lit it at 7.30pm. It got warm very quickly and with _no_ smoke (unlike the kitchen which I also lit today and which also got lovely and warm but which unfortunately was also lovely and smoky). At least we have one warm and useable room and no blanket needed on us legs!

Tomorrow is the anniversary of the first time we viewed the house so we are going out for a meal... not decided where yet. It will also be 99 days since we moved in. Feels like we have been here for ever already. I

PLUM, COURGETTE & GREEN BEAN TART

can't imagine living anywhere else now. I was cleaning my teeth in the garden under the stars last night and couldn't remember the last time I had cleaned them in a bathroom. So much nicer under the stars anyway.

S is still on the roof with his nice straight beams for the framework. They have now given rain for tomorrow (though they said December!!) so he is battling to waterproof as much as possible. I have been digging more of the allotment. Almost down to the cooking apple tree. I will start marking out beds tomorrow and look at what seeds I need.

Love you tons and tons from a very cosy Casa do Campo

Xxxxxx

One of the many things which endeared me to *A Casa do Campo* was the remote piece of land across the sunken track to the east of our house. This I knew, would be my allotment or *huerta*. It had obviously been used as a vegetable plot in the past but when we first viewed the house it was thigh high with grass and innumerable weeds. We had started digging on sunny days during our winter in Galicia. During the summer the ground had baked dry and formed a solid, impenetrable pan. As we had more urgent things to do in those long, hot days I had left working on my allotment until it was cooler. November seemed a good month to get digging again.

My plot was 1500m^2 of tall grasses and interesting weeds. At the top was a walnut tree and a yellow cherry. Down the eastern boundary with Carmen's *huerta* were more fruit trees; apple, peach, plum, nectarine and another walnut tree, growing at a most peculiar angle as if it wanted to touch the river fifty metres downslope. An old but prolific cooking apple and a tangled vine completed the east side. The southern boundary was a line of tall, unpruned chestnut trees. Beyond that was a further overgrown plot of land belonging to we knew not who.

The sunken track, which runs down to the river, forms the western boundary of the allotment with an ivy-clad stone wall and another walnut tree alongside it. It also had a rampant patch of brambles threatening to engulf the lot.

I had tried asking one of our neighbours if he wanted to cut the grass for silage for his cows. The look he gave me, before politely refusing, suggested it was not quite the quality feed he was looking for. So, digging by hand it was.

It was hard work. I had to dig through the mat of twitch grass and other pernicious weeds, take the sod off and invert it on to an ever rising compost pile to allow it to rot and form some nice loam for next year. Then I had to remove all the remaining roots and weeds before moving along to the next sod of grass.

One particular variety of Galician grass is almost impossible to eliminate by hand. This grass grows from small nodules or bulbs which are easy to leave behind. In the dry summer months when all the grass frizzles to a wan brown the little nodules store the necessary food for the plant until the rains bring it alive again. If one of these nodules is left in the soil it will soon regrow forming a thick thatch of grass. Bending down and removing all these nodules was back breaking. I had dug around 30m downhill so far. When I got tired of digging, I would stop and gaze up the valley at the most beautiful view I could imagine. Beyond our house the valley climbs through chestnut woods to the next village, perched high on the hill beyond. The trees were rainbow hued in the autumn sun, the sky a clear blue above. That sight was worth taking a rest for.

Now S had fitted our shiny new stove in the living room he was continuing to dig his leach field. This is a run-off from the septic tank to filter away liquid via a leaky hose. Without getting into the smelly complexities of sewage (I suggest the more sensitive reader moves along at this point), the septic tank separates out solids, which sink to the bottom of the tank, and liquids which pass through a carbon filter (the concrete box that S had been building) and into the leaky hose. From here the liquid 'leaches' out slowly into the surrounding earth, quietly and, we hoped, non-pungently. I was told the leach field had to be 30m long according to some expert somewhere. The way he was going it would be in Eusebio's field soon enough.

Diary Thursday 15th November Mist am, rain pm.
One year since we first saw A Casa do Campo, on a day very similar to this!! Also 99 days since we moved in so a celebration was in order!
Went out to lunch at San Martiño, just outside Taboada. Good parillada grill then had a drive out to the Club Nautico overlooking the river Miño and the big iron bridge. Beautiful setting at the edge of the river. There were a few canoes and small boats around but it was sadly closed today. Then to Toldao to check our windows (well, worth a shot). They have the kitchen window made and are awaiting the glass. Quite positive then! Saw the window and it looked good... if glassless.
Lit a bonfire in the rain and burnt all the brambly bits from the garden. Only rained about an hour and didn't really wet the ground. Lit the new

stove (which behaves perfectly and doesn't smoke) and had an early night listening to music by the fire.

Monday 19*th* November *Mild and somewhat damp! Warm in between the showers. Thankful for the stove to dry our clothes!*
Dear Mum
   Looks like we shall have to stop being smug about our weather. It has rained constantly for the last 48 hours! A small section of the landing ceiling (over the ex-bathroom that Belle knocked down) collapsed in disgust and the floors in the bathroom to be and the end bedroom are soggy... due to there not being a roof over them! Luckily only 2 drips in the living room; one in the corner which S fixed and one coming down the outside of our new chimney (self-inflicted then!).
   We went over to Jen's this afternoon as they also had leaks and called in the 'A' team. S moved a tile or two and put a bucket in the loft. Need to go back and look when it's not raining. Got a shower and a lemon drizzle cake in recompense so seemed fair! On the up side, my newly sown green manure won't need watering in.
   Yesterday we were here minding our own business when a van comes into the village like a bat out of hell, pulls up and out jumps a chap armed with a rifle who runs into our garden. Being rural Spain of course this

wasn't a heist but a hunter in pursuit of his prey!

Now I have no objection to hunting (and wouldn't say no to a bit of wild boar if offered) but this is our house so... S went over to politely tell him not to trample the garden and the man shushed him!! Well, that did me, shushing my fella on our own land. So I laid into him. 'No hunting, this is my garden, you get out... go! go! go!' I kept saying. I don't think he'd ever faced an irate woman before, he scuttled off, head down, saying 'perdone, perdone'. Quite right. Anyway we walked into town for a drink later and on the way back it was very dark and I kept hearing snuffling and started thinking about S' namesake in 'The Thornbirds' being gored by a maddened wild boar. Ugh!

Tuesday: Gala tells me the hunters use their local bar and one of them, called Suso, was telling how he met a mad English woman at the weekend. 'Oh that will be our friend Lisa' said Gala. Looks like I'm famous haha.

Only showers today so managed to move 16 barrowfuls of rabbit/goat muck out of the big barn onto my cabbage patch to be. Concha stopped me and kindly pointed out that I was too late for planting now. I said 'primavera' (spring) loudly and she seemed happy! Also bumped into her this morning on the way to the shops. She was chatting to a girl in a car (possibly the vet) - in the middle of the road. I stopped the car, smiled and nodded and they kept chatting. I crept a bit closer and waved my hand. They waved back and carried on so I edged right up to the car. Concha came over and yelled 'Tienes prisa?' Are you in a hurry? Weeeell not really but I would like to get into town before the shops shut for lunch so on balance 'Si!' Just as well as they were still chatting (in the middle of the road) when I came back half an hour later. 'These English, always in a hurry, always busy. Tut tut!'

S has managed to get the section of the roof over the bed/bathroom more or less watertight now after a small setback this morning when his box of tools went skiing all the way off the highest point of the roof and onto the grass/stone below. His old Black and Decker drill miraculously still works as does the battery one, though the casing is cracked, and his glasses were fine in their metal case. I was on the allotment at the time and had a moment of panic as I heard a slither and an 'Oh no!' As I said to him, 'that's just the sort of over-exaggerated comment I would expect from you if it had been you slipping off the roof!!'

Wednesday. It's raining again! S has re-cemented round the chimney in the living room so fingers crossed it won't leak anymore. I managed to finish my allotment pathway of old magazines and straw, and

PLUM, COURGETTE & GREEN BEAN TART

to muck the onion patch with another four barrow loads of manure (very old and very dried) out of the barn, in between the showers. We also finally got that old stone trough out of the storeroom and just outside the terrace gate using old bed spindles (the woodwormy ones) as runners. Them there Egyptians knew a thing or two. Just need to get it up the slope (which currently resembles a river), through the gate and down the road to the other barn door. We couldn't go the short route through the barn as the step out of the storeroom that side is now far too high even for Egyptian technology.

That reminds me, this morning we heard a thump from the road and ran outside to find a huge stone had slipped down the banking from the chestnut grove opposite and rolled across the road to just next to the old washing trough. Remind me not to park the car that side! We're not moving it!!
Love you tons and tons
Xxxxxxxx
P.S Just found a salamander on the track as we were outside cleaning our teeth before bed. Brought him into the kitchen so I could take some photos for identification before letting him waddle off. So beautiful.

Diary Friday 23rd November Cloudy but dry
Up and straight to Jen's. S spent all day on <u>her</u> roof! Given lunch in exchange and returned home

around 5.30pm. Played scrabble and tried to get warm. Fire doesn't seem to be heating the room up tonight.

Diary Monday 26th November Sunny but strong wind
To Toldao to check window status! Showed us the nice kitchen window again (still sin glass). Said glass maybe arriving on Dec 3rd. Have no green aluminium for the other windows and don't know when that may arrive. They said 'perhaps a month, mas o menos.' Mmm, 'more or less' sounds dodgy.
Back to town rather dispirited. Wish we could ship out our window guy from Rochdale. Absolutely positive it didn't take him this long to make a window!
Bought a new outside tap at the construction yard and asked José about the guys coming to look at the kitchen range. He kindly rang them and said they would be over in the afternoon (they weren't).
Made 3 apple and walnut cakes and some walnut candy from dad's old 'Chocolates, Sweets and Toffees' book (funny that he never ever cooked but loved making sweets). S carried on making frames for mid-section of the south roof over the 'tool' room.

Diary Tuesday 27th November Sunny
Man arrived to inspect the chimney around 5pm. He lit it and of course there was smoke everywhere. Muttered '¡no tira!' continually under his breath then said we needed a fan in the chimney and to make an angle of 45° at the base of the chimney as it is too square. Frankly, that sounds like rot but what do we have to lose? Said he would return tomorrow and left us with a nice smoky kitchen.

PLUM, COURGETTE & GREEN BEAN TART

Diary Wednesday 28th November Mist and cloud. Cooler.
Men arrived (not same man as yesterday) to look at the chimney and to um and err a lot. Brought a sack of plaster stuff with them. Mixed the tiny bit they needed to change the angle of the flue at the bottom of the chimney then threw the rest of the sack into the store room. S managed to rescue most of it after they had gone. They broke the piece of metal covering the flue on the floor so made a cover out of a tile they wandered off to find. One grabbed our Telegraph crossword to light and stick down the flue (until I wrestled it off him) and then used about half a bottle of extra virgin olive oil to loosen the damper plate half way up the wall. When I managed to rescue my olive oil and throw him a sarcastic 'Gracias' he just replied 'de nada'. Note to self... sarcasm is wasted on Galegos.
Fire still smoked of course. The men said we needed a new stove, or a taller chimney or a fan in the base of the chimney or that the boss will be back tomorrow. Great, look forward to it, thanks... oops more sarcasm!

Diary Friday 30th November Mist am
Jefe didn't turn up yesterday about the cocina. Didn't think he would somehow. Up early to drop Jen at the airport. Left us with a key and a list of jobs to do at her house.
Piddled making lunch (beef stew and apple tart) and cracking walnuts for cakes. Carmen appeared carrying a large tray of roasted chestnuts and exhorting us to 'eat them while they are hot'. Couldn't possibly eat them all so I made a pot of my chestnut pâté with some of them and took it over to her. Don't get me wrong, I do like chestnuts and I really appreciate our neighbours' kindnesses, it just seems so much

hard work. Bending to pick them, spiky bits in your fingers, peeling the things, giving half of them to the birds 'cos they are wormy. I think I actually prefer walnuts! Ssh!

Wondering what the fuss was about, I read up on sweet chestnuts and found they are traditionally an important crop in Galicia. The trees provide fuel for burning, wood for building and fruit to eat.

As a fuel, chestnut burns hot but not too fast with less tar than many other woods. As a building material, like oak, it is very weather-resistant and fades to a beautiful grey outdoors. Indoors it becomes a rich mahogany chocolate. It warps less than other woods and has a remarkably narrow outer sapwood layer. The dense heartwood remains impervious to the ubiquitous woodworm beetle. Virtually all the wood in our house is sweet chestnut and I was amazed when I started to sand it how beautiful, silky and rich it is even after years of neglect.

The tree thrives on being pollarded, the new growths springing up invigorated. The old twisted trunks somehow support the new growth even though they look incapable of even being alive. The roots are well entrenched in the tough granite landscape. Sweet chestnut trees can live for two hundred years or more, at times the main trunk splitting almost in two, at others forming wonderful caves and hollows.

Most of all, sweet chestnuts (*Castanea sativa*) provide a supply of carbohydrate rich food in the winter months. The Romans introduced sweet chestnuts to Britain although they rarely ripen properly there. A staple ration for the Roman legions was a type of nutritious porridge they called *pollenta*; dried chestnuts ground and mixed with milk. In central Galicia we have a perfect climate for sweet chestnuts and still have a number of traditional dishes similar to the Roman *pollenta*.

Botanically, along with cashews, hazels, and acorns, sweet chestnuts are true nuts – a one celled fruit with a dry shell. By contrast walnuts and almonds are edible kernels, Brazil nuts and pine nuts are seeds, and peanuts are a pulse (related to peas with those lovely pea flowers in a stunning orange-yellow).

Chestnuts also differ from most nuts by being starchy and low in fat. Compare the nutritional value of chestnuts and walnuts below:-

Per 100g	*Chestnuts*	*Walnuts*
Calories	194	651
Protein	3g	15g
Fat	2g	64g
Carbohydrate	42g	16g

The high carbohydrate value means chestnuts are a valuable source of energy. They were a staple food not only for the Roman troops but also in the inland regions of Galicia. Along with maize, chestnuts can be used as a flour and wheat wasn't widely grown here. Our *Galego* friend remembers carrying sacks of maize to be milled into flour as a child and did not eat wheat bread until she was five years old. Interestingly, I'm told there is a high incidence of gluten intolerance in the Galician population which may be related to the non-consumption of high-gluten flours in childhood.

Chestnuts cooked in milk (*castañas en leche*), which I tried at our student farewell meal in

NOVEMBER

Santiago in September, are still a popular dessert here in Lugo province and of course roasted, chestnuts serve to abate hunger and keep energy levels high for all that chestnut picking and dancing which happily still goes on here. I was starting to believe the chestnut thing was not all hype after all.

DECEMBER
¡Tira!

Christmas at *A Casa do Campo* promised to be a very different affair to that in Monterroso the previous year. Even without the *cocina* working properly our kitchen was warmer than the rented flat, with air vents in the kitchen one could crawl through and which were perfectly sited to blow a cooling December draught around the ankles. The wood-burner in our living room, even with plastic sheeting still tacked over the gaping window panes, awaiting the ever elusive window man, was warmer than the minute storage radiators in the flat, which cooled down just in time for lunch.

We had also managed to make a real home in the four months we had been here. I felt settled and fortunate being able to look at our stunning views across the valley to the hillside beyond, interesting in all its seasons. The greens of summer had long since given way to bare branches, though many trees were still grey-green or yellow with lichen, keeping the valley vivid and alive. I listened to the sounds of the night without any car engines to spoil nature's symphony. Now that I was used to the squawking, snuffling and rustling that went on outside our polythene windows it was amazing. And, as I watched the stars overhead, constantly moving position but always in such a profundity without any light pollution to dim their brilliance, I couldn't imagine living anywhere else.

Saturday Dec 1st Drizzly and damp but Very mild.
Dear mum
  Thank you for my cards! Haven't opened them yet, honest!
  Great tits and robin are enjoying the chestnuts and grubs we put out. Have a wren there too now. Are there more birds in winter or do we just see them more often now it's cooler and they are hungry?
  It's difficult to believe we've only been here 4 months. I've quite forgotten what it's like to stand in a bathroom cleaning my teeth instead of watching Orion over the hórreo! Mind you, I think we have achieved a fair bit in the time. The allotment is ready for spring - the green manure is growing nicely and I have dug a bit more to put in some corn and cabbages for the chickens when we get them.
  We are over the middle bedroom (on the south side) with the roof now and I've tiled what I can (i.e. where it's fastened down) on the kitchen side and over the bathroom/bedroom on the west side. Our new little stove in the living room is toasty, and someone has been to examine the cocina. His conclusion? Buy a new stove! Very helpful!
  The few days of rain have helped in the garden. The soil is at least damp now (not

PLUM, COURGETTE & GREEN BEAN TART

as waterlogged as yours from the sound of it, thankfully) and lovely to dig. All the weeds are growing back too of course haha. It's still warm enough to have breakfast (brunch for you!) on the terrace. Very pleasant for December.

I have started enlarging my herb bed next to the terrace. I barrowed a load of rabbit or goat muck (the owners of that horrible hair we found?) then found some big stones to make a low retaining wall but they are a lot heavier than I thought to lift. I might have to get the heavies (S) in to help me finish it!

In between roofing and other pursuits the lad has made a smashing rustic brace and ledge gate from some bits of wood he found for the top opening on the allotment. That should stop the cows wandering in uninvited.

Monday 3rd Dec. Thought I'd finish this after my birthday day and beat you by sending our Christmas card early! Had a lovely birthday. The lad did me boiled eggs for breakfast. We had lunch at home as we had been out on market day. Did go out to La Scala in the evening though and tried the 'posh' wine (1.30 a glass!) with bacon butties for tapas, yummy! Two more strangers came up to us, one to ask if we liked Galicia and living here; the other to ask if our chimney was drawing yet! (Yes definitely, and sadly no, respectively).

DECEMBER

I took some sweeties to the market meet-up on the first to share with everyone. Augusta, the hotel owner, it turns out, has the same birthday as me so we popped in for coffee and cakes yesterday afternoon between lunch and boozing time!

Today was exciting. We got fed up looking at the battered washing machine sitting on the terrace so S connected the hosepipe and plugged it into the new electrics on the terrace and bingo it actually works! I had to stand with a bucket emptying it until we can sort out a pipe for the rinse water but much easier than hand washing everything!

This evening I had my favourite birthday present. We called at Jen's to check for leaks in her roof for her and I had a bath! Such luxury. I had been dreaming about having a bath!!

We have had a rash of visitors this week. First a 'vecino' from the next village called Manolo who said his cousin speaks English and lived in Canada... not sure what he came for, a nosey I think haha. Then a young lady shouted through the gate to ask directions to the mill as she was doing a survey of some kind. 'You are the English aren't you?' She said. Then two old ladies came by. They live in the next village and are mother and daughter. The older lady told me she was 92 and they were just going for a little walk! What with the Israeli couple from across the valley back in October, it's all go around here isn't it? Oh to be famous!

The Galp gas man came back too, with our contract. After all the shenanigans with the other company it seemed too easy. Must say thank you to Luisa for sorting it out.

Could do with Aunty Jean over. We are trying to source a pig as it's matanza again and we thought it would be nice to buy one locally for our meat. Pepe at the hotel said he knew a friend selling one but it was 150kg... bit big for two! We have had our new big chest freezer delivered so I can store our pig joints when we get it. The freezer arrived Sat morning with a chap and I think his two sons. They carried it in and unwrapped it all and even made sure it worked. And no delivery charge either. Pretty impressive.

Wish you could send some coal over! Wood burns lovely but it doesn't stay in unless you keep feeding it. OK if we are here but if we go to the bar it's a bit nippy when we get back. Mind you windows would help with that too!
Lots and lots of love
Xxx

After the non-arrival of any semblance of rectangular apertures containing glass, the non-functioning kitchen stove or *cocina* was still our biggest bugbear.

DECEMBER

The wood-burning range is a traditional source of heat and cooking in most rural *Galego* homes, as it was in many British rural properties once upon a time. The Galician range has one major difference however: they are generally built into a large marble-topped, brick or stone-built work unit positioned away from the wall so that a warm seating area is created behind the range. The unit dominates the centre of the rural *Galego* kitchen. It is worktop, dining table, TV stand and even sleeping platform on occasions. The idea of a central unit is an excellent one and when we were redesigning the house I really couldn't improve on it for our kitchen. I can comfortably seat ten people around the *cocina*, some of them even get a free heated back support if sitting near the chimney. But, herein lies a problem with the design. Having the range in the middle of the room means that the chimney cannot go straight upwards through the ceiling as in a 'normal' situation. Instead, the warm air (and smoke) has to be forced around the top of the oven box and then downwards into an enclosed channel in the floor, dug beneath the stove. Only then is it directed into the chimney which is often enclosed within the back wall of the kitchen. This creates an amazingly warm area behind the stove both at floor level and on the knees and back. It is an excellent design for heating the oven and the unit retains the heat long after the fire is out, acting as a huge storage radiator. But, as mum said the first time she saw it, "smoke doesn't go downhill".

However, we knew that it could and did, and that the *cocina* design worked beautifully. We had sweated behind the range in our Spanish estate agent's kitchen on more than one occasion. Logic does indeed suggest that smoke will not want to go downhill so a strong pull is needed to encourage the smoke in the general direction of the chimney.

PLUM, COURGETTE & GREEN BEAN TART

This was the bit no one had taught our *cocina*. The smoke, when we lit it, billowed everywhere and from every orifice, even from places where there shouldn't have been a gap. It steadfastly refused to go round the oven box and downwards no matter how we chivvied.

Ever since we had first attempted to light the rusted, old, battered, and rained upon stove the previous year locals had been following our progress closely and offering advice and encouragement.

Carmen, our ever helpful and wonderful neighbour, had shown me how to light the *cocina* and how to clean it using a donkey stone – a large block of compressed stone or sand – to scour the rust from the top. Our friends Cris and Steve had produced a written sheet for us from their landlord to explain how to put lighted newspaper down the chimney through the small damper hole to create a draw. We had even tried building a small fire in the channel at the base of the chimney to warm it and create a draw that way. But all to no avail.

Diary Thursday 6th December Dull and damp
Invited by Luisa to learn about pig butchering. After the first hour I was even allowed to help!! Most of the pig, other than the back legs which become Jamones, seems to be chopped up for chorizos. All the skin is removed and deep fried as a sort of pork scratchings. The fat is removed, salted and wrapped in a big mound to cut up and use in stews throughout the year. The small intestines are washed for chorizo skins, the large intestine and gut for callos (a tripe and chickpea soup). The liver, heart, and kidneys are eaten fresh but the head and trotters are salted. The head is first cut in half and cleaned obviously. The ears, snout and tail are delicacies to be savoured alone.

DECEMBER

We had the tenderloin or pork fillet grilled for lunch whilst butchering... absolutely delicious. Luisa also gave me the liver to bring home. Had a great time. Looking forward to having a go with ours when we source one, though I have some different ideas about cuts...

Diary Sat 8th December Drizzle am but lovely sunshine later
Thought so. S made a much better job of the herb garden wall than me. Will have to buy more herbs in spring or beg some cuttings from people. I have a rosemary and a sage bush growing nicely and the mint from the UK although there is loads of wild mint around here anyway. Maybe English mint will be an invasive species here like Spanish bluebells are over there. As if we didn't have enough to do here, S spent all yesterday at Jen's again doing her jobs list! I felt a bit annoyed but then thought, well, I get a bath and they have been so good to us so can't complain really... well I can, but to myself as S doesn't see a problem at all.
I have cleaned and painted all the kitchen walls now (and boy is there a lot of smoky, stained, mouldy wall to clean and paint!) in the hope that looking nice and sunny will persuade the cocina to work! S cleaned it all out. All the old ash and tar and clinker in the chimney, so it should flipping work. No one can say it is dirty now anyway.

Monday 10th December
Dear Mum
 Me and my big mouth. Less than two hours after we rang you on Saturday and said how sunny it was, the rain started. And the wind. Not exactly gales but pretty windy for

our little valley. The fire roared, the plastic on the roof flapped about madly, the stones holding it all down rattled and then started to slide down the roof! We had visions of the plastic all being in the river by morning but luckily all was well apart from a slightly damp middle bedroom where the plastic covering the ridge had flipped up. Luckily we haven't done anything in there yet and all the tools that we keep in there were in the other corner on the old table.

It was so windy on Sunday that we decided to try the stove again as our neighbours have said that you have to wait for a windy day. It certainly burnt better, with less smoke (but not much less, sadly). Still, I managed a lovely chicken and rice casserole and an apple fen cake in the oven. It cooked them beautifully so there is nothing wrong with the stove itself even if it is rusted to pieces. Had to wash the smoke out of my hair afterwards though!

Our next trick is to get a rotating chimney top or at least a Chinese hat. Not sure how that will help but we will try anything at this stage! It was so lovely to actually use it to cook on, and the kitchen was so nice and warm (and smoky) that I really want it working properly now.

Spotted a coal merchant today too. Not far away. We saw his van outside a house on the road from Jen's and I bravely knocked on the door. He sells coal for 10€ a sack. Not really sure what that equates to as yours comes in tonnes. How long would a standard coal sack last you? Can you work it out for me? Might be useful to just keep the fire in overnight anyway.

Forgot to tell you I had two lovely 'e' cards (electronic, sent by e mail) from brother. Didn't pick them up 'til Friday. Nice surprise!

Did some more washing on Sunday using the newly working washing machine. S was emptying the rinse water down a pipe hole near to the new herb garden when suddenly he saw something swimming in the warm soapy water. He scooped it out... a salamander! They are so beautiful. Glossy black with orange markings. This one had quite different markings from the last one we found (did you know that you can identify individuals from their markings, like fingerprints?) and was a female. Possibly gravid... certainly fat! We think we had woken her up from hibernation as she was a bit groggy for a while but then wandered off to find a quieter, and drier, place to sleep.

Those soap nuts from Lakeland work well, eco-friendly and they get the clothes clean, and nice and soft (and don't harm salamanders!) Thank you.
Love you tons and tons
XXXXXXXXXXXx

PLUM, COURGETTE & GREEN BEAN TART

Diary Tuesday 11th December

A completely dreadful day. A load of men were working up the track. "For the new motorway" jokes S. He wound me up so much I made him walk up there with me to find out what they are doing. The man joked they were making a swimming pool. Very funny.

"It's for the motorway" he says.

For goodness sake will everyone stop messing about! "What is it really?"

"The motorway."

I was getting fed up with everyone's jokes at my expense when S pointed out the sign on the van door... Autovia Lugo a Ourense.

Fifty metres from our house they are going to build a motorway bridge across the valley. My valley, my piece of paradise and they are going to build a great big stinking horrible motorway right next door. What's a real joke is that I turned down a house right next to a new motorway and that I felt pleased we hadn't bought the one in the hills because of a possible motorway nearby and now we will have one of our very own. The irony of it.

I don't know what to do. I realise it's our own fault not getting a survey done or checking all possibilities (although there are so many new roads being built in Galicia with so many possible options for each one that it would be difficult to find a property without some Sword of Damocles over it. Not that that helps a jot). I've sat all afternoon just staring at the view I've loved so much. The steep valley with chestnut trees, vivid green with lichen hanging from their branches. The shape of the beloved oak, probably over 300 years old and probably about to be chopped down, a few huge, stately pines canopying it all. My view that I have stared at as I've been digging the allotment. Breathing in the clean air and just watching the buzzards wheeling overhead. I can't

DECEMBER

believe all this is going to be destroyed for a motorway that Galicia does not, in any way, shape or form, need. We don't have anything like the number of cars that are on the roads in England. Not a quarter of the number. We have very few road lorries transporting unwanted foodstuffs from one place to another for no reason than to transport the same thing back again. We don't have any bloody traffic other than tractors and they can't use motorways anyhow. It's madness, it's European money, and it's going to destroy my valley. And I can't do a thing about it.

Diary Friday 14th December Sunny and heavy overnight frost
Okay, brooded enough. Spent the last 3 days doing nothing, staring at my beautiful view and feeling as if my world has ended but it isn't helping. I can't do anything about this idiocy but as S says - ever the practical rationalist - it could be months or even years before it starts. They may even run out of money (ojála - if only). Meanwhile, we have a home to build and work will take my mind off blasted motorways.
It's been really frosty the last few days. So bad S hasn't been starting on the roof until it has thawed (around 11am), after nearly sliding off one morning. It's a long drop on the south side! The allotment has been frozen solid in the mornings too and yesterday we had no water until 3pm as the pipe from the well had frozen. It's a bit of a poor design as the pipe exits the well on the north side about eight inches above floor level and connects to the stand pipe for the outside tap. It would be pretty impossible to change and gets no direct sun. S lagged it today with some pipe insulation which helped and he says he will build a hut over the exposed pipes.

PLUM, COURGETTE & GREEN BEAN TART

Daft thing is that when the sun comes up properly it's lovely and warm. I had an outside bath and hair wash today and it was nice and toasty in the sunshine. And with a great view. At least I won't be able to see the motorway from that direction... but I'm not thinking about that. The men were back today measuring and banging stakes in. Maybe I'll do a Swampy up the oak tree, S can feed me sandwiches and tea.

S has managed to cement up the outside of the old kitchen chimney from the roof... maybe the gaps are stopping it drawing properly. Won't hurt anyway. He says he will buy a Chinese hat for the top and raise it an extra couple of metres as some of our experts say it is because we are in a valley that the chimney can't draw.(Everyone else's seems ok but we will give it a go.) Paid for the stuff the stupid chimney men had used! Popped into builder's yard for some bits and a very sheepish José said they had bought the tiles and plaster there and had told him to put it on our bill. No wonder they just threw ¾ bag plaster in the store room and broke 2 tiles! Not José's fault so of course I paid him.

I have dug more of the allotment and moved more muck across there. Just keep wishing my view isn't about to change completely. Don't think about it Lisa. And don't mention it to mum.

Monday the something - 17th? Writing this in the sun on the terrace, waiting for the kettle to boil.

Dear mum

It was great to talk to you on Saturday, and a so much clearer line from the roof! No, I won't slip off, don't worry. Good views from up there too, will take you a photo of me sliding down the roof... only joking!

DECEMBER

Had a lovely party at Jen's on Saturday. My chestnut pâté and walnut truffles went down a storm with the English and Spanish alike. Had plenty of opportunities to practice my Spanish too! It was nice to see so many people mingling and all the different foods everyone had brought along.

Have another party on Thursday. Mark has organised a meal for all his 'clients' and kindly included us even though we couldn't buy from him in the end! We will call into Lugo on the way as apparently there is a big DIY store (better leave plenty of time then, haha!) and a second hand shop too.

Cris & Steve (who are buying on the coast) are going to help us to try and register the car as Spanish. He is a bit of a computer buff and has been looking online for how to do it articles. The car insurance is still causing problems. After much toing and froing the agent says we have to have the car registered as Spanish before they will insure it so we will have to get cracking on sorting it out before our UK insurance runs out in August.

Put our 'Christmas tree' up today. It's two branches pruned from the apricot. Look very pretty as they have red tips. S says 'how can you tell it's a Christmas tree?' 'Tinsel, baubles, pressies underneath and a fairy on top of course!!' We have had two wallets from the construction yard (to go with the brollies, hats, calculator and tape *measure), 2 part lottery tickets from the gas man and 2 bottles of perfume from the chemist (I didn't even buy anything in there!) Also have a pile of very expensive coal which somebody sent in the post!!! Xx and some chocolates. Oh and Aunty Jean and Uncle George's pressie which I haven't opened yet.*

Planning to go to the Chinese restaurant again for Christmas day. Enjoyed it so much last year. May even stay overnight at our favourite little B&B, The Gran Via, so we can have a drink. The bars seemed quite lively as we were leaving last year.

Friday 21st Had a good time at Mark's dinner do yesterday. Between 35 and 40 people turned up. Didn't realise there were so many Brits here! It was held at the Rio Ladro, the country house where we stayed when we first house hunted with Mark almost 2 years ago. How time flies!

We knew some people like CJ and Gala. Others were new to us. There was a nice, older couple. She got a little tipsy and was asking everyone to visit them as she misses the company. Bit sad really. He is a radio whizz, used to make and sell crystal radio sets. Interesting as the hotel has a radio museum so Rick could give us a sort of guided tour! There was a couple who live in California and are having their house renovated for them (though most people here seem to be doing the renovations themselves). There was a lovely young couple who live on the way to Lugo and are self-renovating. They have a large van which they offered the use of. She even gave me a card which read 'Richard and Jayne, Big Van', in case I forgot! The couple who bought our 'other choice' house near Becerrea, Anne and Simon, are farming organically. S says they are the original hippies - they used to be off grid in Ireland and in Catalonia. They have invited us over for Boxing Day dinner. They moved here in April so a bit ahead of us, and told us that their stove smoked so much when they first lit it that they had to sleep in the car! Also met a number of people who never meant to stay in Galicia but had been caught by the 'bug' and ended up buying here. One couple were on their way to the US by boat! We also found a statistically interesting fact. There are more Brits who have bought houses here which are number 6 than any other single number. There were five couples at the lunch with addresses that read - numero 6, somewhere or other (including us of course). Bizarre.

Give our love to everyone for Christmas. Think of us walking the walls at Lugo whilst you eat your hand picked chestnuts with your dinner. Glad Jen managed to get them to you. We hope that you will be over here for next year's celebrations.
Love you tons Xxx

PLUM, COURGETTE & GREEN BEAN TART

P.s The field mouse in the kitchen is still evading capture despite our efforts with humane traps, though he has managed to eat a fair bit of the bait! He is so cheeky. Yesterday he ran up the pipe from the gas bottle and sat on the worktop watching us eat dinner! He is very fast and seems to live under the stove.

> *Sunday 23rd December Mist am then sunny and warm*
> *Carmen came round today with half a chicken and a bottle of wine. She mentioned the other day something about 'medio pollo y vino' but I thought she was maybe inviting us for lunch or something in the New Year. I expected that, as usual, everything would become clear if I just said yes. It did! So we have a nice fresh half a capon (recently killed) and a bottle of albariño for dinner. Cheers Carmen and thank you.*
> *I've spent the last couple of days stripping all the horrid whitewash off the 'guest' bedroom ceiling. The ceiling itself is wide chestnut boards with thin fillets of wood in between to cover the gaps and anchor them. A few are a bit woodwormy but overall it looks amazing. I can't wait to polish them up. Even managed to finally find some methylated spirits for my polish recipe. It's called alcohol de queimar or burning alcohol. Also got a load more mouse traps for Jerry and his wife Geraldine… yup, there are 2 of them now!*

Jerry, Geraldine and later their entire mouse family, gave us an idea about the smoking stove. S had found some mouse holes at the side of the stove where they were coming into the kitchen. This made him wonder how they were getting *inside* the stove in the first place. Behind the wall of the kitchen, and behind the chimney, there is another, small stone storeroom, accessible only from outside. Unless you are a mouse of course.

The wall on the storeroom side was quite badly damaged and not mortared properly. Using a mirror and torch S looked down the chimney from the kitchen side (through the damper in the wall, which we call a *tapa* or cover). He thought he could see a hole through to the store but couldn't be sure without knocking a hole himself in the chimney between floor and *tapa* level.

Oh, well, we had tried everything else so go ahead!

He knocked a small hole where he thought he had seen the damage and lo! The mice had made a lovely run through from the outer storeroom and into the chimney itself. From there they could get into the channel under the floor and into the kitchen.

Most importantly, what this effectively meant was that because there was a hole from the storeroom into the chimney, the air was being drawn the wrong way, into the chimney from the back and thus into the kitchen. This meant the flue couldn't draw and the smoke wouldn't go up the chimney.

We had done it!!

S immediately cemented up all the run holes he could find and then re-bricked his hole and cemented over the kitchen wall. All we had to do was wait for it to dry.

§

Meanwhile, it was Christmas and Lugo awaited us.

In the four months since we moved in, our only trips to Lugo seemed to have been to chase paperwork and get tangled in Galician red tape, which was a shame as Lugo is a town worth getting to know and enjoy.

Our nearest city was made an UNESCO World Heritage Site in 2000. It was declared the 'finest example of late Roman fortification in western Europe'. A compact city (the area outside the walls is of little historical interest and even less architectural interest) the centre of Lugo, encircled by the thirty to fifty feet high stone walls is less than a kilometre across but abounds with tiny alleyways, tapas bars, museums and cobbled streets.

Lugo was probably originally founded by early Celtic peoples (Lugos is the name of a Celtic god) but, as the Roman Empire swept across Europe, Lugo was conquered by Paulinius Fabius Maximus of the Imperial Roman Army and renamed Lucus Augusti.

Lucus Augusti became an important Roman town, in what was then known as Gallaecia, due to its court of justice or *Conventus.* Following the Roman conquest of Iberia, life became quieter for a while and Lucus Augusti thrived as both a commercial town and a centre of justice. The town expanded down the hillside. Huts, hovels and even larger manor houses were built higgledy-piggledy all around. But both local and Germanic tribes continued to attack the Roman settlement on occasions until, in the 3rd century AD, the decision was taken to fortify the city.

Lugo is one of the best examples of a Roman walled city still extant. The walls totally encircle the old town, being some 2.2 kilometres in circumference and the only complete walls in existence of this era. They loom impressively as you head towards the centre of town and the *Ronda Muralla,* as the ring road around the walls is called. At their inception, parts of the walls with two-storey towers (of which only one of the original 85, *A Mosqueira,* remains) would have stood over 15 metres high. The walls are wide enough to allow a Roman Century to march in formation around their tops. There are ten named gateways through which one can enter the city. Of those, five are Roman, the rest created later to improve access through the city. From the top of the walls in a couple of places (where ugly new blocks of flats have not been built, obscuring the view) it is possible to see right down the hillside to the river Miño, demonstrating the defensive position of Lucus Augusti.

It is said that one cannot dig in one's garden in Lugo without coming across some Roman artefact and each time some building work goes on, another historical find is made. Sadly, some years ago, and before it became a World Heritage Site, these finds were often covered up or destroyed to save hassle and extra work. Nowadays you will see examples of discoveries around almost every corner, often below ground level and covered by a sheet of toughened glass to preserve them. Behind the cathedral (which I actually prefer to the more ornamented Santiago Cathedral) there is a Roman bath which was discovered during repaving works. Around six feet long and still tiled in blue and white, it brings history to life. The Cathedral of Santa Maria itself was built in the 12th century AD though the main façade is much later. Inside it has a quiet elegance and impressive stonework.

In the process of creating a defensible, walled town, many of the homes which had grown up on the edges of the town were destroyed. Traces of these homes can still be found. When a new auditorium was being built for the University of Santiago near to the cathedral entrance, a wonderfully preserved manor house was discovered together with a temple to Mithras, a Roman/Persian deity. Cleverly, the auditorium was built above the archaeological remains, the lower floor being one of my favourite museums, *El Domus.*

After the Roman Empire crumbled, Lugo was sacked by the Visigoths and eventually left to decline until, by the 8th century AD, it was all but deserted. There were attempts to revive its fortunes but its big break came in the middle ages, when Lugo became a pilgrim town in its own right as well as a way station on the *Ruta Primitiva* to Santiago. Part of the reason for Lugo becoming a pilgrim town was its special dispensation to allow the consecrated host to be exposed to the public 24 hours a day. An occurrence unusual enough to earn Lugo special attention.

In the 18th century Lugo began to host the fairs of San Froilán, a festival which continues to this day in early October. It became a provincial capital in 1833 and, following its status as a World Heritage Site, twinned with the Great Wall of China in 2007. There's nothing like thinking big!

Lugo loves to celebrate its Roman heritage and, like most Galician towns, to create an excuse for a party. There is a Roman festival every year in June. *Arde Lucus* is a riot of colour, sound and re-enactments of battles between barbarians (or Celts) and the Roman legionaries.

In December, the streets tend to be running, not with Romans nor barbarians, but with water as the gargoyles on the cathedral spew rainwater onto the heads of unsuspecting tourists or pilgrims walking the primitive, or original route, of the Way of St. James.

As we found out to our cost the previous year, Christmas Eve tends to be a family celebration in Spain when the main Christmas meal is eaten and families come from far and wide to be together. By contrast, the evening of the 25th December is a time to go out with friends and celebrate.

Lugo was buzzing that evening! We had had a lovely Chinese meal for lunch and a walk through the streets of Lugo, avoiding the gargoyles wherever possible. We had returned to our guest house for a warming cuppa (boiled in our own kettle which follows us everywhere) followed by *Armageddon* dubbed into Spanish. I'm not sure who does the voice over for Brucie Willis, but he doesn't sound right at all. And having a mate called AJ as an abbreviation is fine but in Spanish it becomes *A Jota* which ends up being a non-abbreviation! Still, it was good fun and prepared us for a night on the town. We managed a couple of bars that evening, both with excellent local wine and double tapas. (A Lugo speciality, and one of its highlights, is a tapa from the huge, circulating trays with your drink *and* a tapa from the kitchen.) The second bar, a *pulperia*, or bar-restaurant specialising in octopus, was so good, and the *polbo da feira* from the kitchen so meltingly wonderful that we stayed for four rounds. We watched the barman flame-grilling *chorizos* for another customer over a miniature barbecue on the bar. Afterwards we walked, only slightly wobbly (the amount of food consumed with the wine helps soak up the alcohol, honest) back to the *Pensión Gran Via*.

Sunday 30th December. Mild, warm and sunny. Lunch outside.
Dear Mum,
  Had our first proper electric bill today. A bit expensive as I had been using the electric cooker to heat the kitchen up. Still not too bad though. Not had our council tax bill yet. Our friends' was 62€ for the year so we had better start saving now eh?!!

PLUM, COURGETTE & GREEN BEAN TART

Think we have found a pig! Our friend and neighbour at the bar has pigs and is happy for us to have one so long as we help with the matanza or actual killing. Can't say I'm madly keen but I suppose it's a bit hypocritical to want to eat the meat but not be willing to take part in killing it. It will be interesting to see how it is done here anyway. I've heard and read lots of stories about matanza so will see if any of them are true.

Will need Aunty Jean then for sure to help with making the black puddings (and to help S eat the tripe).

Our produce is keeping well. Lots of walnuts left. S cracks a jarful for me every now and again when I think he looks bored drinking his tea with nothing to occupy him! Both the cooking and the eating apples are still keeping well in the barn. The cookers purée beautifully and the eaters are still nice and crisp in those boxes you stored them in. Means the apples are good keepers too. Would love to know what variety they are. If I ask Carmen she says 'frutas'. Or 'flores' for flowers or 'pájeros' for birds... not helpful!

We also found some lovely tasty mushrooms under the walnut tree. They are bright lilac and called Amethyst Deceiver because they vary so much. Still, they are pretty distinctive. (Note to reader: I did an ecology degree with a module in fungus identification and have spent many years studying fungi, please don't try any mushroom without being sure of its edibility. Pharmacies in Spain are excellent at identifying fungi. Some fungi are deadly.)

I hope our new hazel 'contorta' will survive the floods in the orchard. Must think where to put the kiwi vines when we get them. Apparently the flowers are fragrant so it would nice to have them somewhere we sit out in spring. Perhaps in front of the long barn.

Monday 31st December. Misty all day
Happy noo 'ear to you, you one-eyed B...

Am sitting outside the garage in town waiting for the mechanic Fernando to return. They said 'one hour' around one and half hours ago! Cris & Steve found we need to look at right hand drive headlights for the car before we can get it MOT'd here and therefore registered. Hoping he can source some for us.

Plan to have a wine in town for New Year's Eve then (when everywhere closes up for their family meal!) back here for the beeps with a couple of black sheep beers from our ever shrinking store. Leg of lamb for dinner yesterday. Done in the stove! Which... Tara... now works!!

What a wonderful New Year present. Unlike this mechanic who still hasn't returned. It's now 6pm, dark and the fog is getting thicker so think I'll go home to the lad and

PLUM, COURGETTE & GREEN BEAN TART

warm up a bit.
Love you tons and tons
Xxx

At last we could respond to that oft asked question. "Does it draw?" with a resounding "*¡Si, tira!*"

It appeared that himself's clever idea had worked and we finally had an old and rather rusty, but working and (relatively) smoke free range cooker. After all the advice we had received over the last few months and all the people who had tried to help with various suggestions...

"Try putting lighted paper down the chimney." If I had a peseta for each time I heard that one I'd have, well, quite a few pesetas.

"You need a taller chimney." Any taller we would need to warn aircraft coming in to land at Santiago.

"The chimney is too square at the bottom." Less said the better.

"The stove is rusty." True, but it draws now doesn't it?

For all the well-meaning advice not one, single, solitary person hit on the truth. Not until Jerry mouse and all the mouse babies lit a light bulb in my clever partner's brain.

So we have decided that if, in the future, someone should tell us that their *cocina* doesn't draw properly, we will give this piece of advice...

"Have you blocked up the mouse runs which go all the way through the chimney from the storeroom behind and into the stove and cause the air to be pulled into the kitchen rather than drawing it out through the chimney?"

"You have? Oh, well then try putting some lighted paper down the chimney."

JANUARY
Matanza

Our New Year started with a death. Or actually with two.

We had been summoned to our friend's home at 3pm on January 2nd to participate in their *matanza* and to take away with us a pig dinner - or a few dozen.

The day dawned bright and cold. We bought salt, sausage skins and two big cream coloured buckets (they had to be cream for pig not the more common black ones. A bit like with the blue chestnut buckets, there is probably a good reason). We scrubbed the kitchen worktop and scrubbed a big, lidded tub for salting the hams. We even scrubbed our blue boiler suits and our wellington boots.

Diary Wednesday 2nd January Sunny
Into town early to see the mechanic about the headlights. Not there again! Back to do some sanding of beams (and fingers) in the 'guest' bedroom whilst S took about 200 nails out of the shutters and scraped the larger beams. Just leaving for the matanza when we got a call from the new window man, Bernardo, who Augusta at the bar had recommended. Said we were going out. He will come tomorrow. Inspired by someone actually contacting us we called at the garage

again. Fernando is in Lugo, not expected back, try tomorrow. Off to matanza.

Matanza: Day one. There were two little piggies in a field up the hill behind the house. Somehow they were persuaded to have a lead put on their back legs and we proudly walked them (well, they actually walked us as we were behind) down the road to the garage where the act would take place.

I waited outside with piggy two whilst piggy one met its end, quickly and quietly. As piggy two led me inside it caught the scent of its friend. A little of the blood, which had missed the pot, was pooling on the floor. As quick as a fat piggy can, piggy two ran – straight at the pool of congealing blood to lap up the remains of its companion. Greed was this little piggy's undoing as, before it could react, a chain was around its rear leg and it was upside down hanging two feet off the ground looking rather bemused, and maybe even resigned. Its end came before it had a chance to think what was for lunch as José plunged his huge knife through its throat and straight into its heart.

It was all over within 15 minutes of catching the pigs with no squealing, no showmanship and no messing about. A necessary job, done well.

The carcasses were let down and laid onto clean straw at the side of the garage in a small field. More straw covered the bodies like a shroud before a rather large, industrial-sized flamethrower appeared in José's hands. Flames leapt from the straw and I could smell the unmistakeable scent of roast pig. The flames shrivelled the tiny coarse hairs from the pigs' skin and turned it dark brown. Before the skin started to bubble and crackle José turned off the flamethrower and with cast-iron hands twisted the nails from the trotters, throwing them to the dogs.

JANUARY

Next, a jet washer came into play. Carefully, covering the whole animal from snout to tail, and paying particular attention to behind the ears, the piggies were showered clean and began to turn a sparkling bright white before our eyes. S was even allowed to wield the jet washer for a while.

Once clean and thoroughly shaved by the Spanish barber, piggy one and piggy two were rehung, side by side in the garage. The next step was to remove the innards. Liver, spleen, and kidneys went into clean boxes to take away. We tried the spleen later and can say with some certainty that it is perfectly good cat food (though even the cats weren't actually interested). The stomach and intestines came out onto a huge wooden slab to untangle before cleaning. The heart and lights (lungs), together with the attached tongue were hung on a rail ready to be washed.

The carcasses were left hanging to dry out before being weighed. We, meanwhile, had the unenviable task of washing the tripes in our local river. The river at the bottom of our valley is, in January, flipping cold let me tell you. Mind numbingly and finger numbingly cold. To stand in this freezing river up to your ankles, and to bend down in order to clean pigs' intestines by allowing the current to wash through and invert them, is a type of masochism I, for one, do not wish to repeat. I don't even *like* tripe!

Eventually, the torture was over for the day and we retired to defrost our blue fingers by the fire at home.

§

Matanza: Day two. The following morning we both went into town to collect our piggy. And to chase Fernando the mechanic, who miraculously, was in. Sadly he couldn't find any headlights and asked us to return on Monday. Killing a pig seemed so much more straightforward. Butchering not quite so. The first problem was trying to explain what I wanted. No! I don't want all the skin removing first. *"Con piel, con piel"* I shouted as the knife started to slice away all that lovely crackling. I had perfected this particular phrase at the butcher's in town so was ready for it. We Brits like the skin on a pig joint to produce the wonderful crispy crackling that makes roast pork special. *Galegos* can't see why you would pay the same price for skin as for meat so have it removed (along with all the fat) first *por favor*. I also wanted the pig halved along the backbone so I would have loin joints from each side. I had noticed that normally José cut alongside the backbone on each side leaving the knobbly spine, devoid of much meat, to be cut into rings for soups such as *callos* or the famous Taboadan *caldo de ósos.* (Of which, much more later.) We eventually, with much hand waving, deduced this to be called *estilo de A Coruña,* or Coruña style for reasons that, as ever, were unclear to me.

Whatever it was called José wielded his axe in a frighteningly professional way, neatly and effortlessly cutting the piggy in half.

He removed the back and front legs for *jamones* and his five year old daughter showed S how to rub the legs vigorously to stop the blood pooling and spoiling the taste. If it seemed odd to our English sensibilities to have a five year old in such close proximity to a recently dead animal it obviously didn't to anyone else, and she seemed unaffected by the horror. When S paraded around being 'Grasshopper' with the pig's eyeballs in front of his own she giggled until she fell over.

Our piggy was looking less like an animal by the minute. The head was removed next and plonked into a big tub to be washed and salted. Or, in my case, washed and then boiled for chawl or brawn.

JANUARY

To try to explain that was, at this stage, a step too far! The brain was carefully extracted and popped into a plastic tub. A tiny plastic tub. Luisa thought the tub I had brought hilariously large for the walnut sized brain. Another treat for tea.

The trotters and tail were added to the bucket containing the head. These delicacies, together with the ears or *orejas*, are a big feature on *tapas* menus throughout the town around *matanza* time. It still amuses me to hear a bar full of people asking for their *tapitas* (small, free tapas)...

"¿Tapitas?" "Orejas", "orejas", "orejas", "orejas", "cheese?" That will be us there at the end, the English.

The remaining carcass was chopped into loin roasting joints by the axe-wielding José and the belly/ribs rolled up for further butchering at home.

At last we were ready. Unfortunately S had taken the car back home to await Bernardo, window man number two, so I was stranded with 60 kilogrammes of pig to cart home. José, of course, stepped in to offer me a lift, thankfully leaving the axe behind.

Back home we started straight away butchering piggy two. I thought it may take a while and I wasn't wrong. Even with José having done the hard work and the two of us cutting and freezing it took us until after 9pm to have what we needed in the freezer.

The loins went in as joints. The ribs I removed to use as Chinese spare ribs or barbecue ribs. The deboned belly we then cut into four pieces for bacons. The front legs I had decided to hang Spanish style whilst the large back legs I cut into smaller joints for English cured hams. I put the collar in to cure too and we cut up all the leftover bits, or things I couldn't find a use for, into cubes for stews, pies and sausages.

PLUM, COURGETTE & GREEN BEAN TART

The cleaned head I put into my biggest pan, with its snout only slightly sticking out of the top, with herbs and salted water to boil for my pressed chawl. The fat went into a separate pan to render down for dripping and to use in my big chip pan. (If vegetarians visit, I do oven chips, honest.)

The *cocina* was proving immensely useful as I could fit five huge pans on it and of course, since it was lit anyway, it all just bubbled away for hours on end without me having to do anything!

Thursday Jan 3rd Very wet, all night and all day. Good job we did our matanza yesterday

Dear mum,

Piggy done at last. I'm sitting in the living room with the smell of gently drying chorizos (they are hanging from a wooden pole above the fire. Look like extra Christmas decorations!) We were given them to bring home from Luisa's previous pig. I think they were worried as I had said I wasn't doing chorizos with our pig! Very kind and typically generous of course. I've found a sweet cure recipe for the hams. I'm not really set up for smoking them and am terrified of spoiling so much meat. Though I have hung the two front legs as we ran out of space in the big chest freezer.

Stefan, Annie and the kids (who bought just down the road) dropped in for tea. The youngest kept asking me if we had <u>really</u> killed a pig and wanted all the gory details whilst eating our pork scratchings (also from Luisa's pig). He said he liked chorizos, but had second thoughts when I explained what they are wrapped in! I told him God made intestines that shape especially for chorizos. He forgave me enough to ask for another apple and walnut cake. Apparently the last one went in 10 minutes flat!

Odd, the different attitudes to keeping and killing animals between English and Galego kids. The bar owner's daughter helped with the whole process (including washing the tripes in the river, Aunty Jean would have enjoyed that one... I didn't) at age five! At least she knows where her meat comes from (and she could tell me what each part was going to be too). She is learning English and chanted a bit of humpty dumpty with me!

Found there is an indoor swimming pool nearby in Chantada! Plan to go and have a look tomorrow. Miss my swimming and a shower would be nice as I think I smell rather piggy after all our butchering today!

Oops, the music has stopped and I'm told it's 3 minutes to pumpkin time. Will carry on tomorrow.

Monday 7th Jan. Just back from yet another party! Maribel, our Spanish estate agent, had invited all _her_ clients (and had very kindly included us). A wonderful time was had with all the Brits and Maribel's family. And Gala, simultaneously translating from Spanish to English for us _and_ from

Ukrainian to Spanish for her mother! Such talent... I am incredibly jealous. Maribel has a beautifully renovated house. The kitchen is vast with a big cocina throwing out so much heat. Like ours, you sit behind it to eat. She even has a little gate on one end to keep the draughts out. We had to keep playing musical chairs as those directly behind the range couldn't stick it for long haha.

Other than doing the pig and partying we have also succeeded in getting the big stone trough all the way round to the west side of the house using that tried and tested Egyptian method of levers and sled tracks. Sadly minus the 5000 slaves, but it worked! We used old poles for rollers and a couple of bigger beams for levers. Took us a while with me running round to the front to move the rollers whilst S levered the thing up. Downhill was more fun than the uphill bit! It looks very nice in place by the big barn doorway and is full of water after the rain again last night!!

We have been trying to get the new headlights for the car (right hand beams) but it seems to be rather hard work! We have visited the mechanic in town I don't know how many times. Finally today he actually measured the headlights (after saying he couldn't get any!) It's only an Escort for goodness sake, how hard can it be to find headlights!!

JANUARY

Also still trying to sort some windows! Had a chap came by last week but not had his quote yet. The original company seem hopeless. It all seems highly complicated.

Have also decided the swimming pool will be a regular Friday trip. It's a lovely pool. Very clean and bright and there is a sauna as well as the showers. So we get exercise and a Friday bathnight clean up too!
Love you
Xxxxx

Matanza: Day three. We started off re-salting the English hams before curing them for eight days. The head meat had cooked beautifully and was falling off the bones. Extracting all the tiny bones before pressing the wonderfully soft and flavourful head 'cheese' is a real labour of love. S declined my romantic gesture of the teeth for a necklace so they had to be tossed as I honestly couldn't think of another use for them! Sad really as there wasn't much of piggy that didn't get used that week.

Had I known, the following month we would see uses for *dientes* (or *dentes* in *Galego*) as well as other parts of the pig in the famous *Festa do caldo de ósos* in Taboada.

Next came the sausages. We minced up some of the pig we didn't have another use for. Some bits were a little on the stringy side so maybe I should have been more particular about which bits to use. We live and learn. I had decided on apple and leek flavouring for the sausages. Boiled chopped leeks and cooked pureed apple were mixed together with plenty of salt and pepper. I squidged the mince and the flavourings and added a load of breadcrumbs (this wasn't a neat recipe as I was making it up as I went along. I suppose I ought to have recorded it at the time but my hands were full!) We then tried to stuff the intestines. Not as easy as it looked. I had bought a manual mincer and sausage stuffing machine but it over minced the meat and the mixture seemed to go everywhere as we tried simultaneously to hold the intestines on the tube, fill the hopper, push the mixture into the tube and turn the handle. That was four hands. Oh and to twist the sausages as they came out, and hold the machine down. A nice eight-armed *pulpo* to help would be handy... groan!

Somehow we managed, without too many injuries or too much domestic strife, to get a decent bunch of porky fingers sitting on a plate. Phew!

Diary Friday 11th January Very wet all day and all night
What a wet few days... again! Really windy and stormy overnight. Hardly slept a wink! Drips everywhere and the noise from the plastic flapping at the window openings was deafening. I was so annoyed that we called in at Toldao about the windows (again) on the way to the swimming baths tonight. Had a real rant in a sort of mad Spanglish. He seemed indifferent and still no glass (or green aluminium) looming on the horizon so I don't feel guilty getting other quotes any more.
Rang Bernardo, window man 2. 'Quote mañana'. Mmm, he said that before too.

Sunday 13th January Soooo soggy!
Dear mum
Glad we live at the top not the bottom of the valley after last night. Very soggy, the river is roaring away and all my precious soil is flowing downhill to join it. Oh well, I think we have had all last autumn's rain in

the first two weeks of January. Hope this isn't a foretaste of the year... will have no soil left soon!

We lost the huge dead walnut tree that stood by the chicken shed last night in the wind. It went very quietly getting hooked up on the small apple tree near the track. Very rotten and no roots at all. Good job it didn't fall the other way or it would've flattened our nice newly (but not very professionally, since I did it haha) rendered chicken shed. We spent the morning cutting logs off the trunk. CJ offered to bring his chainsaw over for the bigger bits. We will have wood for years!

I wonder if this will be a slow letter or an express one? I post them all in the same box so very odd.

As it's not outdoor weather we have been cleaning up the ceiling and beams in the end bedroom (the guest room). It looks lovely. Polished up I think it will be smashing. Should've asked brother if he can plaster as neither of us can and the walls need knocking off and redoing.

S has been sanding the beams, well, grinding them really. He is getting all the hard but woodwormy and rough outer layer off. He has got through 2 grinding discs already but the beams look good once they are smooth. I have cleaned the wooden, chestnut ceiling. Have found that soap filled Brillo pads work wonderfully to get

PLUM, COURGETTE & GREEN BEAN TART

the old whitewash off. The ceiling is, of course, gorgeous. Why on earth would you want to whitewash it in the first place? S is making some new fillets for the odd gap where one has rotted away.

I've also been mopping and mopping the kitchen floor. It is starting to show red in places so I think it must have been painted at one time. Dread to think how much cow poo has been trodden in since then haha

S has swapped some of his over-ordered red pine (for the stud walls) for some plasterboard with Stefan and we have found a place which does wider rough planking so may soon be able to put a ceiling in the bathroom and a floor above for the hot water tank then, who knows... maybe a bathroom of our own! Of course windows would be nice too though they seem to be a distant dream at the moment!

As the stove is working so well I thought I would have a proper go with the donkey stone Carmen gave me. Found we also had one in the house which we had been using as a doorstop... oops! Anyway it was very dusty work but cleans the rust off the top well and I can just about see some shiny bits underneath now. Don't care really if it's rusty as I am just happy that it is working.

I am certainly practising my range cookery. Trying to remember the advice we got at that Aga evening at Grice's - do you remember? I can juggle lots of pans on the top now, just have to remember: boiling directly over the fire box and simmering at the far end. My Aga pans are the best and my Le Cruset Marmitout casserole of course. It cooks a roast like nothing else, holding in the heat and all the taste. My apple pie worked well today. The oven gets quite warm if you keep stoking it. As does the kitchen though that would be even warmer if we had windows of course! No problem with air circulation anyway!

Had some of the pig's liver for dinner. Ham pie tomorrow. I prefer the flavour of the boiled ham we did although I suppose the baked one is more like sandwich ham in texture. When I sliced up the baked one for our butties, I found it wasn't cured in the middle so it's a pork/ham mix! Either it needs longer than the book says or our ham was thicker. Oh well! Had our once a year treat of hearts yesterday. We were generously given both pigs' hearts so greedily had one each. The cocina did them perfectly. I did leave Luisa the lights in exchange... seemed a fair swap! The freezer is overflowing already. You had better visit soon to help us eat some.

Tuesday evening - in living room; fire roaring away and singing in the wind, rain pouring down the plastic sheeting covering the window frames which are rattling nicely, and listening to the polystyrene insulation banging up and

PLUM, COURGETTE & GREEN BEAN TART

down (will have to fix that or no one will be able to sleep in the end room!). Poor Annie down the road lost a window last week in the wind, her eldest son hadn't closed it properly and it blew open in the night and smashed. She says she ran into his room to find the curtain blowing horizontally and him still fast asleep. At least having a window break is not an issue for us as we still Don't Have Any!! We do have another chap apparently coming tomorrow to measure up. Yes, well, we shall see.

We invited Annie over to share our ham pie as I had made far too much. Her husband is in the UK selling their 4x4. The youngest told me he wanted to learn how to make cakes as he likes mine. I promised him he could come over next time I am baking for a 'lesson'. Gave him another cake to take home in the meantime!! Annie said she feels guilty she doesn't bake much but then again as I told her she really does get stuck into the DIY stuff.
Love you tons and tons
xxxxxxxxx

Diary Tuesday 15th January
Lunch in town then to Jen's to sort leaks (again). Had a cuppa but then dismissed as they had other friends coming over for tea. Not sure the workers are allowed to mingle with other guests... even if we do know them (it was only Cris & Steve). Odd. Came home to light the fire but the room doesn't seem to be heating up very well. New wood maybe, or lack of windows!

JANUARY

Our window situation was becoming critical. Plastic sheeting covering the gaps was fine in summer but our poor little stove was struggling to heat the living room in the January gales. The *cocina* of course was working wonderfully but we were still losing most of our heat through the empty window panes.

I despaired of Toldao ever actually coming up with any windows and we started to smell a possible cash flow problem (why else would they be unable to get any glass after four months?). We asked Augusta at the hotel, our go-to person for all our problems, for advice.

Wonderful as ever, she contacted a number of companies for us.

Bernardo, window man two, came the day we did our *matanza*. S had left early to speak with him. He had promised a quote in a couple of days. I had rung Bernardo a few times since. Each time he was in the car and promised to send the quote when he got to the office. Nothing arrived. Then he stopped answering my calls. Having a wild idea I rang from our other mobile. He answered immediately then fell silent as he realised I had caught him out. He mumbled something half-heartedly about being in the car but I had my answer – if he was now ignoring my calls he didn't want the job. I didn't have a problem with that, but just flipping say so!

Window man three was from Melide and I didn't even get his name. He was bolshy, didn't listen to what we wanted, didn't measure anything and actually seemed more interested in wandering round the garden examining the stone troughs and our *hórreo,* which he said was worth 12,000 euros. Yeah, well that's nice but I'd prefer windows at the moment (and we were told by Mark that *hórreos* are listed buildings...). We dismissed window man three as a time waster.

PLUM, COURGETTE & GREEN BEAN TART

Luckily, Augusta wasn't finished yet!

The next day we collected Augusta to visit a fourth place, in Agolada. She helped us with translating as usual. The chap, another José, said he would visit the following day to measure up. We also popped into more scrap yards on the way back. No headlights but they would ring (really?!) if any came in.

To my surprise window man number four actually turned up. Well, not the actual same man but the same firm. Paulino measured up everything carefully and said the quote would be three days.

Even more amazing, Paulino hand delivered the quote within a week. He was very diligent and helped us to overcome a problem with the openings. We had wanted to keep the old wooden internal shutters. They were woodwormy, had interesting carvings on them and were unique. I loved them! If the windows were on the outside of the windowsill they couldn't open as tilt and turn; if they were inside, the frame would take up most of the window space.

We pondered and eventually decided it would be better to scrap the shutters and the inside windowsill and have the windows fixed to the facing wall inside the rooms.

Paulino came back to look at our idea and agreed it was feasible. He told us one month "*mas o menos*" so we reckoned on having windows by March.

Diary Thursday 17th January Drizzle all day in Lugo
Ordered our tarima for the flooring. Funny I can only remember the Spanish name once I've learnt it, had to ask S what it was in English! Floorboards... twit! Anyway it will be quince dias. The girl looked most put out when we started laughing and told us "it <u>will</u> be 15 days." She

obviously hasn't heard the 'about a fortnight' refrain as often as we have over the last five months!

Tried to buy a headlight at the scrap yard on the industrial estate but it was broken... he said we could have it cheap but doesn't seem worth it for a single cracked light. And we still need two. Just seems too difficult for words!

Priced up Rockwool and plasterboard from a place on the industrial estate. Okay prices but they wanted 64€ delivery! Bought a load of electrical wire etc. from Aki instead and a pair of goggles for S (swimming... why didn't he get some last week? Who knows?)

Saw a sign for a menú del dia on the O Ceao industrial estate so decided to try it. As usual the sign was confusing. When a sign indicates left at the next roundabout, I sort of assume it will be the <u>next</u> roundabout rather than the one we passed just before the sign! We drove around for a bit and I was getting hungry and fractious, when we spotted a sign for 'Los Tres Amigos'. Not the one I'd seen advertised but I didn't care. No menú del dia displayed either and it looked a cut above our usual haunts. I bravely asked the chap if they did a menú. He thought for a while and said okay. A bit more than we usually pay but I was hungry and didn't bother to ask what we got for the price.

He started by bringing the bread, wine and water (the holy trinity of a menú). Then came a raft of starters; empanadillas stuffed with seafood, prawns in garlic, mushrooms (also in garlic), and fried Padrón peppers (the Russian roulette of peppers). There was a hiatus and S asked if I thought that was it. How did I know? But the portions had been generous enough for a ración and it was a posh place. I was just considering asking when our waiter returned with two huge

PLUM, COURGETTE & GREEN BEAN TART

plates filled with pork chops in a wonderful cream sauce (most unusual in itself) and the ubiquitous fries. Stuffed full, our plates were cleared and a homemade flan (how do you say flan in English? Oh yes, crème caramel!) appeared. Just right after a huge meal. Must remember to get lost more often!
Spent a load more at the Chinese cheap shop on the way home buying an extension cable of 50m and a light.
Home 5.30pm. Lit fire and assessed our day's spend!

Diary Sunday 20th January Sunny and warm
Fired up with success that we may soon have windows we decided to take the afternoon off and walked up the track past the house, down past the second water mill and up the other side of the river to the top of the hill where there is another village. Crossed back over the river and walked home the other way. About an hour's walk and very pleasant. The motorway looks very close from the track where the markers have been left. Really am trying not to think about it but I just keep seeing trucks and dirt and noise and... go and do some sanding of a beam. That takes my mind of it. Decided to start knocking some of the grotty cement render off the outside house wall on the motorway side to see what the stonework will look like exposed. Mark told us all Galician houses were rendered as Franco had a wasp phobia and the insects like to nest in the mortar in between the stones. Sounds like rot but a great story nevertheless. Our wall has nice big stones, some rosa granite others the grey granite and quite square. Should be good cleaned up... eventually. Better staring at a wall than looking toward the motorway anyhow.

JANUARY

Tuesday 22nd January 9.45pm Very warm and sunny during day!!
Dear mum,

You will want to know that today I wore my shorts for the first time this year and I think I may have got sunburnt! We ate dinner outside complete with sunglasses, sun hat, and said shorts. Lovely. Someone told us ages ago that Galicia has weather in 15 day cycles and I hope he's right. Two weeks of solid rain and now, hopefully, two weeks of sunshine!

Planted 300 onion sets today. The garlic is over 8" high so hopefully it will do well. It 'feels' like spring at the moment anyway.

We popped into town to check my emails earlier and to put my 'English classes' notice up now I am a 'qualified' English teacher haha. I put one in each of the bars that we frequent and one in the library. Have one of the barmaids and her sister interested already so may have to do some work soon.

Do you remember the old boy with the beret (you helped him on with his jacket when we were in Scala bar back in Oct)? It was his birthday today. 100 years old! I gave him a kiss as I couldn't think of the appropriate things to say. He seemed happy with the gesture anyway! Hope I can still totter into Scala for a vino when I'm 100! (May even get my own cushion too).

The range is still going well. Did Sunday dinner lovely. Roast loin of pork. Ever so

PLUM, COURGETTE & GREEN BEAN TART

tender and moist (mind you, the quality of the pork helps too… only fed on home grown produce and no chemicals or antibiotics) with roast apples from our store. My plum sponge rose lovely, despite running out of baking powder and having to use bicarb and the oven being way less than 200°C – though who knows as I don't have a thermometer and am not sure how accurate the cooker one is. I'm starting to wonder how necessary it is to have exact oven readings for things anyway! Mrs Beeton says: 'to test for a range cooker without regulator: hot oven; a piece of white paper put into the hottest part of the oven turns a rich brown in 3 minutes; fairly hot oven (200°C) it turns light brown in 3 minutes; moderate oven the paper turns yellow in the time and in a warm oven it does not colour.' She also says a hand put into a hot oven will sting after 8 or 9 seconds… think I prefer the paper trick haha.

I cleaned up the brass rail at the front of the stove the other day. Using wood ash (plenty of that) and lemon juice. I dipped half a lemon shell into the ash and scrubbed. Comes up brilliant. Did I say I have started cleaning the top up too? It is slow but definitely getting the rust off.

We have been tiling the back (south side) of the roof. S has also been sorting out the skylight over the attic room where poor Les was entombed in Oct. Tell brother we will soon have a job for a competent plasterer (the bedroom walls which we knocked off before our weekly swim and sauna last week...though we had to have an extra-long shower before going into the pool or we would have clogged up the filter with plaster dust). Tell him, no wages but bed and board available!

Thursday. Sorry, this will be late again as I thought it was Wednesday today. Doesn't time fly!? I hope your back is better. I assume something you had been doing previously precipitated the incident with the sock? Should I ask, or will I be mad at you?

Actually had a quote from the other window company (Agolada) today. Much less than Toldao (our original company) so I rang Toldao and asked if they had the windows yet. No. So I told them to forget it. Thought he would argue that they had made one window (minus glass of course) and I was ready for him, but he didn't seem at all bothered so I think it is for the best.

I have sowed lettuce and planted tulips and Iris reticulata in front garden and some violas in a tray in the barn. In a couple of weeks or so we should have quite a show of blossom if the rain holds off. Apricot, peach, apple, cherry and plums are all showing big fat buds and even the robin has got himself a wife... well, he's not chasing her away and she keeps wiggling her bum at him so I'm guessing they are

PLUM, COURGETTE & GREEN BEAN TART

going steady at least! Spring must be coming.
Love you tons and tons
Xxx

Diary Thursday 31st January Sunny and warm. Lunch outside again
Made a batch of cakes. Apple and walnut ones okay but the chocolate one sort of ran all over the oven! Tastes okay though. Planted some land cress and some primulas. Then looked at the end wall I am going to point up in the bedroom. Sorted a bucket of small stones ready to put into any gaps. I think I'm nervous to get going!
Popped into town to book a table at Bar Mencia for Sunday's festa do caldo de ósos, ('pig bone stew fair'... sounds better in Galego I think!) May get more ideas for what to do with our growing freezer full of piggy two!

FEBRUARY
Pig bone stew

If I thought that the festival season would be over after the long, hot summer, I was happily mistaken. Galicia loves its fairs and festivals, and *Galegos* love their food. Combine the two and you have a perfect day out.

A *Galego* can never be far away from his next meal. Pre-lunch drinks always include a *tapita*; a small, usually free, plate of something tasty. Lunch is huge and three courses. (When we first walked the *Camino de Santiago*, we could no more manage a full *menú del día* than fly. By our fifth month of permanent residence, we seemed to have evolved somewhat. Maybe the portions were getting smaller, or we were more up to the challenge!) Dinner is another full meal, eaten late, with more tapas beforehand to stave off hunger.

Galician festivals, even non-food orientated ones, normally include some food somewhere, whether it be a hot dog stall or a *parillada* (grill) set up on the village green. Even more fun are the single foodstuff themed festivals. Padrón has its peppers; Cea, its famous bread; O Grove, the Exaltation of Seafood and O Carballiño its octopus festival. Vilaba has its capon fair just before Christmas and we have our pig bone stew fair on the first Sunday in *carnaval*.

PLUM, COURGETTE & GREEN BEAN TART

Friday 1ˢᵗ February Frost overnight, sunny and warm now.

Dear mum

Thank you for your letter. Can't believe January has gone already. Your talk of Christmas meals and visiting here before next Christmas makes it feel like the year is rushing past... or have I fallen asleep and missed it all like Rip Van Winkle?

It's been lovely this last week. We even had a picnic down by the river in Monterroso today. It's very peaceful there at this time of year.

There was quite a crowd at the hotel for the 'ex-pat!' club this afternoon. Jen and her dad, Stefan from down the road with the whole family. His youngest has settled into school really well and loves giving us new Spanish words he has learnt. He is picking it up so quickly. Wish I could have learnt Spanish at that age, would've helped so much! Stefan's eldest has left school (he only had a few months to go when they moved over anyway and was struggling a bit I think) and has managed to get an apprenticeship locally with a plumbing firm. It's nice to see them doing well (and a real boost to the age demography locally too haha). CJ and Gala were there too, then when we got home there was a note from Anne and Simon (cats and dogs) to say they had popped in to visit us so I invited them to the next market. Might as well get all the Brits in one place eh? Ha.

Had a nice swim afterwards though probably not a good idea after a Galego lunch. I'm surprised I didn't sink!

We have been tiling the roof (still). We are running out of old tiles, sadly, as quite a few are broken so we may end up buying some new ones unless we can find someone throwing some away. Certainly the village seems to have a few shiny new roofs since we started! Think we instigated a trend! Our new-old roof now looks the oldest in the village.

S has fitted the skylight in the attic room. It looks much brighter than with a sheet of glass over the hole though you will need to be seven foot tall to actually open the window!

Talking of windows! We have ordered the ones from Agolada for the two bedrooms, the bathroom to be and the kitchen. Decided to leave the barn doors and the sunroom for now as there is work to be done on those and if they have a smaller order maybe they will make them quicker! The man seemed very conscientious and even revisited with different suggestions to make the most of the small window openings we have. We have decided to have one pane of glass in each instead of the traditional six smaller panes as the new frame already takes up so much room and it's a shame to spoil the view with lines. Your bedroom has

PLUM, COURGETTE & GREEN BEAN TART

a lovely view of the water mill on the river at the moment while the trees have no leaves on. It will disappear soon though once they all leaf up.

We have also ordered a second huge Velux (now S says he knows how to fit one) for the big barn roof on the mezzanine level. That one will only take four days to arrive from Italy so why do ordinary windows take so long?!

S just beat me at scrabble. Twice in a row. I am forgetting my English. Can't do the quick crossword at all anymore! Think I'll go to bed. It's pumpkin time anyway xx

Saturday 10pm. I hoed some of the allotment ready for planting this morning. Noticed the sweetcorn (thank you for sending them) says that the two types - one is 'sugar-enhanced', the other 'extra-sweet' - shouldn't be planted together so I will put one lot in the garden though I'm not sure now if I should plant ordinary corn (maize, for the chickens) with sweetcorn. Will it cross and turn the sweet one starchy?! Is there anything in your gardening books about it?

Very frosty overnight. I suppose that is the downside of clear sunny days in winter. Luckily I had taken my pansy seedlings in last night. The land cress and primulas I sowed are indoors too. I have bought some lime for my cabbages but it's too early to plant much else yet. The sun is deceptively *warm but it was white over this morning.*

No reply from my text to you. Hoping your back is better now?

Tomorrow is the big fiesta in town... the bone stew fair. We have booked a table at Bar Mencia and invited Jayne and Richard, the couple we met at Mark's do (big van). They said this was one of the first houses they saw when they were buying so are interested to see what we have done. They found it confusing with all the different half-levels and stuff. Theirs is a much squarer house with a room in each corner. I remember Mark sending us details about it. Funny how we all viewed the same properties but have chosen different ones. Just as well I guess!
Love you tons
xxxxxx

A *Festa do Caldo de Ósos* or the pig bone stew festival (it really does sound better in *Galego*) is held in Taboada each year on the first Sunday in *Carnaval*. This is another of those dates that one needs to be born here to be able to work out. *Domingo de Carnaval* (or *Entroido* in *Galego*) is seven weeks before Easter Sunday, or the Sunday before Pancake Day if you are English.

The fair is strange, quirky and fabulous fun like most *Galego* festivals.

The day starts early (around 11am) with a parade through the town and speeches by the mayor and civic dignitaries. The opening of the market follows. This is billed as an 'exhibition and sale of products of the countryside and derivatives of the pig'. Including (but not exclusively), *chorizos*, shoulder, hams, *toucino*, and *dentes*. Thankfully, for those of a more sensitive nature, there are also artisan breads, cheeses, honey, local wines and *augardente* or firewater (or literally tooth water).

There are, of course, refreshments to be had. Specifically, a bowl of the famous *caldo de ósos*, served as a *tapa* in most of the local bars and at the market itself in a special 'beer' tent, washed down with local wines of the *Ribeira Sacra* region whilst listening to the local *gaita* group (a Galician folk dance and musical group with traditional Galician bagpipes).

At 2pm everyone retires to the local restaurant of their choice (usually booked up well in advance) to partake in a special *menú del dia*. Taboada is tiny by British standards having a town population in the region of three thousand. (The council area, of which Taboada is the administrative centre, has five thousand souls and covers an area of 147km^2.) However we are blessed with ample facilities. There is a school, health centre, social centre, town hall, library, post office, and far more bars and eateries than the population size suggests might be needed. At last count we had twelve bars or cafés and four restaurants. On *festa* day, nine local restaurants and bars offered the special *menú*. We had chosen the local restaurant of our friend and all-round helpmate Luisa – the Parillada Mencia.

Pig bone stew is much nicer than it sounds, being a slow cooked broth of chickpeas, potatoes and pork or ham bones (usually those backbone pieces that are left over after the 'Spanish' method of butchering the pig) together with the *Galego* seasonings of garlic and paprika. Done well, it has a delicious and rounded flavour.

All the restaurants compete to produce the best *caldo* each year and Luisa's would have been cooking since early morning in one of her huge metal pans before being brought to the table in giant tureens to be dished out by the participants. Each time a tureen empties, it is miraculously refilled like a Galician horn of plenty.

Of course, being Galicia there is also the holy trinity of bread, wine and water included, and the *caldo* is not the only course but merely an appetiser.

Once everyone declares themselves well and truly stuffed with soup the tureens are whisked away to be replaced by great big platters of pork ribs and potatoes. These *costillas* are roasted in the oven, this time with carrots and peas, white wine and garlic. And again the platter is refreshed each time it looks dangerously close to being emptied, even to the point of some unwitting victim having the last rib ceremoniously plonked onto their plate so the platter can be removed for refilling.

Finally, everyone again declares themselves sated.

Only dessert to go! For this special *menú* there are normally two desserts; fresh local cheese with honey or/and *filloas*: a type of thin pancake traditionally made with pigs' blood and totally delicious.

Only coffee left and one can escape to quietly sleep like an overstuffed armchair.

Diary Monday 4th February
Musings on a Mediterranean diet:
The wonderfully Galician pig bone stew fair has had me pondering the Galician diet in general – the very antithesis of the heart healthy, olive oil and vegetable laden, 'Mediterranean' diet.
The Galician food pyramid would consist of: meat, fish and potatoes; wine and augardente; grelos (turnip tops) and toucino (pig fat). And yet I know of many Galegos well into their 90s. The chap who celebrated his 100th birthday in January is far from unique (though he does have

some concessions to age... like his own cushion waiting for him in the bar. Something like I would imagine the king to have, if he were to sit in a rural bar sipping coffee that is). So what is going on?

Checking out the so-called Mediterranean Diet, it seems that, sadly, the original study was flawed. It focused on two poor, rural communities in Crete and Sicily in the 1950s. The diet of these communities was probably only one factor in determining the inhabitants' longevity. Their genes would have been another and lifestyle a third. In these communities people worked all day in the fields in the fresh air, ate long, leisurely lunches with family and friends, and had a siesta in the afternoon. They had no long commutes in filthy city rush hours. No snatched lunches at a desk in an air-conditioned building. None of the stresses of a modern-day life in the rat race.

Stress is known to be a leading factor in heart attacks and, taking out the obvious dietary differences, we could be talking rural Galicia today. So my new fame will be the Galego anti-stress diet; lots of hoeing in the fields, two hour lunches with plenty of vino and lots of friends, a nice, relaxing siesta then more digging followed by more wine and tapas down the local with a noisy game of dominos (very vocal, good for alleviating stress). I think it will be a winner!

Why do the Spanish eat so much pig? Certainly in Galicia, the menu board is not exactly vegetarian friendly. A local sandwich menu might read; *jamón Serrano, jamón York, salchichon* (sausages), *lomo* (loin), *chorizo* (spicy or not), *bacón*, cheese with ham, cheese with *chorizo*, cheese with bacon, *jamón con bacón y lomo*, spam, spam, spam, spam...

Two explanations leap to mind:

FEBRUARY

The first is simple. In a rural setting, a pig is one of the most useful and efficient converters of food waste into quality meat (historically anyway, heaven help anyone daring to feed scraps to poultry or pigs now – oops, slipped on the way to the landfill your honour). It is one of the best meats for smoking or salting to preserve it and it tastes good. Pigs can be kept, if not morally then certainly cheaply, in a small space. Their manure is excellent for the vegetable patch, they grow from a tiny piglet to something approaching one hundred kilogrammes in less than a year and of course each and every part can be used. Even the teeth it appears.

The second reason is more complex and more fascinating. When the Catholic monarchs Isabella I of Castile and Ferdinand II of Aragon evicted the Moors in the 15th century they gave the remaining Muslims in Spain a choice. Convert to Christianity or die. One way to prove one's conversion was to ostentatiously eat pork, a meat banned by the Islamic faith. Although eating pork is no longer a requirement to live in Spain, one of the hangovers from this time is the sheer amount of pig products still on a menu. *Tortilla de patatas* anyone?

Diary Tuesday 5th February Drizzly and mild
Into town early for shopping. Everything closed! A festival day, again. So came home! I'll learn one day... maybe.
Did a couple of mortar mixes pointing up the bedroom wall. Have found that using my fingers to push the mortar into the holes works best though it ruins the gloves... and shreds my fingers on the granite. Just can't get the spatula to do the same job somehow! Seem to spend more time collecting the mortar off the plastic sheet on the floor. Also spent ages finding stones to put into the gaps. Especially now I have taken

the old corn husks out. Maybe I should just have left them in?!

Monday 11th February. Hot and sunny!
Dear Mum,

It has been so warm the last few days! I have been in shorts and even managed a topless sunbathing session one lunchtime (must get that tan topped up. Haha).

I have decided to plant the 'chicken' corn on the allotment and one of your packets of sweetcorn up by the house to be sure they don't cross. I will save the other packet for next year. We have cleared a bit on the west side near to the house which is actually nice deep soil unlike most of the 'garden' around the house. I will use it as a flower garden after the corn is out. Funny you should mention a stall on the market here as a group of us were discussing just that last week (after a few lunchtime vinos at the bone fair it has to be said). The plan is there, we will have to see what actually grows before we decide to implement it! Had a good time at the fair despite the weather suddenly turning on us, though we didn't stay for the Charleston 'big bang' as the orchestra was billed (think it was a typo and they are the Charleston Big Band but then again, these bands do have very odd names).

Jayne & Richard came and Cris & Steve who are buying on the coast and are helping us register the car (when we find some headlights that is). J&R are living in similar conditions to us though their kitchen is in an ex-chicken shed (but it is a very nice ex-chicken shed with proper windows unlike our kitchen). We got to talking about life before septic tanks and rain coming in roofs, and being able to sit outside in winter (usually anyway!) and of course market stalls. CJ wanted to come too but Gala said he needs to lose weight so he wasn't allowed!

Our table was reserved with a note saying 'los ingleses 6'. The chat carried on afterwards in our cosy kitchen (the stove had stayed in whilst we were at lunch) until about 8pm. Very nice day.

Rich lent us his kanga hammer (a big stone breaker drill) so S has been playing with his new toy today digging a trench alongside the west wall of the house for the bathroom waste pipes to join up with the existing pipes from the loo in the living room to the septic tank. It is much quicker compared to the hammer and chisel he used before but incredibly heavy. I can't even lift it up!

They (J&R) are driving back to the UK this month to get some plants so I asked if they could pick up some ash whips for us. We had an idea to grow some for coppicing for firewood and haven't seen any here. The one S had in the UK grew so quickly. This means I have been attempting to clear some *of the long grass from down the bottom end of the allotment so we have somewhere to plant them. I now have a large pile of straw for the chicken shed!*

I was over in the allotment hoeing for my spud patch this morning when Eusebio turned up on his tractor to tell us off for buying 'plastico'... not because it's environmentally bad (which it is I know) but because we could have picked it up for free. That is also true as the plastic used to wrap the silage bales is usually just ripped open and left to blow away in the wind until it tangles in a tree. Anyway, we agreed with him and then managed to negotiate for a tractor load of cow muck (he was clearing out the barns when he stopped) for 20€. He dumped the muck but didn't take the money. Now I don't know if he wanted more. If he was joking about the 20€ and I have offended him. Or if I just got the entire conversation wrong... which is most likely. Tried to mention it to Concha later (at least she can hear me) but she said it was up to him. Very helpful!

Forgot to mention, we were pulled by the guardia civil on the way back from the fiesta meal and S was breathalysed! First time ever! Of course he had only had one glass of vino anyway and a 3 hour lunch so it read 0-0. Quite clever of them to stop people coming from a fiesta after lunch though and the officer was even bright

FEBRUARY

enough to choose the <u>driver</u> of the vehicle!

Whilst S has been playing with his kanga drill I have been pointing up the exposed stone wall. I am very slow and not particularly good but it's your bedroom I'm practising on so as long as you leave your glasses off it will look fine haha.

Also bought another huge tub of woodworm killer so I'll soak the beams S has cleaned up, and the ceiling too before I polish it (looks smashing cleaned). S is re-erecting the wall between that bedroom and the bathroom to be and swapping some floorboards around so we should have all good old ones in the bedroom. Then a plasterer and some windows and hey presto!

Weds 8pm Lovely and sunny again. Just off for a vino in town. It must be spring, we had a very pregnant salamander in the garden yesterday (same one as from the washing machine hole) and two deer in the field below the house. Also saw our first skink of the year emerging from a hole in the garden and wondering where all the long grass went!

I have been sanding and polishing the door to the bedroom whilst S puts the door frame back in. We have to use the same frame as it is warped to the shape of the door!! The door looks really nice polished up. Just need some new glass. CJ says they found a place up a dark, narrow track with no signs and a dilapidated farmhouse at the end which, inside, was an Aladdin's cave of glass and mirrors. Then again, he's a lot more adventurous than me!!

We also collected the Velux for the big barn today. Well, we didn't as it wouldn't fit in the car so they agreed to deliver. Only problem is managing to pay. Everyone else seems to settle up at the end of the month or at some point in the distant future whereas we like to pay when we collect something or, shock horror, when we order something! We are so very foreign!
Off for our tapa
Love you tons
Xxx
P.S Had a delicious ham hock with mash, and baked apples with chocolate sauce for lunch yesterday done in my lovely range cooker. I love my cocina so much!
P.P.S Can you post us a packet of Yorkshire tea please? Down to our last one. I was going to order in bulk online but the postage for a dozen packets was the same again as the tea. Will just ask visitors to bring us a packet over when they come. R&J (big van) said they would bring us some back from the UK but a packet to tide us over would be good. It hasn't lasted as long as it did in the UK. Probably 'cos we are having more tea breaks and certainly we have more visitors!

The bone stew fair was not the only local festival on in February. It was also the Arzúa-Ulloa cheese fair, the weekend of 15th/16th. This local, creamy soft cheese has a *denominácion de orígín* status and can only be made in a select number of local dairies. The cheese fair is organised by the *comarca* (or district council) of A Ulloa. This consists of three *concellos* or local councils; Monterroso, Antas de Ulla and Palas de Rei. The fair rotates between the three councils. Sadly, but not surprisingly for Galicia, these three *concellos* find it hard to ever agree on a mutually acceptable date for the fair, so it always a pleasant surprise to find a poster advertising it!

We went down to the cheese fair, which was being held in Monterroso that year, on the morning it opened. It didn't open until 6pm. I checked the poster. No it didn't mention that at all! I decided I'd never be a local if I couldn't work out what time *feiras* and *festas* started!

As cheese is one of my favourite things in the world to eat, we popped back in the evening. (See, that's wrong too - it's not evening until about 10pm. We went at 6pm, still afternoon.) Anyway, the fair was open and we got some freebies but there was no cheese! That was the following day apparently. So, a cheese fair without cheese, incredible!

There were some freebies though! S is hopeless at fighting off the old ladies for free giveaways – far too polite, so I had to do the grabbing. I got a very nice pinny and a couple of tee-shirts with *queixotetilla* on them (tit cheese – for the shape.) The old ladies were pushing and shoving and grabbing armfuls of stuff like they had no clothes at home. We bought a saw blade (I know, it wasn't just cheese related) and got a free baseball cap thrown in. Next minute a chap came over, and seeing our cap demanded one too. He didn't even buy anything!!

PLUM, COURGETTE & GREEN BEAN TART

Determined not to give up on trying the actual cheeses we returned on the Sunday morning.

There seemed to be less stalls than the previous year when we had visited with Jen, the weekend we came over to sign for the house. It had been May that year and warmer weather. It had also been in Antas de Ulla which, despite being a tiny *concello* always puts on a good *feira de queixo.* I sampled what must have been every cheese in the *cupola,* as the round building in the centre of Monterroso town is called. We bought a smoked *San Simón* 'tit' cheese and a soft cheese with walnuts in it as well as an Arzúa-Ulloa cheese from the dairy *Diqueixa* and a delicious goat's cheese from a little old lady.

There was a French stall selling cheese aged in caves, somewhere or other. As the lass 'womanning' the stall had wandered off, one *Galego* chap came and helped himself to a big wedge of a dirty looking cheese to taste. He put it in his mouth and immediately spat it out on the floor to hoots of laughter from people nearby. The stall holder rushed back in a furious temper to berate him. It seems you are supposed to remove the mouldy, earth covered rind before eating the cheese. Leaving a *Galego* alone next to any foodstuff is like leaving a kid in a sweet shop, they are going to have a try!

Later that day, Carmen came over with more eggs and some wonderful sweet dough things called *orejas* because they look like (but thankfully don't taste like) pigs' ears. She kindly included the recipe too.

I ended another lovely weekend by ringing mum from the roof. I'd found it was a much better signal up there – smashing views too. It would be a shame when the roof was finished. I decided I would have to climb out of the new Velux to ring her.

FEBRUARY

Monday 18th February Cloudy but mild today
Dear Mum,
 Anyway we still have suntans before anyone else! They are apparently beginning to get worried about the water situation over here already. You wouldn't think it from the rain in January but the rivers haven't fully refilled over winter as autumn was very dry (if you remember from your sunbathing in October) and this should still be our wettest time of year. S is happy though as he now has the last bit of the roof at the front off (over the big barn).
 Could do with a spot of rain for my seeds - can't possibly water everything running back and forward with a watering can, though the onions are poking through water or not and I have some Lollo Rosso up that I planted in January! We may have our own lettuce when you come over if nothing else. (And eggs too if we manage to get our chickens next month) Just hope all the rain doesn't arrive in April!
 Wednesday: Sun and showers. Still mild. First blossoms are out. Peach I think... or apricot, whichever we decided on!
 Just got your letter, thank you. What do you mean September? I've told Carmen and Luisa that you are coming in April now! They both asked if you were staying longer this time. They said that if you are coming for such a short time 'you may as well go

PLUM, COURGETTE & GREEN BEAN TART

and visit the doctor' at least I think that's how it translates! I suppose it's not considered a proper relaxation if it's so rushed (people tend to have one month holidays here). Anyway you have no excuse for not staying longer if you are coming on your own eh?! I know I said on Saturday that we had thought about driving over but the car isn't likely to be re-registered anytime soon (we are still headlight hunting. The Ford garage wanted 300€ for a pair!). We will probably leave visiting until Oct/Nov when we could also bring walnuts and things over for everyone. So we will be very pleased to see you in April.

Planted my leeks in pots yesterday and some parsley and land cress in the allotment. Parsnips next I think. Yes, I will try tomatoes and peppers. I have some Gardeners Delight tomato seeds I bought in Wilkos before we left. Should do okay in big pots in front of the long barn I think. Carmen kindly came round with some Calendula plants, Gladioli bulbs and some other frondy leaved plants and some eggs. We had six (small) eggs for breakfast and I planted the flowers in my triangle near to the terrace. The Iris reticulata are all up and flowering now. Look lovely. We then dug a semi-circular flower bed out on the west side, under the garden wall to the orchard, for the Gladioli. I've added some annuals (Cosmos and Nigella) too. We are trying to make that bit more garden-like to discourage the tractor from using it to turn round in. We rolled the two huge stones which fell out of the wall in November, until they were level with the newly sited stone trough so they make a kind of low wall, then strimmed the grass. It seems to be working so far. May dig more beds and put the bench outside under the walnut tree too.

Tell Belle we will try to keep some chorizos (or cinzano - which I think sounded better mum!) for her - maybe we should make some of our own next year if they are that expensive over there and sell those on the market too! I daren't tell Luisa. She is still recovering from me saying wine is around £3 a glass in UK and No Free Food. She thinks I was joking about the tapas.

We have asked her to grow us another pig this year. She likes giving me recipes and is very patient listening to me mangling her language! Oh and tell Belle that she specifically asked if my sobrina (niece) was coming back as she has a very nice cousin who is single...

I'm sorry Kate is having so much trouble with the kids, though I was 37 by the time I decided what I wanted to do for a living so I can't comment! Talking of work... they are hoping to start on phase II at Whitemoor. According to Davey Millar it will probably be November before they are ready to start

PLUM, COURGETTE & GREEN BEAN TART

moving newts. He promised to let me know when they have a contractor.

Richard & Jayne found some ash whips (to plant at the bottom of the allotment for coppicing) in a nursery near to Lugo and kindly bought us some. We now have quite a network of friends who will look out for things you need and help each other with renovation problems. With the exception of Stefan (who is a special case) no one charges for help. Instead we have a sort of reciprocal agreement; help for help. Very nice, very new age!

Had a go cleaning the walls in the big barn (whilst the roof is off to allow it to air out). They look lovely though you have to stand quite close to get enough power and I was covered in water, dust, goat or cow poo, spiders and bits of granite. S kindly took a photo for posterity!

Lots of love

Xxx

Book that ticket - no excuses - looking forward to it. Xxx

Diary Thursday 21st February Mist early then very hot and sunny

Decided to have a go at hot water crust pork pies. Spent all morning in the kitchen. S on the roof. Up there all day putting the frames on for the next section (Northwest) and cementing the gap underneath.

Later: Pork pies look ok! I poured in stock made from the trotters so should jell nicely. Strimmed grass through the trees and finished removing grass on west side corn plot, then did a bit more pointing on the bedroom wall. Finished 7pm. Lots of washing up, hope the pies are worth it! (Late eve: Had pork pies for supper. Taste ok, though the pastry could have been a tad thinner.)

The last weekend in February we had yet another outing. This time it was to the city of Pontevedra on the west coast of Galicia for the inaugural meeting of the Anglo-Galician Association. Anne and Simon came with us so we had plenty of opportunity to learn about the wisdom of 'Saint Bob' (Flowerdew). We didn't mind as they are both very knowledgeable about all things organic and it helped pass the rather long and convoluted journey up and over the mountains. The scenery from the tops was astonishing. My ears popped and refused to clear all day which made listening to the group interesting. The venue was in Pontevedra old town. The centre of Pontevedra is a picturesque city with some fascinating stone buildings which we vowed to return and look at another time. After the meeting, which was lively and loud with plenty of opinions about the group aims and an eclectic mix of ideas, we adjourned for lunch at a local hostelry. As one of the Spanish members said, "You can't have a meeting in Galicia without food!"

Tuesday late February?! Pleasant and sunny evening. On our terrace at 6.45pm with a last tea before washing up and watching final Lord of the Rings film on DVD.
Dear Mum,
  We have had an afternoon planting 48 ash trees at the bottom of the allotment (3 to go, gained one extra). Had to give up on the

PLUM, COURGETTE & GREEN BEAN TART

watering though as the well couldn't cope. It did rain a bit this morning but has been incredibly dry through February. Probably only 4 rainy days (will check diary*) so we are being careful not to overload the well as, being spring fed, it fills slowly if the feed itself is slow. Seems okay so far.

*2 drizzly days since 6th Feb!

The blossom on the early plums looks lovely. The apricot is just coming out. Our first daffodil opened today and the first shallot (of the ones you sent, thank you) is up too. Spring is here, rain or no rain.

The little plants Carmen brought over are looking happy. She brought another dozen eggs over yesterday. Will have to find her some plants to swap. Talking of plants, I hope you are bringing a big suitcase: two cuttings of your Rosa rugosa; one Amelanchier; any primulas you have spare; Viburnum; Pyracantha; any spare rockery plants. The house leeks are doing well but I don't think the Campanula survived the winter. The glory vine is happy in a pot on the terrace, growing up an old fork, and has buds on. I may plant it near the grape vine so it can scramble up that. Will see what you think when you come.

We also made a trellis yesterday for the black grapes in the space in front of the chicken shed. That I cleared in October. Now we just have to wait for them to grow and produce some grapes for us!

FEBRUARY

On Saturday (oops no, Sunday... probably). Anne & Simon (cats and dogs) came over and we all went to Pontevedra for the inaugural meeting of the AGA (Anglo-Galician Association). It was very enjoyable with a good mix of English, Spanish, French and even New Zealanders. The next meeting is at the end of March at an Italian restaurant (Oh, I forgot the Italians) overlooking the Miño and Portugal. We plan to make a weekend of it if it's nice still.

A&S brought us over some Jerusalem artichokes to plant so I've put those in. My potatoes are chitting nicely in the barn. Carmen has her cabbages in already and they were liming the field down the valley today, it was like a snow blizzard. He must have limed the whole of the valley... villages and all. S says a bucket of water each and they would have had their houses whitewashed for free!

Wednesday. Very wet! Well, at least we didn't have to worry about watering in the rest of the trees. Think they will be fine haha.

S has been trying to make a chicken enclosure between the downpours but every time he went out the rain got heavier again so only half done so far! I chickened (Groan) out and went indoors to clean and polish the living room door. Looks very nice as usual. I've also started on the kneelers. May be able to get you to reupholster them

PLUM, COURGETTE & GREEN BEAN TART

when you visit? S says we could put legs on them and have two chairs. Philistine!

I was happily sanding the door to a backdrop of Jesus Christ Superstar at full volume when Stefan and family (Tattoos, nearest neighbours) turned up. Luckily S persuaded them that I wasn't really in pain just 'singing'. It's easier to sand hard whilst singing loudly… at least that's my excuse!
Love you tons and tons
Hurry and book your ticket. Plenty of planting left to do. And remember, don't smile at the security guards and under no circumstance try to chat to them!!!
Xxxxxxx

Diary Thursday 28th February Hot and sunny but had real rain yesterday!
The rain brought out another salamander. Different one with lots more markings and 2 big red spots on her tail and base of the legs.
Posted our letters this morning and bought posts for the chicken shed enclosure. S dug in the posts while I made two apple and walnut, and a sesame orange cake. Biryani and dhal (non-curried!) for lunch.
CJ called with his chainsaw to cut up the old walnut tree this afternoon. Repaid with tea, orange cake and small walnut tree to plant! S made a door for the chicken enclosure, (he's working really hard, hoping to get chickens on Saturday at Monterroso market). Put paper and straw inside the chicken house, mended/redesigned the nest boxes and put everything inside ready. Just need the hens now!

MARCH
Chick chick chicken

One of the big draws of Galicia, other than the wonderful people and the erratic climate, was the ability to be able to afford enough land with a nice derelict house on it to realise our dream of self-sufficiency.

I had extensively researched what was required. How many potatoes need to be planted for two people for a year, how many cabbages, how much corn for the chickens, how many trees to provide firewood etc. etc. I filled pages and pages of my notebooks. It appeared that three hectares was the target to be completely self-sufficient so we started looking for properties with that amount of land. Let me tell you that is a Lot of Land! Forget football pitches and other useless comparisons, it's just a lot. A lot to weed, a lot to sow, a lot to harvest, a lot to dig and a lot to care for.

We regrouped, realising that we wouldn't have the time to look after so much land and to simultaneously self-renovate a house (which we both wanted and needed to do to keep in budget). Three hectares would basically be a smallholding. For instance, if we grew wheat we would also have to harvest and mill it. If we had cows we would have to put them to a bull or use artificial insemination. We would have to milk them and to have them slaughtered. Sheep escape. Goats eat everything. And pigs?

We saw a lovely sow at a local farmers' market. She was huge and white and we soon realised that if, come killing day, she didn't want to participate we would struggle to convince her. As we stood admiring her curvaceous two hundred pound figure, her statuesque ten foot length and her dazzling sharp teeth we caught each other's eyes and a terrible, vivid picture formed in my mind. S approaching her on *matanza* day, the heavy wooden 'pig killer' in his hand; me approaching from the other side with a bucket of food, wheedling, hemming her in. The sow watching us balefully with those little piggy eyes and... charging. The food scattering as I run. S manfully standing his ground, woodwormy old mallet in his raised hand before...

No, cross pigs off the list too.

We set our sights lower. Grow enough vegetables, fruit, and nuts to sustain us year round. Raise chickens and rabbits and buy a pig from our friend. Not quite self-sufficiency but a reasonable compromise.

Chickens were always one of our must-haves for our new, *vida dulce* in Galicia. The garden chicken boom in the UK was just starting when we left and trendy, designer chicken houses could be had for less than two thousand pounds. Mum regularly sent us lovely photos of them from *The Telegraph* newspaper. They were works of art. One, an egg-shaped hen house measuring two feet high by around a foot diameter, was apparently suitable for three hens. It looked both impossible to clean and totally impractical. It also seemed a perfect shape for a fox to roll away for a late night snack. Our chickens would have an inexpertly rendered, old brick-built shed with wonderfully quirky Galician perches inside – long pieces of thick tree branch sitting on four splayed legs at just the right height above the floor. Not the Ritz maybe but a pleasant *pensión.*

I read up on chicken care: on what to feed and when, what illnesses to look for, and at what age I would get that all-important first egg. I read stories glorying in incompetency. Foxes taking hens at night because the hen house door was left open and owners going away for weekends and forgetting to feed the hens. I read expert advice telling me hens will only lay when there are more than 14 hours of daylight and need artificial lighting in winter if one wants year-round eggs (no-one told ours). I listened to accounts from friends saying you can just throw a few scraps at them and get ten eggs a day (no one told ours that either).

In reality, all my reading and research prepared me not one jot for the arrival of our first three point-of-lay brown pullets.

Monday 3rd March Dull with sunny bits and quite breezy
Dear mum

Our hens have arrived! Pepe from the hotel helped me to choose them on Saturday from the market. The guy put one into a small cardboard box. I went to take it off him so he could do the rest but no... he stuffed all three in the same tiny box! They seemed none the worse for it when I got them home complete with water trough and chicken feed. We put them straight into the shed as my book says to keep them inside for 48hrs. This gave S time to finish the fence now it has stopped raining.

PLUM, COURGETTE & GREEN BEAN TART

Today was the first day we let them into the compound that S has been working very hard to get ready and fox proof. I can't believe what had been thrown in there. Old drinking glasses, tiny bottles used for animal injections (I think), door handles, broken vases and about a ton of unidentifiable bits of broken glass. S has dug down about 2 feet and is still finding bits!

They were lined up at the door when I opened it and were soon running up the ramp to the pop hole and flying back down again wings outstretched. Probably the first time they've had chance to flap around properly! Anyway they have quickly got used to it, and us, and especially the idea of food. When I walk past with the washing up bowl they all come running. We shall have to modify the warped old wooden door to the shed though. It wasn't a problem yesterday when they didn't know there was an outside, but today, 5 minutes after shutting them in, there was a cluck and a head appeared around the closed doorway! They are apparently 18 weeks old so we look forward to our first egg in a couple of weeks. Should be getting 3 a day by the time you arrive in April.

Needless to say the chickens have been a bit of a distraction to getting any work done! but S has fixed a sensor light in the hallway downstairs. We bought it last week in a smashing lighting shop in Lugo. Almost left after two minutes as the first lot of lights were all 500€ plus. Luckily we found the cheaper end. This one is a metal, hanging light like an outdoor lantern and was 31€... except it wasn't, as the girl knocked off 10% and then gave us a bulb for free. I'll never understand the Galician attitude to pricing. Either no price tag at all, or if there is they change the price at the till! Oh well. Will take you there when you visit. Some lovely Tiffany lights too, similar to your dragonfly lamp. It should be much safer going up and down the stairs now and might even chase some of the bats away! Only problem is we can now see how mucky and bumpy the walls are so I've cemented the worst bits and will get some more white paint to brighten it up! May have a go at the living room walls too as at least two of them will be staying long term.

I've started sanding down the back door for painting. I love the little sliding hatch in it, I must ask Carmen what it was for. It makes me think of someone asking for alms at the monastery gate. The wood is surprisingly good for saying it is an external door. I fancy a nice dark red or burgundy colour for it. Will paint the utility door to match. It will look good with some red geraniums on the steps.

Had a message from a friend who wants to come over and help. We said she would be

PLUM, COURGETTE & GREEN BEAN TART

welcome though the hotel might be more comfortable than the house if she wants hot running water (or running water!). I was thinking of jobs for her (plenty of those). Eating out could be tricky mind as she is vegetarian. Hope she likes tortilla as there's not much else. Even the lentil soup has pork and chorizo in it. Glad I'm not still vegan, don't think the Galicians even have a word for that sort of extreme behaviour haha.

Can't wait to cook you some meals on the range, just hope it doesn't get too warm to have it on by April. It was very warm sitting behind the stove eating today - the first time we haven't eaten al fresco in ages. I made pizzas, and cookies for afters!

We certainly have plenty of firewood now that CJ has cut up the dead walnut tree that had fallen down. I can get to the allotment without climbing over the thing and we have lots of logs for S to chop up. Also found a huge grub inside the tree. At least 2 inches long and as fat as my finger. We think it was a stag beetle grub. Would send you a pic but don't think you would like it much... the chickens on the other hand loved it!
Love you tons and tons
Xxxxxxx

Diary Friday 7th March Frost overnight. Sunshine day, warm!
Finished filling the gaps in the back door and sanded utility door for painting. S screwed the

MARCH

electricity junction box on in the attic space, and got thoroughly filthy with cobwebs and dust and bat poo, then nailed on the bathroom beams for new ceiling.
Carmen found me on the allotment. Gave me another dozen eggs plus Saxifrage, Cyclamen and Dahlias to plant. Wish I had something to give her back!
The rough planking for the floor in the loft arrived together with all the floorboards for upstairs. Luckily I was in town when the chap rang for directions so I guided him in. We stacked the wood in the attic, the bathroom, the bedroom, and the hallway – it does look a lot, hope we haven't over ordered! And only six weeks... just slightly over quince dias then!
To swimming pool to clean up! Bought paint and primer for the walls and doors on the way. Back to Scala after. Fielded questions of 'where have you been?' José bought our vinos! Again.

Diary Sunday 9th March Sun, rain and cloud
Today I painted the hall ceiling (and myself) then, energised, tarted up the (temporary) living room with more white paint. Needed some sand for the cement render as the stuff we had was too coarse. José at Xesteira very kindly gave me a bucketful for free yesterday! I do love this place. S has been busy making the stud wall in Bedroom 1 (well, between there and the bathroom). I remember the first time we visited the house and leant against that wall to look at the view – the whole wall moved! Neither the top nor the bottom of the brick wall was fixed to anything. Think his stud wall will be more secure... at least I hope so!
Lunch Gammon (ours, good) and pineapple (not ours!). Apple crumble. This afternoon we cleared a space between the leach field pipes and planted out the strawberry plants we bought at the

PLUM, COURGETTE & GREEN BEAN TART

market. The idea is that they will get some moisture from the leach field run off. Think the rest of the time (and most of the week) has been spent chicken watching!

We decided, in the interests of being able to eat them if necessary, not to give the chickens names but numbers. One, two and three had sergeant, corporal and lance-corporal stripes on their legs to identify them. The numbers lasted about as long as the felt tip stripes. Number two became the very un-PC 'Fatty' due to her habit of eating anything in sight. A slowworm, mice, my fingers, were all food. Number three was a spectacular jumper, managing to raise herself a good three feet (that's a metre for the youngsters out there) from a standing start, especially if this meant she could reach the grape vines which provided shade over the summer. So full of grapes was she that her name became Veronique after the chicken dish of the same name. And number one was, and always will be, Number One.

Rural *Galegos* in general have a different attitude to animals than the squeamish British. We feel it is barbaric to kill an animal for food whilst happily buying some packaged piece of water-filled cardboard on sale at £1.99 down the supermarket. There are still many of our friends who can't believe we really kill things to eat, though they themselves are far from being vegetarians. Our neighbours keep animals for food. They are looked after accordingly and killed when necessary. Although not animal lovers, in the sense of keeping animals as pampered pets, our neighbours are not without feelings for their livestock.

One day, Carmen came to the allotment where I was working. She slapped a chicken onto the granite step and shouted "*Mira!*" Look at this! Taking in the situation at a glance I realised the chicken was dead. It wasn't a difficult deduction, it had no head. "The third this week, what are we going to do?"

We decided to set up a trap, guessing from the bite marks that the perpetrator was a weasel or pine marten. I duly went to an agricultural supplier in Monterroso and explained the problem to the young female assistant.

Her eyes grew round as she blurted out "I know what that is!" She said something in *Galego*. "Oh yes! Farmers have many problems with them taking the milk of a cow."

"Really? But how is it called in Castilian?"

"Oh, they are only in Galicia. They have much danger to chickens."

I wrote down the *Galego* name and showed it to Carmen when I delivered the trap. She looked bemused and shook her head.

"What is it?"

"Small animal, spiky, many times is run over."

Ah! That will be that well known dangerous animal, the ninja hedgehog then!

(Although we never did catch the chicken-killer, an RSPCA inspector friend did later tell me a gruesome story of finding a hedgehog devouring a litter of new born kittens so maybe they are not as harmless as we both thought.)

Tuesday 11th (so S tells me) March Wet but mild

Dear mum

Boy is March staying like a lion! It has been quite wild here the last few days. Really stormy last night. It isn't often windy but when it is you can hear the wind roaring up the valley maybe 5 or so seconds before the big pine tree starts to move and then you brace yourself for it to hit!

The hens are getting more used to the great outdoors. They were out for 2 hours in the pouring rain yesterday and seemed to quite enjoy it though they looked like drowned rats! They were fluffing their feathers for ages. Today we let them into the garden for half an hour before their tea. They had a great time. Straight for my flowers of course. I found Fatty with a tulip flower in her mouth looking for all the world like Ermintrude from the Magic Roundabout and not at all embarrassed at being caught! They explored all the barns and the terrace. In fact they were fine until they spotted me taking their food bowl out of their compound (to fill it up). They all ran at me clucking madly and flapping their wings in an attempt to move quicker. They then followed me back to the wooden box where I keep the feed. Fatty jumped into the box and wouldn't get out. Number one followed me back to the compound and started eating the corn quite happily. Number three followed but couldn't find the door to the compound and stood clucking sadly and watching her sister eating all her dinner. Fatty was still on the terrace and had to be carried back! At least they put themselves to bed now though they still sleep together in the nest box rather than on the perches. (Maybe they never had perches before?)

MARCH

We went to Agolada to chase the windows today. They still haven't got them and Easter is upon us so it may be a little longer yet before we have draught free openings. I <u>was</u> hoping they would be in for you to see! Oh well, maybe next year haha.

The bedroom is starting to look good. S has the stud wall up on the bedroom side and two wall lights wired in (though they are not connected to the mains yet as we ran out of wire!) We hope to start rejigging the floor now to make it sound whilst we are waiting for the windows to appear!

I have finally finished painting the hallway so at least the bumpy bits are bright and clean when the light comes on. We also have half a floor in the space above the bathroom to be, where the water tanks will go. (I helped lift the rough planks up and boy were they heavy! Suppose they have to be solid to take the weight of a full water tank.)

I've also finished polishing the two kneelers and the old door to the big barn. Am hoping you will be able to re-upholster the prayer stools for me in April if I buy some material. The old stuff is a bit on the worn side. It also has some candle drips on it (as does the little potty cupboard above where the kneeler was). Obviously they were used for the purpose intended. The old door from the lobby to the big barn is lovely wood but so hard, my sander doesn't touch it. The

PLUM, COURGETTE & GREEN BEAN TART

barn side has been rubbed smooth and oiled by years of (we think) goat's rubbing up against it. Oh, that reminds me. Pepe came round with his son who speaks some English. He was telling us about the family; there were 11 of them in the house and the animals below. I asked him about the goat hair in the downstairs barn. 'Oh, no' he says 'it's human hair'. Aaargh! Turns out one of the family was a hairdresser and made wigs so he kept the hair for that. Yuk yuk yuk. So glad we threw it out now!!

Planting has slowed with the inclement weather. My red shallots and onions are growing well. Still no carrots up nor yellow shallots. The peaches are in flower and a very beautiful pink colour. Used up the last of the cooking apples from the barn last Sunday. Bit soft but not bad for 5 months storage. Made a lovely crumble anyway! Today we had Chinese ribs done in the oven whilst we were out. They were perfect. Rich and falling off the bones. We'll have to do some for you. Not long now!

Love you tons and tons

Xxxxxxxxxxxx

PS We have every confidence you will manage fine on your own. S says you will no doubt start chatting with your seat neighbour on the way over. And Santiago airport is so small you can't get lost.

XXXXXXXX

Extra kisses for the journey!

MARCH

Diary Wednesday 12th March Sunshine! Reasonably warm too
Posted mum's letter. Planted 7 rows of spuds (75). Carmen called over the wall to say she had some col (cabbage) for me. Then planted 4 rows of 8 col plus 3 rows of 8 repollo (a different cabbage I think). They look awfully big to transplant. S watered them in while I dug trenches for a further row of spuds ('house' spuds) 105 spuds planted in total... should produce enough for us.
Let hens out while we cleared the nettles near their house and had our dinner outside on the terrace (can keep an eye on them that way). Sowed 6 red and 6 white cabbage in yoghurt pots (red in plain pots, white in fruit pots... just realised would have been more logical other way round!)

Diary Saturday 15th March Sun, wind and rain
Into town. Bought a roll of chicken wire to hem 'em in as they are eating everything in the garden, especially my flowers. S is going to put a fence around the fruit trees to give them a secure run. They will still have plenty of space, and shelter from the trees and I get to keep some flowers! They will be safe from the cats and foxes too.

Our main pest, or eater of chickens, we actually found to be the beautiful but deadly buzzard. This killer soars on thermals many metres above the chicken run then plummets silently to snatch a meal. Chickens are not the smartest birds in the avian world and will often watch as the buzzard tears into their fallen comrade instead of running as fast as their little legs will go.

Our chickens started as free range then, as my flowers started to disappear, we put up a one metre fence. They jumped it. Two metre fencing

PLUM, COURGETTE & GREEN BEAN TART

followed but this didn't stop the aerial attacks. We bought nylon wide-mesh netting for the top which worked until a goshawk managed to dive straight through the mesh taking poor Danni on the very day she laid her first egg. The mesh became chicken wire which then had to be propped up, which then became a full construction project running into hundreds of euros to the amazement of our neighbours who told us that chickens only cost a couple of euros at the market. True enough, but despite the fact that we would one day eat at least some of them, we didn't want something else to do so. We felt we were losing the war. We did have one triumph over the buzzard... but that was all way in the future and is another story!

Sunday 16th March. Grey & windy but warm in the sunny bits!
Dear mum,
  Had an interesting day out today. Happened to see an advert in the local paper for a visit to some petroglyphs (Neolithic rock carvings) nearby. Cris & Steve accompanied us. There was an historian there who gave a talk about the carvings which I managed to understand... a bit of. Another chap kindly translated some of the talk. It seems they really don't know the significance of the carvings. Some look like people or animals, some are mazes, Celtic looking designs or just squiggles, and some are modern day additions (like a man with a top hat on!) but it's amazing to think of someone 4000 years ago carving a doodle in a rock whilst watching his sheep.
  Of course, being Galicia, after the

educational stuff we all adjourned to a local restaurant for lunch. We skipped the afternoon lectures as I wouldn't have a hope of keeping up, and after huge mixed grills and vino I might have fallen asleep anyway!

Popped into town for a vino earlier this week and immediately ran into the usual problem with paying for drinks. José was in the bar so we managed to get him a beer for a change and left before he could buy one back. In the next bar (we have to share our custom around!) one of our neighbours who we have hardly even met bought our wines. Don't think we have ever got to pay in that bar... seems to be our vecinos (neighbours) haunt!

Our bathroom (to be) now has no floorboards on it as we decided to knock them off on Friday (before our swim luckily as we got a bit dusty). We bought some chipboard to put underneath the new floorboards for a bit of extra support and insulation. Unfortunately we have come to the conclusion that we don't have enough good boards to keep the existing old floor in the guest bedroom either. A lot of the ones that look good from above are woodwormy below. We will try and save the best ones for the attic room (Belle's room)

The cabbages Carmen gave me look a bit happier after the rain yesterday but they do still seem very big for transplanting. The problem is that everyone will take note if they die. As I planted the spuds Carmen was asking: why do you dig with a spade instead of hoeing, why aren't you cutting them in half, why are you planting rows east to west instead of north to south? The problem is I know the answers: I know how to use a spade not a hoe, I have plenty and they won't get diseased so much if they are whole, the ground slopes north to south so I'm hoping making trenches across the bed will help retain water in summer… but I can't always explain in Spanish so I just stand and look dumb instead. At least she was impressed with my onions so one gold star this week!

(Good Thursday!) Cloudy but at least the wind has abated. Hope it improves for your visit. So far March has been nowhere near as good as February, weather wise.

As you see I haven't posted this yet so you get two weeks in one. Everyone here packed up for Easter on Tuesday so no mail etc. Today is Jueves Santo or Holy Thursday. Carmen has had lots of visitors so I had the bright idea of thanking her for all her help by making some Easter biscuits and taking them over. She said they enjoyed them very much and promptly returned with a dozen eggs and a bottle of Albariño (local white wine). 'To drink with the tortilla you can make with the eggs' she told us! It can be so frustrating trying to give anyone anything over here, they are all so kind and generous. But the eggs are very welcome as the girls have yet to lay any. That ditty dad used to sing keeps going through my head… 'chick chick chick chick chicken, lay a little egg for me'. I've tried singing it to the girls but it hasn't worked so far (though number one did have her wings over her ears yesterday for some reason haha). S keeps threatening them with the pot but I think he's joking as he enjoys playing with them as much as I do!! When we come outside now they fly at us from wherever they have been making mischief and start pecking our legs. I think it must be chicken for hello! (Or they were fed using on-demand feeders and are pecking at the paint spots on my trousers.)

Now, things to bring on your visit. Walking shoes, some warm slippers in case we have a night in - the floors are a bit chilly, especially with the gaps in the upstairs hallway! We have plenty of overalls, fleeces, and brollies, and I have saved you a nice red cap for working in. We went swimming this morning as the pool isn't open in the afternoon being a holiday (again). If you fancy a dip bring your cossie though S says we won't <u>have</u> to go swimming that week as you may let us use your shower at the hotel haha.

If you have time and space could you bring us a Saturday Telegraph. All of it would be nice, though probably more than your weight allowance, but the crosswords definitely and the money pages please. Also, an odd request for a 76yr old I know, but could you get me a couple of packets of Tesco's own brand tampons! Of course they do them here but they are much more expensive! Thank you! Jayne & Richard (big van) are bringing the heavier goodies back, including real ale for S (which I hope he might share with me).

I have been busy baking cakes as we have a VIP visitor arriving on April 7th. Also been tidying up! See how many new/different things you can spot. A kiss for each one.
Love you tons and see you soon
Xxxxxxxxxxxxxxx

Diary Friday 20th March Sunny but very breezy so feels cool
Took back door off (well, S did... it is very heavy!) Coated it with gloss paint. Wasn't windy when I started, now there are leaves flying around everywhere and sticking to my nice new paintwork! Looks very red – sort of pillar box red rather than the burgundy I expected. Maybe it will fade on drying! S meanwhile painted the attic window tunnel. The tunnel (with the bit of Perspex ledged on top) was, according to Carmen, originally part of the chimney from the lareira or open fire in the store room below, which explains why the walls in that room are so smoky black. It now makes a perfect skylight window for the attic room. In fact we like it so much S is thinking of putting another one in there. It will be quite bright eventually, unlike

MARCH

when poor Les stayed in October! Actually, considering how cheap the skylights are and how quickly we can get them compared to the 'normal' windows maybe we could just put them everywhere!

Diary Saturday 22nd March Snow, rain, hail and sun... oh and an icy wind!
Perfect Easter weather! Undercoated utility window. My hands were frozen! S continued making the new chicken fence to keep them in and off my flower bed! Made a very clever 'pop hole' for the compound. A small opening in the wire fence with a dangling wire door curtain they can push through but which hopefully will deter predators. They soon got used to it though number three stood watching it flap back and forward for ages before diving through. Reminded me of myself at school skipping games... now! now! aaargh!
Managed to plant 32 sunflowers in between the hail and rain storms! Thought it would be getting better by now! We created some ingenious cloches for them using the copa de chocolate pots. S melted a hole near the top and made me some thin wire stakes with a hook on the end. Invert the pot over the sunflowers, stake it down with the hook and hey presto! Only problem is that I am 18 short... (MORE CHOCOLATE POTS FOR PUDDING THEN (S))

Diary Sunday 23th March Sun am then cloud wind and rain (of course)
Think the weather is conspiring against me, look... 8th, sunny, washing on, rained. 15th sunny, washing on, rained. 23rd, sunny, washing on, rained. Could be a useful trick in summer.

PLUM, COURGETTE & GREEN BEAN TART

Diary Wednesday 26th March Another wet and windy day!
I tried to dig a trench for the new asparagus crowns. Got absolutely drenched while doing so and the trench filled with water so decided it would be prudent to wait a bit! S very sensibly was inside doing his electrics now we have bought more wire. It's so humid the stonework is all running with water. The terrace looks like someone threw a bucket of water over the walls and floor. I tried to clean up that old chestnut bedframe instead. It took the rest of the day as the varnish is really sticky (probably the damp too.) Think the bed will look really nice in the guest bedroom, though S will have to extend the side rails as it is only 5'10" long (and 3'10" wide... sort of Galician shaped).
Lunch: Tortilla Galega using some of Carmen's chickens' eggs

On the final Saturday of the month we left the chickens to fend for themselves whilst we went to A Guarda on the southwest tip of Galicia to meet with the Anglo-Galician Group. They had arranged a meal at an Italian restaurant run by Anglo-Galego-Italians. The restaurant was just behind the beach in an old pine forest. The setting was stunning. Sand and trees, a piney, salty tang in the air and a slight breeze ruffling the waves. Although we left home in thick fog it was sunny when we arrived in A Guarda. After two and a half hours driving we needed to stretch our legs so a bracing walk on the beach was called for.

That gentle breeze was deceptive.

A Guarda sits on the Galician promontory overlooking Portugal to the south. The river Miño forms the boundary between the two countries from Tui (up river) to A Guarda, where it discharges into the Atlantic. The estuary (south) side of the beach was lovely, warm and sheltered. But once we turned the corner it was like another world entirely. The Atlantic wind was so fierce I had to hang on to S to keep upright and retain my dignity!

There were around twenty of us for the meal, a delicious and very generous Italian *menú* with lashings of local *vino* and lashings of chatter. We had booked a room overnight. The restaurateurs, Sheila and Luís, had a couple of charming log cabins in the woods next to the restaurant. We had a blissfully long, indulgent shower followed a couple more glasses of wine in the bar chatting to our hosts. We knew we would sleep well.

The Galician spring weather had other ideas. A devil of a storm brewed up overnight. I lay in our cosy bedroom thinking of the huge pine trees towering over our little log cabin. I imagined them crashing down and turning us and the cabin to matchwood. The wind howled, the trees creaked and groaned and the rain hammered on the roof but incredibly by morning it was sunshine again with only a few dead branches to show for the maelstrom.

Since the day promised to be glorious we decided to visit Santa Tecla (or Santa Trega in *Galego*). This hill, which overlooks the beach and dominates the town of A Guarda, has a restored *castro* on it. Feeling lazy, we drove up. Halfway to the top was a payment booth. We were just thinking of walking instead (which was free) when the guy said twenty cents - for the car and two passengers. Thinking of the amount that would be charged for such a historic monument in the UK, I had a hard time not laughing out loud. I don't want to spoil it though.

Santa Trega was discovered accidently in 1913 during construction of the road which goes around the hill. Only around half of the *castro* has been excavated but it is still one of the largest Celtic Bronze Age settlements found in Galicia. It sits 200 metres above sea level with fantastic views to the town of A Guarda below, the wild Atlantic to the west, the Miño estuary to the south (and Portugal beyond), and overland toward Tui and Ourense to the east. There is an archaeological museum, chapel, and restaurant on the top but best of all are the restored Celtic buildings. Generally groups of round houses (although some later ones were Roman inspired and therefore square) *castros* are found all over Galicia. The buildings are made of stone with a heavy wooden prop in the centre to support the mainly thatch and wood roof. Some of the houses at Santa Trega have been partially rebuilt so you can look inside. I sat in the gloom in a Celtic roundhouse pondering on the life of an ancient Celt compared to our rather easy life in Galicia. Then I thought: 'they didn't have any problems with window men because they didn't have any windows. They didn't have problems with chimneys not drawing because there was no chimney, the smoke merely circulated around the little one roomed house'. I suddenly felt an odd kinship with these ancient peoples.

Back at the restaurant we ordered a takeaway pizza to eat on a sheltered part of the beach, nestled below the pine trees. We sat watching the boats bobbing in the estuary and the little island at the very mouth of the river, called Ínsua, where we could still see the ruins of the 15th century defensive fort.

The drive back was somewhat longer than the outward journey due to the fact that we took a slight detour, round and round Ourense, with its mind-blowingly confusing one way system.

S, who was navigating, was pointing below. "We want that road down there."

MARCH

I, driving, politely replied, "how do I get to it when everywhere is one way?"

Just when I had given up hope of ever leaving Ourense we popped out on the Lugo road.

We finally arrived home rather later than expected to find we had had two eggs laid in our absence. There would be home-produced eggs for breakfast and a good end to the month!

APRIL
Galicia is a world

I was incredibly lucky growing up. We lived in a post-war council house in a rural spot with a big garden overlooking fields of cows. Dad was an enthusiastic gardener in his spare time. A member of the *Auricula* society and a lover of bonsai, he was also a great vegetable grower. After he was forced to take early retirement from the colliery when I was only 16, he and I spent many happy hours in the garden. When our elderly neighbour asked if he would look after her garden too he jumped at the chance to grow even more of his own produce for our table. We grew *Romanesco* broccoli years before it became trendy. I podded fresh peas and dug for potatoes. I learned to hoe, to weed and to enjoy the taste of home-grown.

When I first moved to London in my teens, I lived in shared houses. One was a huge Edwardian pile in Muswell Hill. My tiny bedsit had access to a vast, derelict and totally overgrown garden at the rear. One day whilst I was at work, mum, who had come to visit, decided to clear the whole thing using a piece of broken glass she had found. I returned to an exposed crazy paving pathway, a nettle-free area to plant and a slightly crazy, nettle-stung but contented mother. Over the next two years I grew the most amazing tomatoes, onions, and even peppers in that sheltered and fertile,

APRIL

south facing garden. Each time he visited, the landlord would say he was going to lawn the whole thing. Thankfully he never did. I continued to enjoy my produce and the sunny garden in equal measure.

Many years later I had my own allotment in Leicestershire. Leased from the council for the princely sum of £10 a year, it was also overgrown and had the added joy of no piped water. In summer I had to lug buckets of water from the house a mile away. I cleared the land and planted fruit bushes and horseradish. I grew mangetout and shallots, brussels and sweetcorn and, on finding a nest of chickens' eggs one day in the middle of my carrot bed, dreamed of keeping chickens of my own.

If I thought that all of these varied and wonderful experiences would prepare me for my *huerta* or allotment here in Galicia, I was sadly delusional.

April Fools' Day! Sunny and warm
Dear Mum,

Keeping fingers and toes crossed that this weather will last for you.

We have just finished tea. Goat's cheese, our walnuts (still bags of them left), and two nice crunchy apples. Have eaten all the fresh cooking apples (some still in the freezer) but the eaters are keeping very well, especially the ones in the plastic bags you made holes in and hung up. Gala says theirs are all rotten. Reckons they were frosted in the garage. We had pork and apricot (the ones you cut and dried, also keeping really well) stew today for dinner. Found the cocina

PLUM, COURGETTE & GREEN BEAN TART

makes a mean rice pudding too with a good crispy skin. Yum!!

Looking forward to getting some fresh veg from the allotment. The veg they sell in the greengrocer's is generally good but very limited. Only found parsnips once last year and I couldn't explain to Carmen what shallots were even having looked up the Spanish (eschalots). Goodness knows what they will all make of the artichokes!

I know I am being watched planting and hoeing in the allotment and notes are being made. I am dreading getting it wrong with the phases of the moon which all the neighbours stick rigidly to. Is it new moon or full moon? I planted onions at full moon but that was wrong apparently, according to Anne. It should have been new moon. Mind you they have pushed their way through despite my error!

Thing is, it's the reputation of England and all her farmers on the line here - a very big responsibility is this!! I'm sure the ash trees were planted incorrectly, Eusebio hasn't spotted them yet but he will, he will!

Oh yes, big news! We have discovered what the big building at the end of the road is... Stefan told us but we didn't believe him. It is a big supermarket, agricultural supplies and hardware shop. How long have we lived here?!!! They don't exactly advertise by, for instance, having a sign saying supermarket, or a door you can see through, or any little hint that it is anything but a factory. S says it's probably a huge chain like Tesco's so everyone knows. I think Galegos are just born knowing certain things, such as the timings of festivals - like a sort of racial memory.

Will post this tomorrow along with the letter S wrote to Les. He has taken around 2 weeks to pen his. He might be slower writing than me but much neater. If my writing gets any worse I shall have to start typing my letters. Problem is fingers can't keep up with brain! Ha!

We have been trying to find accommodation for Les and family for the summer. Managed to finally find someone at the campsite in Monterroso but it worked out quite expensive for car, tents and 4 people so we asked at the 'hostal' nearby. He offered 3 rooms with their own bathroom to share for 40€ a night so if they are happy we will book that.

Your room is booked here in Taboada of course. The lady asked how you were and is looking forward to seeing you again.

S has been making a set of stone steps, round the back to the garden on the west side, with some huge granite stones. Looks very professional and covers the sewer pipes.

We had two of our very own eggs for breakfast on Monday (laid whilst we were at the coast...nice surprise and very tasty). Hopefully now they have learned how to do

PLUM, COURGETTE & GREEN BEAN TART

it we will have plenty of eggs for you to try in a week's time! Now the chickens are settling in well we are going to look for some rabbits to complete our menagerie.

Wednesday 2nd April. Had our fifth egg today so building them up for you! I have been busy painting the utility (to be) door and windows with nice shiny red gloss paint to match the back door. Hope you like them.

Better post this or you will be here before it arrives. We need to get on with some cleaning anyway as we have a very important visitor arriving soon.

Love you tons and see you (very very) soon
Xxxxxxxxx

PS don't forget our paper if you can fit it in. xx And the jar of marmite, but in your hold luggage as Jen had hers confiscated at customs as liquid (only if you melt it I would think but you don't argue with the airport security... do you mum?!)

Diary Thursday 3rd April Hot and sunny after the mist cleared 12pm
Had a surprise call from the land registry office in Chantada to say our papers are ready for collection (wow! Only seven months). We went straight there... just in case they changed their minds. 850€ Ouch! Didn't have enough cash on us as I had thought she said 85€ on the 'phone (I obviously still can't do numbers), so had to go to the bank. Apparently it is so expensive because there are 7 separate parcelas or plots of land (I thought they were adding them together at the catastro? So what did <u>they</u> do then?) I give up.

APRIL

Still, we are all registered and legal on all the bits where we need to be, I suppose that's the important thing (though I <u>would</u> like to know what the Catastro office did).
Back home in time for morning tea. Painted a second coat on the utility windows then took the back door off again and did a second coat on that too. S continued making the stone steps over the sewer pipes.
Lunch: Veg stew with walnuts in it.

Diary Saturday 5th April Hot and sunny
Ooo hope this lasts for mum! Spent the last couple of days cleaning for our VIP visitor. Yesterday I cleaned the terrace and swept all the cobwebs off whilst S finished fitting the last full sheet of chipboard for the bathroom subfloor. Today we have cleaned, polished and vac'd the living room. S gave the car its biannual wash and even washed the old net curtains which we are keeping for an extra layer of insulation across the window openings in the living room!
Lunch: Pasta with home-made pesto, using our walnuts and parsley and Galician cheese, followed by cookies and cream for stamina! One egg at 10am.

Diary Sunday 6th April still hot with a breeze pm
Had four of our own eggs soft boiled for breakfast with toast soldiers, scrummy! We swept the kitchen and hall then cleaned the kitchen from top to floor (which is becoming redder with each mop). Our bacon joint with cabbage and mash for lunch and honey and walnut tart for afters. One egg laid at 6pm. So much for Katie Thear and the self-sufficiency guy saying hens only lay in the mornings. Obviously our hens don't read the same books! Just finished tidying up for mum and We Are Ready!!

PLUM, COURGETTE & GREEN BEAN TART

The sun was glorious that first week in April, once the early morning mists cleared. We could still see white puffs lingering above the Miño as we drove home from Chantada on the Thursday, creating a perfect candy-floss stripe directly above the river. We had found that whenever we had a cool night following a warm day the mist would blanket our valley all the way along our little river, the Rio Moreda, back to the great Miño. Usually, the sun burnt off the mist by 11am at home, chasing it back towards the river. The closer one was to the Miño, the longer the mist lingered. CJ, just a kilometre from us as the pigeon flies, often saw the sun an hour later.

§

Galicia is an interesting place in which to garden. It has an Atlantic climate on the coast, with warm damp summers and mild damp winters. In the mountainous interior there is a more alpine climate, hot, dry summers and cold winters. Into this one inevitably has to throw climate change. My neighbours repeatedly tell me that the weather has changed since they were small, when it rained all summer and was snowy all winter. Even discounting normal, fallible memories, we can see changes ourselves. We have not had a really heavy snowfall for five years. The village *lavadeira,* or washing trough, has not had any water in it since before we arrived. This latter partially because of a lack of maintenance but at least in part due to lower rainfall. That first year they were concerned about the water table as early as February.

Added to the uncertainties of climate change are the *Galego* 'microclimates'. When we first arrived we laughed at Mark, the estate agent, and others, who would declare each property we saw to be in a 'microclimate'. They can't *all* be microclimates we reasoned. Well, actually, they can. Chantada, just 15 kilometres south of us was totally flooded one day. Water flowed down the streets and lifted manhole covers up as it forced its way through the drainage system. We had not a drop. Our friends Jayne and Richard, not 20 kilometres north, once had a hail storm so violent it punched holes in their newly fitted guttering. We had a slight rain shower. One day we heard a howling noise and a tight but vicious mini-tornado whizzed through our tiny hamlet just missing my fruit trees but destroying more of the same at a neighbouring village the other side of the river. On the coast one can grow lemons, avocados and even bananas. In Quiroga, an inland town in a valley near to the Castilla y León border it is mild enough to grow oranges, and olives commercially for oil.

And so it goes on. Galicia is a land of complete contrasts.

There is a beautiful poem by Vicente Risco which begins: *Tú dices: Galicia es muy pequeña. Yo te digo: Galicia es un mundo y cada vez que la recorras encontrarás cosas nuevas...* Freely translated this reads: 'You say: Galicia is very small. I say to you: Galicia is a world and each time you return to it you will find new things...'

Risco's evocative poem sums up this amazingly diverse and complicated land perfectly. Every valley, every hill, every *aldea* and every *lugar* is unique, with its own flavour, its own traditions and its very own climate. This was also the land where we had chosen to garden and to try self-sufficiency.

In the Lugo hills, sitting at 500 metres above sea level, we have our own challenges. The altitude means that even in summer, when day time temperatures can be in the high 30s Celsius, the mercury can drop as low as 7°c overnight. Even more problematical, the seasons are not linearly progressive as in say, the interior of Germany or

PLUM, COURGETTE & GREEN BEAN TART

the United States. One day in April can be spring-like at 24°c, the next can struggle to make 8°c. These temperatures bounce back and forward with no by your leave. As I write this in July it is 37°c, the sun so bright it burns your eyeballs. Yesterday it was raining and thundering so violently it was dark by 5pm and didn't top 20°c.

That first year, the March winds, hail, frost, and snow gave way to April sun followed by rain, rain and more rain...starting the day mum arrived for her visit.

Diary Monday 7th April Mum arrives SCQ... Rain! Typical.
Put Chinese spare ribs in the oven for dinner and fed the hens then off to Santiago. Flight landed on time. Picked mum up, had tea at the airport then to Leroy Merlin to get more electrical bits for S and a solar light for the garden. Popped into the bathroom shop to look for a bath but nothing caught my eye as a match for my imaginary tub which should be big enough for two and be a real statement piece for our new bathroom to be.
Home for 2.30pm. Ribs done perfectly! Only needed to stir fry the veg and cook some rice. Brilliant. Last of honey and walnut tart for pud.
Mum and I viewed the estate (in the pouring rain), and the works in progress indoors, then watched our hens eating my tulips one by one as S continued making the fencing. Ran mum up to the hotel. Two eggs. (First egg from number two?)

Mum was staying a full week this time. We had planned to do lots of sightseeing with her. It rained solid for the first four days of her holiday.

Mum, of course, didn't care. She helped me to bake cakes, watched the chickens in the rain and sat, huddled in her coat, in the kitchen. Despite the warmth of the *cocina* the kitchen felt damp and

APRIL

poor mum had arrived with a streaming cold. I later learned that the doctor had thought she might have pneumonia and advised her not to travel. My strong-willed mother as usual knew better than any doctor. She had travelled anyway.

Diary Wednesday 9th April
Today we have been to Lugo. Mum said her hotel room was cold so I mentioned it to the lady this morning and asked her to turn the heating up. Visited the Roman baths in Lugo near the river. Builders seemed to be in. We knew it was the right place by the stink of sulphur but there was no light so it was impossible to see anything at all! Not sure if electric was off, the bulb blown, or it is just like that normally. Nice modern spa hotel above though. We sat and had a tea and watched the dressing-gowned clientele parade about.
Had lunch at new place we found out on the industrial estate, Juan's. Really good menú (with vegetables) and homemade puds! Mum attacked the arroz con leche (rice pudding) with gusto! I think she is feeling a bit better.
Called over to Anne & Simon to collect two more hens (one a beautiful white Wyandotte) and a cockerel (and a load of home grown veggies). They gave mum a quick tour. They have done a load of work on the place and have some great (different) ideas for the rest of the house that I hadn't thought of when we viewed it. Back for 7pm then out for English lesson in Antas while mum and S waited in Bar O Farelos. Brought my student over to them for some 'real' English conversation after. Think mum confused her when, sympathising with Maria's bandaged arm, she said that she also had a 'wonky wrist'. Well, they want to learn 'real' English don't they! Dropped mum back at the hotel.

PLUM, COURGETTE & GREEN BEAN TART

On the Thursday, it was still pouring with rain but we had our second surprise of the month and some very welcome news.

After only three months (and fully seven months since we had first tried to order some windows) we had a 'phone call from Agolada to say they were coming that very morning. Two charming lads arrived promptly at 10am and fitted the first window, in the kitchen, quite quickly. It looked lovely and was soon toasty warm with the *cocina* going. Mum even took her jacket off for the first time this trip.

Unfortunately the upstairs windows weren't so simple. They didn't fit! The three windows were all ten centimetres too tall for the openings. I couldn't believe this. After all this time they had made the windows the wrong size. How could that even be possible? The two fitters seemed unconcerned as they rang the office for advice and stood smoking outside. After what seemed like an eternity they came back with a choice: we could either wait for new windows to be made the right size or the men could cut the stone embrasures to fit the windows they had brought. A silly question after this long – cut the stone! The two fitters immediately brought out a large angle grinder (obviously kept in the van for just such an occurrence) and started cutting a chunk out of our bathroom window sill. As one finished cutting, the second lad fit the window into the now perfect sized opening whilst his partner moved to cut the next stone sill. Besides the usual two hour lunch break, the two men worked solidly, declining all offers of tea, coffee or snacks until 8pm. All the windows were in and we had three nice neatly cut windowsills. Paulino seemed happy when he came to check.

"They have made a good job, no?" he asked, smiling. "*Tenéis una vista preciosa.*"

APRIL

Yes, it is a beautiful view and I couldn't help but wonder, just a little, if Paulino hadn't deliberately mis-measured the openings, knowing we would be left with slightly bigger windows, and therefore a better view of our beautiful *vista* – as if!

"I forgot to tell you with the windows coming," said Mum as we drove into town that evening. "When I got back to the room last night I thought I had been thrown out!"

"What? Why?"

"Well, it was empty. The room. My clothes, my toothbrush, everything. I was going to ring you then the lady arrived. She was wearing nothing but a silk teddy! I didn't know what to do! She kept shouting at me and pulling my arm so I thought I was being evicted."

Mum has a vivid and quite illogical imagination sometimes. To be fair most 'normal' Spanish to a non-speaker sounds like shouting, especially if the woman was trying to make a reluctant mother understand something.

"Well, what happened?"

"She dragged me downstairs to another room. All my stuff was there. They had even laid my nightie out on the bed."

Of course mum had no idea what was going on. When we took her back that night the lady explained she couldn't get the heating to work properly in the first room so had just moved her... lock, stock and clothing!

We had a good laugh, and three vinos in town, paid for by José (again).

Friday 11th April Big ball of yellow in the sky!
Just finished washing up from our party. Invited CJ and Gala and our vecinos Carmen and Daniel over for vino and cakes. Very enjoyable evening and incredibly hot in the kitchen with the nice new window in. Carmen was full of good words

for what we are doing, which is always nice. The Madeira cake, macaroons and nugget went down well (as did the vino). CJ gave mum a lift back to the hotel so we didn't have to stir! Apparently her new room is far too hot haha.

Saturday 12th April Sunny
At last! Two sunny days in a row! Have taken advantage of the break in the weather to do some planting. Rhubarb (from A&S) in, onions weeded – growing nicely, a double row of our peas (dried ones found in the house) planted – the first lot are up and growing. Last 14 pots of sunflowers planted and covered. Jerusalem artichokes are growing strongly. Anne says they are a weed if not controlled so will keep an eye on those, though we have plenty of space anyway. S continued the fencing round the new chicken run (with minor modifications suggested by mum). That'll teach 'em! The new chickens are settling in well. The big cockerel is already in charge and has serviced every one of our girls at least once a day since he arrived! He is a handsome brute. Mainly white with long brown hackles on his saddle and neck, a flat top comb and deadly looking spurs. Think number one may be a bit put out as she used to be the boss girl, but they all do as he says and come running when he clucks! The little Wyandotte is really sweet and the cockerel is very protective of her. The other one is also white but not a Wyandotte I don't think. Poor thing has a damaged leg so doesn't run very well and the others bully her a bit.
Had a walk up the track with mum, looking at all the flowers coming out... primroses, some tiny wild daffodils, violets, and lots of things that would be expensive rockery plants in UK, like the 'heavenly blue' and the rock roses. Seems strange to have them all growing wild and so incredibly

APRIL

beautiful. Nothing beats nature for a planting palette.
Up to Scala for drinks. Managed one round but Xesteira José's dad bought the other!

Monday 14th April
Another hot and sunny day so we decided to go up to the petroglyphs near the windmills where we had been with the group. No wind at all, and lovely clear views. Got mum up onto the lookout platform. She didn't realise it was cantilevered out over the not-inconsiderable drop until she got down and I showed her! Oops.
Had a lovely pork roast yesterday slow-cooked inside the Le Cruset in the cocina overnight. Had some of our veg from last year and an apple crumble with lemon sauce. (Our apples but not our lemons... little limón is still too small though it has flowers on.)
Three eggs again. Last night drinks in town and managed to pay for one round. Lost track of who we owe drinks to now!
Did a bit more planting in the morning. Everything is looking good. Am thinking we seem to have the perfect combination of rain and sun here. Hopefully the April sunshine means winter is over now.

That first year I had enthusiastically planted everything early. The February sunshine, and memories of the warm spring days we had encountered house hunting, lulled me into believing the glorious weather was here to stay. It wasn't and it didn't.

I have since decided that Galicia almost has two separate growing seasons. With the judicious use of sunny spots, cold frame, cloches and the polytunnel, I can start planting in early February for a late spring crop of peas, carrots, potatoes and

PLUM, COURGETTE & GREEN BEAN TART

salads. The hot dry summer needs copious watering for my plants to grow (and as we garden on a sloped piece of land any rainfall we do get runs away down to the river below). Winter is too cold for anything other than the hardiest crops like parsnips, Brussels and broad beans, but autumn can last well into November, perfect for the tomatoes, peppers and squashes. We are still learning.

Wednesday 16th April. Sun and showers.
Missing you
Dear mum

Seems very quiet without you! Sadly you left us both with your cold (thanks haha). Had a lovely time and glad you got a bit of sunshine at least. The neighbours have all been having a nosey at what we were planting. I do hope it all grows properly for my sake and that of the British Isles.

Had fun after we dropped you off. We went to Leroy Merlin again, looked at tiles and switches and things, then called at the scrap yards to see if they had any headlights (they didn't). We also paid for our windows. Thinking of ordering the ones for the sunroom and the big barn now as they seem good windows and not too slow to deliver... relatively speaking!

S has finished the chicken run and put the gate on as you suggested so hopefully they will now leave my tulips alone. They still have the whole area under the fruit trees and vines to cause trouble in.

Later: I've got a job! Went into town to

check my emails and picked up a message from WA asking me to do this year's newt monitoring on site at Whitemoor. I've negotiated doing the four visits in two goes. One trip will be at the end of this month. Two weekends monitoring with a week in between to visit you (if you will have me haha) and the second trip in late May.

Forgot to say, my pork stew was cooked lovely when we got back from the airport again. I made a Spanish flan (crème caramel) today with some of our eggs. Delicious, and so yellow! Also did a cake with lots of eggs in it as we are getting pretty much 3 a day now though I have had a couple laid without shells. I wonder if it's because of those dogs from the next village trying to attack them last Tuesday?

Thursday. Breezy. Sun and showers

I've booked my flights and a hire car for 24th April and B&B at The Causeway (I can't resist Brent's huge breakfasts). Also booked the dentist for a check-up while I'm over. Will be up to you on the Monday if that's ok. Book somewhere for lunch for us all. Xx

I have been painting those old metal washstands. They look great cleaned up with a coat of black enamel paint on. Think they will go in the two spare rooms. I already have a basin for one of them. Will have to look for one for the other stand... then some fancy towels to hang on the rails. I know, a bit premature but I can dream!!

PLUM, COURGETTE & GREEN BEAN TART

Had omelette for lunch. It was more like a soufflé, all puffed up! Hope your eggs made it back safely in your bag!

Tried hoeing the corn patch but it kept raining! Still no carrots or parsnips showing. I'm really hoping they won't let me down or England will be humiliated here in Galicia!

Friday 18th Wow! What a wild and stormy night. Maybe winter isn't quite over yet. It's hailing now! We were surprisingly undamaged with the heavy rain and gales last night though the old window frames on the terrace blew over and broke and the (metal) cockerel on the hórreo flew away! Had leaks at the edges of the new windows and S had to re-fix the plastic covering the roof as it kept blowing off. He has temporarily tiled the ridge to hold it down. Also found our Chinese hat from the stove chimney way over beyond Carmen's hórreo. Good job no one was passing. Makes a good Frisbee if a little sharp!

Later: Just back from our swim (we were rather mucky from knocking floorboards off in the guest bedroom). Spotted a poster for a cider festival tomorrow night in Chantada. Offered to take CJ and Gala. I have volunteered to drive, as the least cider liking person in the party.

Pumpkin time. Night night.
See you very soon (again)
Love you Xxxxxxxxx

APRIL

Diary Saturday 19th April Wet again
S dug a trench to try and direct the water away from the garden. I know why they made that big step onto the terrace now! The water whizzes round the corner of the barn, straight onto the driveway, down the path and then swirls at the entrance to the terrace looking menacing before it slowly seeps away downhill to the river.
Took us a while to find the festival this evening as it wasn't in the main square but at the top of the hill. (Sure it didn't say that on the poster hey ho.) Lots of cider stalls. 2€ for a glass then you go around sampling cider from each stall. There must've been 20 stalls but luckily for me only about 2 had anything worth drinking so I didn't feel left out! Most were so sour, bite-a-nail-in-half types. Fun night though and, amazingly for somewhere serving free alcohol, no trouble at all. Saw one young chap a bit worse for wear whose friends had propped him up in a doorway where they could keep their eyes on him. Sweet.

Diary Sunday 20th April (Full page of rain symbols needed!)
April showers have turned into April gales and April downpours! My poor veg will be washed away and the neighbours laughing their heads off at the stupid English!
As it's not exactly gardening weather I helped S in Bed 1 (guest room) stacking the good and bad floorboards for future use. Problem is the good ones won't pull up easily as the lovely old 4" Galego nails are hooked into the wood so the boards tend to break if we aren't careful, whereas the woodwormy ones just leave the nails behind in the floor beams to be prised out afterwards! Oh well. After lunch S put in new beams ready for the chipboard subfloor in there. Think I just piddled away and hid from the weather!!

PLUM, COURGETTE & GREEN BEAN TART

We were late up this morning due to festival hours but still had our scrummy boiled eggs for breakfast/brunch with toast soldiers then roast chicken (not ours!) for lunch, with treacle tart and lemon sauce for pud. This is the life!

As if the weather was not enough of a challenge to a newly-arrived Englishwoman, there was the added, and far more important challenge of keeping up with the *Galego huertas.*

Galegos are very conservative when it comes to food. This is partly a rural thing – not much opportunity to try new flavours and cuisines whilst growing up on a small farm six hours from the nearest curry house – and partly a fierce Galician pride in their own culture and food.

A Japanese restaurant opened, very briefly, in Lugo. The day we visited, there were five of us and four staff. The owner, a lovely chap from Barcelona, was quite cagey when we asked, curious, why he had chosen our town. "Because there wasn't a Japanese restaurant here," he snapped. ...mmm. Not that he helped himself. There was no *menú del dia*, no tapas at the bar to try the novel cuisine (which was beautifully presented in the Japanese style, but so small! Only a single prawn on my seven euro fried rice! Where were the rest of them? The bread, the vino?).

In the allotment it's the same story. We are blessed with a climate suited, not only to temperate vegetables like carrots and parsnips, but also to many Mediterranean ones like aubergines and peppers. But *huerta* after *huerta* grows potatoes, cabbages, corn.

When I first picked my mangetout, our elderly neighbour Iñes asked why I didn't wait until the peas had formed. My cherry tomatoes are considered 'a bit small' and my parsnips 'animal food'.

APRIL

Slowly things are changing. One year S made me a cloche, the next year Carmen had an identical one. The year I started watering into plastic bottles to get much needed moisture to the growing plants' roots, the village was suddenly beset by sunlight glinting on upturned plastic bottles in every vegetable patch!

Maybe the locals are willing to learn from *los ingleses.*

In the local market vendors sell bunches of part-grown carrots and onions to plant or bare-rooted cabbage seedlings, which sit wilting in the fierce heat for half the morning before being bought, then left in a scorchingly hot car whilst the purchaser has a leisurely lunch followed by a nice *siesta.* All the time the delicate fledgling vegetables sit quietly drooping. Then, around 6pm he awakens. Down to the newly-hoed patch in the *huerta* he trots. Along each perfect furrow he goes, quickly laying out the 'cabbagelets', roots toward the valley, limp leaves along the ridge above, then he carefully covers the tender roots and gently waters in the young plants....

Er, no, actually then he goes indoors for a quick *vino* and dinner leaving these young orphan plants exposed and vulnerable to the worst the weather can throw at them. They lie, limp and unloved, for three days then, deciding they may as well make the best of it, they start to grow, and grow, and grow until they rival Jack's bean stalk in height. In fact Jack would have been better with a sturdy Galician walking-stick cabbage for a climbing frame – though chopping it down could have proved hard work!

Consider the tough uncompromising life of a *Galego* cabbage seedling and compare it with that of my own cabbages...

I sow my seeds, two or three to a pot, in good compost, thinning to one strong seedling and growing this youngster on, still in its own warm cocoon until it has six good leaves. On a cool day I make a slit in the soil where it is to be planted. Taking care not to disturb it too much, I tap the young plant out, the rootball and the beautiful soil clinging to it and protecting the roots. I place it carefully but firmly into its slit, tamp down the soil and water it gently. I place a sunscreen above to keep it from overheating and cover it if it's a little cool in the evenings. It is in fact, a mollycoddled, spoilt child of a cabbage. And is it grateful? Does it grow huge, overshadowing my neighbours' latchkey cabbages? Does it return my love and affection by being big and strong and delicious?

Does it heck! My neighbours' cabbages are *rascacielos* reaching for the sky while mine are still a modest bungalow.

Maybe *los ingleses* still have a lot to learn from the *Galegos* too!

Diary Wednesday 23rd April Hot…just in time for me leaving ha!
S has finished laying the chipboard in Bed 1. Bit fiddly as the levels are all over the place (surprisingly for this house!). I decided to piddle with levelling that area next to the horno outside. This is my pet project. It will make a great south facing 'al fresco' sitting area once levelled and tiled. The earth is mainly friable rock so relatively easy to dig out with pick and shovel (Yeah, I'm proud to be a coal-miner's daughter).
Made some cookies and a cake, to put in the freezer for S whilst I'm away. We moved the huge tractor tyre out of the Long Barn so we have space for the firewood when it arrives, then did a tour of the allotment to show S what he

APRIL

needs to do while I'm away. Eyes <u>will</u> be watching him and probably reporting back!
English lesson this eve in Antas then vinos in town. Managed to pay!

(S) Diary Friday 25th April Sunshine
Alone! L to UK yesterday. Lay some floorboards out in Bed 1. Into town for espuma to stick first two down so I can nail the rest. Yard shut at 1330! Nails and drill bits from ferreteria Ínsua. Lunch: 3 egg omelette. Muck out chicken shed, not that mucky really. Order water cylinder; 2 coil, immersion, vented, insulated, plus water butts and cold fill tank with ballcock from J&R (going to UK ? next Tuesday). Chicks and plants.

(S) Diary Saturday 26th April Humid
Buy espuma from Xesteira. Stick down floorboards below window. Struggle to get first line straight then get four more rows done okay. Lunch: chicken broth and mash - eat enough for 2. Seal kitchen window – sealant inside, cement outside. Cement outside entrance to terrace for tiling. Don't quite finish as CJ turns up for chat, tea and cake. Manages to put his foot in wet cement on way in and way out.
Swarm of bees in bathroom. Show them the window. Chicks and plants.

(S) Diary Sunday 27th April Windy pm
Washing machine on. Lay some floorboards. Hang out washing. Colour co-ordinated (should've took photo). Tour of allotment. Take 1/3 covers off sunflowers. Check apples in barn. Build crowing platform for cockerel. Lunch: Tripe, big pan full. More floorboards, almost across the room. Wash hair using hosepipe. Chicks and plants

PLUM, COURGETTE & GREEN BEAN TART

(S) Diary Wednesday 30th April Very Wet and windy
Walk allotment. Spot 3 slowworms. Collect slugs for chickens. Floorboards up to awkward bit by wall. Have to chisel out back of board to step over existing raised board supporting stud wall. Very slow. Tea: Spag bol and broccoli. Knock in posts along track by orchard to stop cows wandering through. Chicks and some plants. Light fire, clean clock glass and pendulum.

MAY
A working girl

(S) Diary Thursday 1ˢᵗ May Wet again.
*Lay floorboards (Bed 1). Have reached as far as the door, Hooray! *Go to the market. 8 tomato plants, bags of maize and pienso for the chickens. Cheese and jam butties by the river in the rain. No one else at hotel for meeting so back to continue flooring.*
*Asked Eusebio if he had some string to put on the anti-cow posts I'd knocked in yesterday. Didn't think he'd understood a word but later there was blue, black and yellow string all along the track!

(S) Diary Friday 2ⁿᵈ May Sunshine
Take Bed 1 doorframe out, chisel stone and back of new floorboard to make floorboard fit then put frame back in. Goat's cheese and lettuce butty. Cockerel outside the new fence. Usher him back in. Mix cement, finish cementing kitchen window outside. Check allotment. Swim and sauna. Tuna pasta. Fireworks (bombas) for a fiesta somewhere late on.

Whilst S was busy at *A Casa do Campo* monitoring my allotment and laying floorboards in our 'guest' bedroom-to-be, I was back in the UK monitoring great crested newts and laying out mats for basking reptiles.

I had only ever wanted to work with animals. My favourite outing as a child was to Twycross zoo of the indomitable Molly Badham and the PG Tips chimps. I dreamed of looking after those chimpanzees, especially Cocoa the famous brown chimp. At 15 I wrote to the zoo asking for a summer job. If I thought they would welcome me into the ape enclosure with open arms I was sadly mistaken. I could take money in the car park but not until I turned 16. In those days I didn't always see the bigger picture. Now, I can see that offer as a possible springboard to a real job: the chance to visit the zoo and talk to the staff, to get known and to demonstrate my abilities and enthusiasm. This was my first 'job application'. I was naïve and disheartened. I also realised I had no transport to get there.

As a teenager I had a book called *Jobs Working with Animals* that gave the qualifications needed for each one. I pored through it on a regular basis.

My next choice, after zookeeper, was RSPCA inspector. I wrote to the organisation to enquire about positions, only to be told, very bluntly, that women were not considered for the job as they are 'too sensitive'. This was probably true in my case but an example of the amazing sexism of the early 80s. Thankfully those attitudes have changed and there are now plenty of excellent female RSPCA inspectors. Hearing some of the harrowing stories from a friend who is one of those, I am pretty glad I was turned down.

The father of one of my friends at school was a zoologist. He was a great chap who gave his time freely to help us to study for our 'A' levels. He seemed, to my young mind, to spend an inordinately large amount of time helping toads to safely cross the road on their annual breeding migration.

Zoologist! That was the job for me!

MAY

I applied to read zoology at university and was offered conditional places at Swansea, Bangor and London. Unfortunately, the year of my 'A' level exams was an especially sunny one, and sunbathing near the old folly behind our house much more interesting than revising. I ended up scraping a pass in biology, thanks to the study days given by my friend's dad, and a slightly better grade in general studies, but not enough for any of my university choices.

My parents and I scanned newspapers for clearing-house places and I opted for a two year HND 'B' Tec in Applied Biology at NESCOT (North East Surrey College of Technology). A very long-winded way of saying I was off to the big smoke to pursue my dreams.

§

I enjoyed both my time at college and the HND course itself, although again I didn't study as much as I maybe should have. London was far too interesting a place. I shared houses and enjoyed living in a city for the first time in my life. I somehow graduated with my diploma and immediately fell to looking for my first job working with animals, for which I felt I was now perfectly qualified.

Jobs, it seemed, were not as easy to find as I had imagined. The HND (Higher National Diploma) was neither one thing nor the other. It didn't have the status of a degree but neither was it as practically based as an HNC (Higher National Certificate, a 'lower' qualification which included more practical experience, of which I had zilch). With an absence of employers jumping in to offer me jobs working with animals, I applied for what I could.

My very first job interview was terrifying. A panel of ten professors asked such loaded questions as: "where do you see yourself in ten years' time?" I still don't know the correct answer to that one. 'In your chair' seems presumptuous whilst, 'retired and living in the Caribbean' a little glib. Whatever my answer, and I cannot recall what it was, the job was mine. I was a junior 'B' MLSO assistant. Another wonderful acronym with which the world is overfilled, and which meant I spent my days scraping agar plates and growing bacteria. It was working with animals – of sorts!

I liked the people I worked with, even my boss Ma Baker, as we affectionately called her (behind her back only), and made some life-long friends at the Public Health Laboratory in Colindale. When a colleague left I was given the responsibility for his work. I relished the challenge, but my hard-won HND was too broad to allow me to progress without taking further exams. I could not apply for his job even though I had been doing it perfectly well for three months. I started a HNC course in microbiology at night school but, disillusioned, had already decided this was not really the career for me. I was 21 years old and it was time to move on.

§

(S) Diary Tuesday 6th May Sun
(L back please collect me at 9.45pm!)
Finish levelling stone step in hall (for now). Town. Petrol for airport run. Lunch: tuna again. Cockerel out again, clucking at the girls to follow him and looking worried when they don't! Put him back inside. First row floorboards down in bathroom. Veg stir fry for tea. To airport.

Diary Wednesday 7th May Hot and humid. Brief, dry thunderstorm
S cooked us scrambled eggs on toast for breakfast. Perfect! It's good to be home. Both had

a look at the cockerel who has been causing trouble while I was away, jumping or flying out of the enclosure. I held him while S clipped his wing feathers which should stop him flying (didn't make any difference he still got out later).

Thursday 8th May Thunder and lightning!
Dear mum
Phew, it's nice to be home! It was lovely staying with you and seeing everyone of course, though I feel like I spent more of the time driving around than actually doing anything. I did nearly 1300 miles in the 2 weeks! Not that I'm complaining. Getting the reptile monitoring at Stansted and the newt monitoring at Corby as well as the monitoring at March were a real bonus and made it worthwhile coming over. (Financially that is… You, of course are always worth coming over for!)

Still can't believe how many slowworms I found at Stansted. Remind me to show you the photo when I come back. There must've been a hundred or more under one mat. Glad they are doing so well. Maybe I should show old Mrs Grumpy who used to abuse us every chance she got for stealing 'her' slowworms! Oh well, it takes all sorts.

The lad has been busy here while I've been a working girl. He has laid all the new floorboards in the guest bedroom (your room). They look sooo good. Really pleased we decided not to try and cobble together enough from the old ones now as the new floor runs all the way through and will look really smart. He has started laying the bathroom floorboards too. The lobby part is interesting as that big stone step (well, the top of the supporting wall below really) is higher than the rest of the floor now the original floorboards are off. He has chiselled some off the top but will still have to somehow bend the boards over it. Should be fun!

Today he had more fun cementing up the bathroom wall to try and level it for tiling. Of course being an old stone house not one wall is either level or square!

The hens are all well. I think the cockerel will be Buzz, after Buzz Lightyear in Toy Story, as he is very protective and well meaning! But a nuisance as he keeps escaping! No egg from the little Wyandotte yet but the one with the dodgy leg is starting to look remarkably like a cockerel!

Forgot to say, Franki did an excellent job as my helper at March. She soon got the hang of netting the ponds and walking in her waders! I showed her how to place the bottles in the ditches for trapping. She only 'lost' a couple but we found them after half an hour of searching the thick undergrowth at the edge of the ditch. My biggest nightmare is of leaving a bottle in and someone finding it months or years later! Happened when I was out with Steve, the ex-wildlife copper once. He was showing me a *pond to trap and there, way above the water line were about a dozen bottle traps on sticks poking out of the bank. The level must've dropped at some point, they looked very old. Oops!*

My allotment has been well cared for and everything is shooting up. Apparently it rained quite a lot the first few days I was away then turned sunny so the carrots, parsnips and weeds are off and away! We have been busy hoeing and weeding since I got back (never ending... must think of a better solution next year. Think I must've left some grass roots in when I originally dug it over). I've potted on my tomatoes, peppers, broccoli and sprouts. Everything seems to be doing well. At least the neighbours can't point their fingers at the English now. They are dying to know where I've been though.

I've done the first lot of invoices for the three jobs. Nice to be earning something! I have a lesson tonight, so with that and the next lot of work I should manage. Good job it's cheap to live here!

We landed early at Santiago. Don't think it's really 2.5 hours from Liverpool. Just an excuse for the blasted Ryanair fanfare - tarantara! Think I will just fly Stansted both ways next time. That way I can do Stansted monitoring on the way to you. It will save some fuel as Pete's saying he can't pay my fuel both ways. Meanie! Mind you

PLUM, COURGETTE & GREEN BEAN TART

since the job is only an hour or so it's not worth it for him really.

I enjoyed our meal at the Old Mill. Tell Aunty Jean to pick somewhere for the end of the month. My treat this time! We can go and visit Uncle George again too. I was so chuffed that he remembered me - and his old Escort! Hopefully it might be properly Spanish next time I see him. Will have to bring a photo!

Will post this on the way into town to see Maria.

Love you tons and tons and see you soon!
XXXXXXXXXXX

Diary Friday 9th May Sun and showers
Both to the allotment again. Sowed runner beans in two wigwams, plus white and French beans, between showers. Hoed the flipping weeds again. S dug the bean trenches and filled with muck. His cement fell off the bathroom wall.
Lunch: Trout and couscous. Rice pudding for afters. (All poor, not a good cook day... or good cement day!)
After lunch both planted nearly 9x5 block sweetcorn (43 corn... 2 short) west of the house. Covered with 'copa de chocolate' pots. To swimming baths then onto CJ and Gala for chat n tea until 1 am.

Diary Sunday 11th May Hot by pm
Boiled eggs for breakfast. Both to allotment again! S dug holes for squash and courgettes and filled with muck. Hoed spuds. Sowed butternut squash, pattypan squash and courgettes (7+7+7).
Lunch: Our ham with parsley sauce. Plum crumble for pud.

S continued in bathroom laying floor and re-cementing wall. Carmen brought round some more plants; an ice plant and another succulent I don't recognise plus marigolds (Calendula). Planted up my hanging baskets. Tried (unsuccessfully) to stop the cows coming into the garden so ended up chasing them around instead. Sowed swede and put sheepswool (from the old mattresses) round strawberries to try and retain moisture. Two slowworms in allotment under plastic. Finished 9pm.

Tuesday 13th May. Rain off and on. Turning into a thundery and wet May!
Dear mum

What a frustrating couple of days! We have been trying to sort out the MOT (ITV here) for the car so we can get it re-registered as Spanish. We were told we couldn't get Spanish insurance until the car is registered here and our UK insurer won't insure us in Spain for longer than a year.

Cris & Steve have been checking online for anything about the process as the Traffic Office here are hopeless. They seem to have no idea at all! Anyone would think they have never seen an English car... or maybe they haven't come to think about it! Anyway Steve found an article that said we could take the car through the ITV without swapping the headlights first (we still haven't managed to find any at the scrapyards. I think we know every scrappie from here to Santiago and back!) The site *said that although the headlights would be a fail, you then have a month to get any failures fixed and a free retest. If we can do that we can at least get the insurance sorted as we can prove we have 'started the process'. Anyway, we went to Lalin ITV station to book a test but they refused our logbook (V5) and sent us away. I didn't know what they were telling me so very frustrated and almost in tears! The garage in town here said they thought the logbook should be fine and suggested we try Lugo ITV. Now these places are all government run so should be the same in theory but we have learned the hard way that if at first you don't get the answer you want, you try a different person!*

So today we went to Lugo bright and early, so we could get everything done before the lunchtime shut down! Lugo ITV were more helpful but we have to get a form, to confirm that the car is a bog standard Ford Escort, from a special engineer!! Seriously. The ITV station sent us to the Engineer's College out of town for the report which then sent us onward to an air conditioning shop - honest - you couldn't make it up! The report will take two days. The chap seemed to think it was probably an Escort so that is promising! (And there's me always suspecting it was a Ferrari really). Mind you it was raining so heavily whilst he was examining the car that all his careful measurements had run all over the page by the time we got back to the office so he had to look them up online... under Escort!! He did say that he thought the steering wheel being on the right could be a potential problem though!

At least we were home by lunchtime for our spare ribs!

We have spent the afternoon sowing the maize for the chickens. S put in posts so I could hang string to deter the birds. It looks quite pretty with silver paper and old CDs flapping about (and the odd pigeon walking in between... oh well!!). I also planted up the rockery bit I made with sweet william and primulas. So a nice end to the day.

Oh and we have ordered the second lot of windows from Agolada. A huge double door for the big barn, for when that becomes my dining room with views to the orchard, and two lots of big picture windows for the living room/sunroom-to-be. It will look so different in there with panoramic views down the valley (as opposed to no view and opaque plastic at the openings.) He _said_ mid-July so I'm hoping they will all be in by the time you visit at Christmas!!

I land at 12.30pm again on 22nd but as I'm doing the reptile monitoring on the way this time I should be with you by tea time. Looking forward to it!

Oh, thought we could go to Burton one

PLUM, COURGETTE & GREEN BEAN TART

day, I want to bring some bits back, if you ladies fancy a day out... maybe Wing Wah for lunch?
Love you tons. See you v v soon
XXXXXXXXXX

Diary Wednesday 14th May Rain and more rain!
Into town to book hire car online for next lot of monitoring work. Met Spanish Jeni, had coffee together and went to see her house. Looks lovely. She promised to send their plasterer over to us for a quote. Went into the bank because of excessive charges on our account. They say we can't have the advertised free account. Not sure why! Wish I could understand better.
S finished laying the floor in the bathroom and started putting up the stud wall to the lobby area. I began sanding the floorboards in Bed 1. Bit slow and very dusty! Had to shift the wardrobe around in order to sand so carcoma'd it (wardrobe) with the woodworm killer. Is it me or are we making up more and more words? Carcoma'd? To paint woodworm (carcoma) killer onto something! A brand new verb!
Made 2 cakes and quiche for lunch (used 7 eggs up). 3 more eggs by 12 noon.

Diary Thursday 15th May Sun and more showers all day, some heavy
Ordered WC, bidet and washbasin from Xesteira. They can't get the huge bath which we liked so will look in Roca tomorrow. Bought yet more chicken wire and rebar. S then spent the day raising the chicken fence. It's now six foot high... see if that will keep 'em in! He also made them a 'bike shed' for them all to hide under when it rains and have fun in. Planted sweetpeas (old

fashioned, mixed) and primulas by the gate and night scented stock by the tub.
Lunch Fish pie and purple sprouting broccoli (ours) and chocolate copas (needed more plant cloches!).
Sowed lettuce 'all year round' in allotment, weeded carrots, parsnips and beetroot. Planted more of the 'flores' Carmen gave me then sanded a bit more of the floorboards in Bed 1. 3 eggs.

Diary Friday 16th May Drizzle
Off to Lugo... again. Collected engineer's report. Thankfully, they decided it was definitely a Ford Escort (not as obvious as it seems as CJ is having trouble getting his Mitsubishi Shogun re-registered as it is badged as a Pájero here so they won't accept it as being the same car! Bizarre.) Took all the paperwork to the ITV station. Got a thumbs up but couldn't give me a date there and then for the test. Rang one hour later to give us appointment for Weds evening... I love Spanish bureaucracy.
Spent lots of money in the Chinese bazaar on what I have no idea! Took 'espuma', which was no good, back to AKI and had an argument as it wasn't returned within the two week period or whatever it was. Explained the foam spray wasn't fit for purpose as it leaked all over the place every time we tried to use it so is exempt from any returns policy. At least that's what I would have said in English. Probably didn't come out quite like that so just refused to move until they swapped it. That worked better. Bought a load more electrical stuff.
Fortified by lunch at our favourite café, Recatelo, we bought a bathroom light in Luz Norte and then went on to find a bath in Roca on the way home. It's huge enough for two. Rounded on one side but flat to the wall. And lovely and deep. We

PLUM, COURGETTE & GREEN BEAN TART

even sat in it for a while (shoes off) to test it. Got some odd looks but you have to be sure eh? Will deliver 'quince dias'. Haha!
To swimming baths. Found a spares shop (recambios) in Chantada... why had we not thought of that before? Headlights would be 200€ (better than Ford if we can't get any from the scrap yards). 2 vinos for a euro at pool café - nice, own bodega. Good day all in all.

Diary Saturday 17th May Drizzle
Lit stove which smoked and smoked. It really doesn't like to be abandoned for a day. Hoed all the paths on the allotment waiting for the kitchen to clear then made 2 cakes and 3 jars of walnut, apple and date (actually dried plums but near enough) chutney. Lunch: Pasta with blue cheese, walnuts and mushrooms. S finished making the frame for the stud wall to the bathroom (lobby end) and piddled trying to get the warped door frame back in. We need to keep it as the door is also warped - to fit the frame of course!
Vinos in Mencia and Jema.

Diary Sunday 18th May Dull and drizzly
Started on lunch after us boiled eggs but stove playing up and not drawing at all (because we have guests coming obviously). J&R arrived at 1.30pm with hot and cold water tanks, beers and other bits ordered from UK. Lunch not ready until about 4pm. Typical really. Will never live it down I'm thinking! Still, everyone enjoyed it when it finally made it onto the table. Roast Pork, roast spuds and veg. Apple crumble and custard. Chatted until about 7pm then washed up and fed hens. Tea and done.

Diary Monday 19th May Hot by pm
Into town hall to order empadronamiento for

traffic office (to prove we live here). Can collect it tomorrow. Rang plasterer Jeni recommended. Can't come before Thursday. Said he would ring me back. Didn't.
Lunch: Bubble n squeak with leftovers from yesterday.
Sanded bathroom floor and filled gaps between boards. Needs a finishing sand tomorrow and done. S found and artistically sculpted some pieces of wood as presents for mum. One piece is an owl, which is beautiful.
Planted up shallow tub with violas and red sweetpeas. S put up hanging baskets for me.

Diary Wednesday 21st May
Made cakes for S and mum and some mint ice cream. S screwed the hinges on the bathroom door (and made it fit!). Bacon (ours) eggs (ours) and potato cakes for lunch. 3 eggs laid by 11am.
Off to Lugo for our MOT. Looked in glass place, Lara, for replacement panes for the window in the bathroom door. Some nice mirror designs in there. Am now thinking a large mirror on one wall of the bathroom may brighten it up more than the marble (... AND BE LIGHTER (S))
The ITV station is a very different set up to MOT stations in UK. Six lanes with officials on each one. Loads of cars sitting on the car park in some kind of order known only to the Spanish. We had to book in at the office then sit and wait in the non-queue. You move into the relevant lane when called and then drive through a sort of MOT obstacle course, checking lights, suspension, emissions etc. Of course it's all in Spanish. S couldn't hear them and I was trying to translate but should have swotted up on car terminology before going in! Incredibly noisy in there with all the cars revving and honking, and the smell is horrid; diesel and petrol and exhaust fumes and

grease. We were there over an hour and the guy actually chucked S out of the car and drove it himself at one point. That was much easier, although he said he hadn't driven a right hand drive before. She only failed on the headlights so not bad for an oldie.
Called at spares shop on way home. Headlights now only 108€ for a pair!

(S) Diary Thursday 22nd May Rain pm
(L to airport 11.30am flight.)
Visit Agolada on way home from airport. Windows for sunroom will open inwards and there is one tilt and turn on each side. Good. Call in bar about firewood as still not delivered. Asks if I will be in tonight. 'Yes'. Says he will deliver 1900. Fit stud wall above bathroom door. Starts to rain very hard. No wood. Tea: Beef stirfry, rice

On the flight back to England I pondered how my career choices, or fate, had brought me to Galicia. At age 21 I had decided microbiology was not for me but I had no idea what to do next.

By a serendipitous accident, which life often seems to throw my way, I met an old school friend on the National Express coach home one weekend. She told me that she was an Occupational Therapist for a local authority. By the time we reached Leicester I was determined this was to be my next career.

Back in London I found out what I could about Occupational Therapy: not an easy task as the local job centre had never heard of it and tried to give me details about Physiotherapy instead. I persevered and eventually won a place to study at my next acronym, WLIHE or the West London Institute of Higher Education in Osterley Park. This was a college chosen more because I could remain living in my bedsit in Muswell Hill with my cat,

MAY

Mister Mistoffles, (and continue working down the road at a nursing home, cooking for residents on a Sunday) than for any particular desire to study in West London.

Having learnt my lesson regarding the power of experience, I applied for a job as an Occupational Therapy Assistant at an old and imposing Victorian asylum in Friern Barnet, Northwest London. This was the notorious Colney Hatch Hospital. For the eight months before the course was due to start I worked and learnt. Most of the learning was how not to do things, but it was learning and I began to have an idea what OT was all about.

The course was in the main fun though I had many clashes with the staff, most especially when they tried to send me for placement well beyond commuting distance. My job and my cat counted for nought. I ignored them and commuted anyway. The placement was horrid, at an old Victorian institution far worse than Friern had been, and the commute horrendous. Nevertheless, I worked hard and I passed and left with another diploma under my gowned arm.

I worked as an OT for various local authorities in London, and later back in the Midlands, for 11 years. I moved into sales, working for two well-known disability aids companies. I enjoyed the jobs but it wasn't quite what I had dreamed about all those years ago. I was restless and I wanted a change.

§

In summer 2001 I took a short break with Earthwatch, badger watching in the beautiful Wytham Woods near Oxford. The woods, owned by Oxford University, are home to many scientists and DPhil. students all examining and recording their own small world. Insects, small mammals, deer and badgers are just some of the ongoing studies taking place in a setting which is at once peaceful and evocative of an earlier age.

The long weekend was wonderfully relaxing and rekindled my desire to work with animals. I was invited to return to help with the next badger-monitoring weekend where the animals are humanely caught, weighed, given a thorough animal MOT and released. It was hard work, starting early and finishing late. There was much heavy lifting and even more fleas. I loved it.

I was talking to Sandra, one of the Oxford University DPhil. students, about my failure to realise my dream of being a zoologist all those years earlier when serendipity (or fate) once more came calling. Sandra asked why I didn't go back to university now and do my degree. Would anyone want me at 36 and three quarters? She persuaded me they would.

I returned home and contacted my local university. Yes, they loved mature students, especially ones with previous qualifications. No it didn't matter that my HND was 15 years old, I should apply. Yes, I could have an interview anytime.

I studied my finances and wrote lists of outgoings; mortgage, bills, food etc. If I could get a part time job as an OT to fit around my college hours, didn't go out and ate frugally I thought I could do it.

Staffordshire University offered me a place to read ecology. I had a wonderful interview with a great lecturer, Paul, who seemed delighted that I wanted to return to university at my advanced age. He pointed out that I had done an ecology module in my HND course. I admitted that I honestly didn't remember it, but he showed me the pass mark on my certificate. Paul went on to tell me I would start the course in the second year as the first year was

MAY

mainly orientation and getting youngsters into work mode. The very same week I had an interview for a part time OT post at Stafford Social Services. My plan was coming together.

§

My daydreams were interrupted by that blasted Ryanair fanfare. The flight had landed in Stansted at lunchtime on Thursday 22nd May 2008. Meanwhile, back in Galicia, S was looking to add to our menagerie of animals.

(S) Diary Friday 23rd May Very wet
Weed one row onions, one row spuds, ½ row maize, rained off. Into town to look at rabbit cages (joulas). Agricultural shop near garage (lad asleep in cabin) measure and check out cages. Leave (lad still asleep). Go to agricultural shop at top of town. No joulas in this week. Back to first shop. Lad awake, mum gives me prices. Cheaper but not as good quality as other place. Lunch: tuna and lettuce butty. Cut wood to make a mobile rabbit pen. About to get ready for baths when leña arrives. He struggles to get trailer through the gate. Goes forward and bumps into old concrete washing thingy. Manages to back through the gate but tractor tyre is holed. Dumps firewood, grabs money and dashes off toward town before tyre goes flat.
To baths. Order headlights. Pick up next Friday. Swim. Party of screaming little girls. Sauna (no light on), very relaxing. Tea: blue cheese and onion omelette.

(S) Diary Monday 26th May Storms thunder lightning
Raining and raining. Rest of firewood not barrowed yesterday soaking so may as well leave

PLUM, COURGETTE & GREEN BEAN TART

it now till it dries out. Clean up in bathroom. Fit plasterboard on lobby side of bathroom wall. Test varnish on piece floorboard that will be under bath. Runny. Floor good colour. Shows up unsanded patches (oops (L)). Tea: Pasta rabbit and tomato surprise (surprise is that it has bones in it! (oops again (L)). While making tea horrendous thunder storm. Stream running down garden, leaks in lounge and bedroom. Put out lots of buckets. Light fire to dry out. Walk to mill 2130 to take photos of roaring river.

(S) Diary Thursday 29th May Wet
Wake up with stiff back after barrowing rest of firewood yesterday. Fit strip light in bathroom. One hour on allotment. Then onto roof to secure ridge tiles. Then to loft space over lounge to check for leaks. Can't find any obvious holes but find lost tape measure. Into town. No rabbit cages till Tuesday. To Xesteira for plumbing pipes. José has half the shop out showing me fittings. Buy what I need. Tea: Bacon and cabbage omelette with baked beans. Lay out tubos for waste pipes. Second coat of varnish under bath.

(S) Diary Friday 30th May Sun showers
Measure and measure and measure then cut hole in bathroom floor for waste pipes. Remove planks dividing big barn from pig barn downstairs. Trim beam and chisel wall until pipes fit. Man arrives with bath 1615 but won't drive wagon through village so trolley and carry bath and panels from No. 1. Unwrap and check for damage (all ok). Pay man. Make cuppa. Get things ready for swimming baths. Chicks away. Drink tea. Xesteira for more tubos and bends (codos). Collect new headlights and chat in English to owner's little girl. Buy new discount card at baths for 10 goes. Tea: Gammon fried onion mash and beans.

MAY

(S) Diary Saturday 31st May Sun
Start to take car headlights off. Take grill off but still can't get to one screw without removing bumper. Put it all back together and take it to the garage. He starts to take light off and comes to the conclusion bumper will have to be removed. Book it in for Tuesday along with oil change and air filter. Back home. Cut tubos to size and fit up to WC ok. Glue lower section in pig barn. Strim half east lawn. Tea: Veggie omelette, yoghurt.

I was 38 years old when I finally got the job of my dreams.

As soon as I had confirmation that Staffordshire University had offered me a place and I had secured a part-time Occupational Therapy post at Stafford Social Services, I resigned my job as a sales representative, much to my boss's disgust. He told me he was about to promote me, to give me more money and more responsibility, and finally, when all else failed, that my new career would be 'cold and wet'. Sadly for him, that was the bit I was actually looking forward to! I handed back my shiny new company car, bought an old banger of a Morris Minor Traveller and set off on my new adventure.

I loved being a student again and found the coursework challenging and fascinating. With less distractions than previously, I found I could really concentrate on what I wanted to do. I spent hours in the university library researching assignments, got down dirty in field trips and took a voluntary job at the National Trust in the Peak District where I discovered the twin delights of surveying ponds and spelunking. For my work placement I returned to Wytham Woods to once more help with the badger monitoring. This time I was a student ecologist not just a lay person. For my thesis I joined an organisation called Operation Wallacea which offered placements in the rainforests of Sulawesi. I took a six week leave from work and went off to survey Indonesian rivers for tadpoles under a stern Aussie called Graeme. The experience was indescribable. The rainforest trees were tall and widely buttressed, reaching for the sky. The rivers, winding through limestone karst, were so similar to my beloved Peak District and yet so vastly alien. The local people were friendly and self-sufficient in a difficult and isolated area (we were on a tiny island 24 hours by boat off the southern tip of Sulawesi, a small island itself, set amongst the thousands of small islands that make up Indonesia). They taught me how to live within nature and to respect it and the wonders it can offer up.

My hard work paid off and, at age 38 and a half, I qualified as an ecologist with a first class honours degree. Deciding I didn't want to work as an employee again just yet, I started punting for freelance jobs and once more serendipity popped up her lovely head.

Whilst I was at university I had joined a number of organisations. At a conference organised by one of these, Froglife, I met Saffra who was recruiting for a project near Manchester. The company she worked for were looking for people to survey various ponds for great crested newts (a European-protected species which mainly survives in the UK and seems to have an affinity for ponds on golf courses). The pay was poor and there was only minimum fuel allowance but this was my dream. I wanted the experience and I liked Saffra immediately.

On our induction day in the Peak District, April Fools' Day 2003, it was hailing and blowing a gale. I was freezing cold and my fingers were numb but my National Trust waterproofs were doing their job. I loved it. I also quite liked the guy who kept us waiting an hour before finally arriving to sort out our rather mismatched group and show us how to net and bottle trap. He had an energy and focus that pushed the foul weather away and, beneath his vivid orange waterproofs with the hood tightened around his face, were a pair of laughing blue eyes.

JUNE
Sardines and green beans

Serendipity, or fate if you prefer, seems to have played a large part in my ending up in beautiful green Galicia.

If I had not bumped into an old school friend on a bus all those years ago, I would not have ever heard of Occupational Therapy. If I had not become an OT I wouldn't have been able to get a part-time job to allow me to go back to university to pursue my childhood dream of working with animals. If I hadn't gone on a badger watching weekend, I would never have realised my dream was still feasible. If I hadn't spoken to Sandra at Wytham Woods, I would not have thought to pursue my dream. If I hadn't met Saffra, I wouldn't have got that first job as an ecologist, or many subsequent ones she organised, which allowed me to dream of moving to Galicia. If I hadn't met Saffra, I wouldn't have met S and then I wouldn't have known Galicia even existed. And I would not have this life, here, in Galicia. Everything is interrelated. Life is amazing!

My second monitoring fortnight was coming to an end. I had had a good time (it is difficult for me to call what I do a job in all seriousness. It is just too much fun!) but I was looking forward to getting home. Galicia felt like it was my home now. And my blue-eyed man was waiting.

JUNE

(S) Diary Sunday 1st June
Washer on. Whites then coloureds. Think bath is far too big! Tidy up, change, go to market. New people there, John and someone? Enjoyable chat. Strim long bit in south garden. Put drying away. Weed last row of maize.
Tea: Pasta, ham veg tomato sauce

Diary Monday 2nd June Cloudy (Santiago)
(L back 11am. Please collect me!)
S arrived to collect me on time, 'plane 10 minutes late. It's nice to be home.
Into Leroy Merlin again. Will be moving in soon. Bought more electrics and wall tiles (white) for the bathroom. Into Santiago for lunch at Manolo's. Discovered boot of car soaking wet where it had rained in. Yuk!

Diary Wednesday 4th June Cloudy and humid
To Lugo again now new headlights fitted (by the garage – bigger job than we expected!). No need to make an appointment at the ITV station this time, we just had to sit in line with our failure sheet on the front windscreen 'til they called us. Passed (only rechecked the bits it failed on – i.e. the headlights). Got a nice window sticker but have to go back (again!) to collect the certificate in 2-3 days to give to trafico. Why on earth couldn't they give it to us there and then??? Said we didn't need anything else anyway.
Had our butties for lunch and looked in DIY shops endlessly. Called at agricultural shop again back in Taboada. No rabbit cages until next Tuesday now! Just as well we don't have any rabbits yet then!
Both carried the new bath tub into the bathroom. Looks perfect to me, if slightly slanted. Nothing is level or square of course! (especially the floor and the walls). S stuck sewer pipes together (I got to

help by holding one!) then fiddled with the bath levels... apparently the tub needs to sit level or the water will run out one end (Who knew haha!!)

Diary Saturday 7th June Hot but cold N wind eve
Made 2 cakes, and stewed lamb for tomorrow's pie. S measured the plasterboard for lobby ceiling. Helped (!) offer up ceiling – crickey it's heavy to hold above your head (well, above mine anyway!) – whilst S marked it, recut it, offered up, remarked, recut ad infinitum! Ouch, Mr Perfectionist! The two pieces needed for lobby done and fitted. Phew.
Pasta, blue cheese and walnuts for lunch. Mowed east lawn leaving rather pretty wildflower bit in the middle.

Home Tuesday 10th June. 9p.m. Hot and sunny Thunder later
Dear Mum,
 We heard a sliding and thudding noise this afternoon and found a sheet of corrugated (not nailed on) had slid off the roof on the west side, taking a load of tiles with it! Good job I haven't planted on that side (and that no one was in the garden!!). We assume it must've been the wind, which has been blowing a bit even though it's very warm - deceptive really as both of us are a bit pink from the sun!
 S has been varnishing the bathroom floor now he is finally! happy with the level on the bath (and has resanded the floor to <u>his</u> satisfaction haha). It looks very nice (the floor). The colour of the chestnut boards has come up lovely. We have bought some wall

JUNE

tiles and the taps from Santiago. I need a border I like now and I can tile in there. No sign of the plasterer still... or the new windows for the sunroom of course!

I've planted the celery Franki got me, and my leeks are in though I think something is eating them. Could be the hoopoe. They are very beautiful and not at all nervous but I wonder if his long beak is pulling my leeks out while he's delving for leatherjackets. Found a male slowworm, a juvenile grass snake, a big skink and a large lizard with a blue head (an ocelated lizard I think, looking at the book, with his courting colours) on the allotment today. All good news for us and bad news for the slugs. I think we have a shrike too. He was sitting on the fence out back. That's not good for the great tit chicks so hope he keeps away.

The chickens are behaving, except for Scruff, the little cockerel with a dodgy leg who was supposed to be a hen. He decided he was feeling grown-up and tried it on with one of the brown hens. Of course he couldn't mount her with his bad leg, and being smaller than she is he ended up dragging her along by the neck. She was screeching and making a fuss so Buzz came running. Needless to say poor Scruff hasn't tried it again but it did look funny. The hen was quite ruffled afterwards.

We are off into Lugo tomorrow again to try and sort out the car registration. Getting

PLUM, COURGETTE & GREEN BEAN TART

there slowly. Wish Uncle George could have seen it with its new Spanish plates. How is Aunty Jean? Tell her we will try our best to get over for the funeral. I'm trying to find a card but you know what it's like here for greetings cards, a cartoon footballer just doesn't cut it really under the circumstances.

Maybe you could both come out in September for a break? Should have lots of fruit then, although the pears and apricots have both succumbed to the late frost so no fruit there this year. We have plums and figs and nectarines and peaches coming; and I think some lemons on my little tree. Aunty Jean would love it here. I have loads of beans growing and the courgettes are starting to form too.

The flower garden is looking good. The little violas I planted are so pretty. There are some in the triangle and some in a hanging basket over the terrace and some in a half barrel near the vines. I've also planted up the hay manger and the other hanging basket which S hung by the big barn doors on the west side. Will be lovely with some real doors in there haha. We have put some string across that side as the cows got in and trampled that little semi-circle I dug out and planted up. Eusebio still manages to turn his tractor round so we may think about a permanent fence and gateway later.

JUNE

Most of the rockery plants you gave me seem established despite the postman walking on them each time he takes a short cut to deliver your letters. S says perhaps you could write 'beware of the flowers' on the envelope in future!!
Love you tons and tons
Xxxxxx
Weds am Just watching the hens enjoying a game of tag - running all around the compound chasing each other. They've stopped now as S banged the food bowls so they are all clustered at the fence waiting expectantly!!
PPS V v hot again

Diary Wednesday 11th June Hot
To Lugo yet again. Collected documents from ITV station. To trafico with our ITV certificate to register the car. Instead they gave us a form to fill out. Needed to pay car tax, registration tax and a fee (for paying I think!!) Off to the tax office in centre of Lugo to pay car registration tax first. Chap put all the details into the computer, hummed and ha'd a bit, scratched his chin then decided the computer had come up with too high a figure for our humble Escort so he put in the price he thought we should pay and somehow worked backwards. Ended up 73.12€ so everyone happy with that. Sent to the bank to pay. The teller tried twice to input name but couldn't find us. Sent us back across town to the tax office. Seems one needs to have a separate <u>tax</u> registration number in order to pay anything related to tax. This is the same as our NIE but a fiscal number so it is a NIF instead! More forms to fill in. Back to the bank and managed to pay. Ran

PLUM, COURGETTE & GREEN BEAN TART

back to tax office as time was getting on and the lunchtime shutdown imminent. Arrived back with minutes to spare. Got our form to say it's all paid. Phew! One down!
Celebrated with lunch at café Recatelo.
Called into J&R on way home to regale them with our story so far, drink tea and deliver cake. Invited us to their village fiesta on Saturday evening.
Home 8pm. No eggs so did a search and found a nest of 5 eggs in the brambles!

Diary Thursday 12th June Hot hot
Into Taboada to pay our road tax at the town hall. Waited one hour then told we couldn't pay there but had to go to Lugo! Did our 'no entiendo' bit and hung around until Pilar said she would fax the details over to Lugo for us. Went to Scala while we waited and checked UK flights for next week. Back to town hall at 2pm. Told to come back tomorrow.
Lunch: Jacket spuds with eggs, coleslaw and salad
Carmen kindly offered to feed the animals for a couple of days while we go to Uncle George's funeral.

Diary Friday 13th June Hot during day but cool overnight
Both to the allotment. S dug trenches for white beans and peas. Moved compost pile and collected first French beans. Loads on. Into town to book flights to UK and a hire car for 3 days next week. Back to ayuntamiento. Eventually, after more waiting and 'no entiendoing', got to pay car tax via the bank in town. Another one down! Boy, this is fun! 27€ road tax for the year after all that.
Made cakes; sponge for R&J, chocolate one for us plus cookies. S continued with the bathroom, putting in a block for the bath leg to stop it moving

JUNE

To swimming baths for our weekly bathnight then onto R&J for their village fiesta. Met the couple that bought that huge house north of Lugo we thought was too big a project. They told us they had kept the mummified cat and buried it under the floor where it had lain for so long. Lively fiesta. Free ribs and sausages. Up until 2.30am partying. J&R's spare bed lovely and cosy but fireworks carried on until after 4am so not much sleep!

In Galicia, festivals are an integral part of life. Our town council has had, at one time or another; tortilla festivals, Celtic festivals, paella festivals, wine festivals, tapas festivals and chestnut festivals. Once, I complained to a Spanish friend about all the late nights we were having partying and how we needed our sleep. Her reply? "Plenty of time to sleep when you are dead."

Galegos seem to know how to enjoy life and make a festival out of almost anything. Every *aldea, lugar,* town and city has its own patron saint and therefore the festival day associated with it. Our local parish one is Santa Maria, on August 15th *El Dia del Asuncion.* There is a mass at the local church followed by a parade and later music in the tiny village square around the long abandoned bandstand. Saint's days are often also accompanied by food. I'm not sure what saint our friends' village was celebrating but the fiesta was fun!

I loved the Galician attitude to partying even if I was not yet up to the reality.

Diary Saturday 14th June Hot
Breakfast with R&J. Collected all the bamboo canes that had fallen back to earth from the homemade 'bombas' last night. Glad we weren't underneath any! Another example of the Galician laid back attitude to life... make a dodgy firework

with fertilizer. Stick it onto a bamboo cane. Hold in your hand whilst lighting. Let go, pray, and wait for the bang! Called to see Maribel about the car insurance now we are finally (almost) Spanish. Had coffee and chat at the hotel in Monterroso. Pepe from the hotel offered to sell us a rabbit doe. Should already be pregnant. Just need the rabbit cage now! Lazy afternoon as tired from our late night! We are so un-Spanish. S had an explore at the beams above the 'sunroom' windows. Neither beam goes full length from pillar to pillar so that will be an issue for cutting the openings for the new windows. Oops!
Showed Carmen chicken feeding regime.
Lunch: Roasted pig's cheeks and veg. Queen of puddings

Diary Monday 16th June Cloud and rain in Lugo
Guess where! Lugo again.
Straight to trafico. Paid their 'fee' and showed we had paid the registration and car taxes. Success! Well, no... there was no 'valid until' date on ITV certificate so they couldn't complete the registration process! Dashed across town to ITV (they really could help by putting all these departments nearby... just a thought). ITV said they couldn't give us a 'valid until' date as we weren't legal at that point – not until it is matriculated (that is, has a Spanish registration from the traffic department)... catch 22 and two thirds! We stood around a bit and eventually the woman just redid the certificate and made up a date. She apologised and said trafico were 'fatal'. I couldn't have said it better myself! I can't believe they haven't come across this issue before! Back across town to traffic office. Happy! Wowser! Can pick up permission to drive and new Spanish registration number any time after Wednesday. Seems appropriate somehow. Sure Uncle George

JUNE

would have been chuffed to bits with his old car.
Chocolate and churros to celebrate then called into police station to see about getting a plastic ID card instead of this silly piece of paper. I had read somewhere that we could have a voluntary identification card (tarjeta identificación voluntaridad). The chap in the 'extranjeros' department listened carefully to my explanation whilst walking us through his office then opened the door, gently pushed us through and closed it. We were back in the corridor! I'll take that as a no then? Two successes in one day was too much to hope for.
Ate our butties for lunch then called into the second hand shop on the industrial estate O Ceao. Nice bathroom wall cupboard in for 40€ so bought it. Spurred on, we also bought a new TV from Eroski. Onward to Agolada to change the window sizes (due to the beams not being all the way across the window openings and S now having to make pillars to support them). Hadn't started windows anyway so no problem to change!
Packed for UK.

Diary Friday 20th June Very hot and probably was the last 3 days whilst we were away.
Arrived home late last night together with our haul from the electrical shop, plumbers' merchants, and Wilkos in UK.
Up early to go to Lugo yet again to collect our new registration number. The car is finally Spanish!!! Back home and into town to check if the 'joula' has arrived for the rabbit. It's in the shop but they can't deliver until Monday! S played with plumbing in bathroom.
Lunch. Quiche with Carmen's spinach and our pork. Salad de la jardín with first fresh peas, some of the millions of green beans that have

PLUM, COURGETTE & GREEN BEAN TART

ripened in the 3 days we were away, parsley, lettuce, landcress, and new potatoes dug from our allotment. Delicious!
Bathnight. On the way to the swimming baths I spotted a van delivering plasterboard. Took down number and address. Not far away.

Sunday 22nd June 8.30pm. Very very warm
Dear Mum,

Have managed to plant out my brassicas at last - Brussels sprouts, green and purple Broccoli, white and red cabbage. A bit of rain given for tomorrow to water 'em in. The white beans and peas we put in last week are all up and the tomatoes seem to be doing okay. Courgettes are growing but squashes and sweetcorn seem to be rubbish. Think something is eating the seeds.

Big news is that we finally have our new Spanish plates. Just need to sort out the insurance now and 'ya está'... done. Uncle George would have been so pleased - the old girl is finally Spanish!

We had a BBQ yesterday. The couple that bought that huge old house north of Lugo that we viewed two years ago invited us. They have done a heck of a lot of work but it is a Huge house and a Huge project. Richard & Jayne came too. Very enjoyable and a very hot day.

Cris & Steve finally have their house ready to move into. They have invited us over for the Ortigueira folk festival in July. Looking forward to that.

JUNE

One piece of very sad news. Jen's dad died whilst we were in UK for George's funeral. Didn't even know he was ill. A lovely man and he did so enjoy it here. Think Jen may end up staying in the UK now as her family are there.

One of the village cats got into the chicken pen today but the cockerel started shouting at it and then Scruff joined in so eventually it slunk away with its paws firmly over its ears!! Yesterday there was a kerfuffle in there and one of the hens appeared with a slowworm in her mouth. Of course we had to interfere. Slugs and snails yes, but not one of the good guys. Anyway we chased her around for a bit. She had swallowed it up to the head then spit it out again so I managed to grab her while S rescued the slowworm. It was soggy but surprisingly none the worse for its experience!

I took Carmen those plants you gave me round and a cake to say thank you. She insisted I come in, got me a beer (non-alcoholic as I said I'd fall asleep) and lots of biscuits which I had to take back for S to try... and I thought *I* was thanking *her*. Carmen said the hens were good and she had collected the eggs for me (other than number 2 who is now hiding hers in another lot of brambles).

Love you tons and love to Aunty Jean. xxxx
P.S Where are you going in July? Was it Weymouth? XXXXXXXX

PLUM, COURGETTE & GREEN BEAN TART

Diary Monday 23rd June Hot pm
Went into town to sort out insurance for the car. 'Linea Directa online' much cheaper than Robin and cover from today so cancelled UK insurance. Noticed a poster just up about some do tonight for San Juan on the campo do feira.
Collected our new bunny rabbit, a huge brown female, from Pepe and bought automatic chicken feeder for when we are in Ortigueira.
Joula finally arrived. Left bunny in temporary hutch until we decide where to site her new home. She seems content on the grass in the 'ark' S made.
Back out to check out what's happening in town.
Lunch: veggie burgers and chips

Sardiñada para San Juan
Tables are set up on the old market place behind the town hall, bonfires are built and the local *bombeiros* put on alert. Huge barbecues are arranged behind the trestle tables and lit around 9pm. As the light starts to fade people begin to emerge from the shadows and the local bars.

Music is piped from the back window of the council offices, boxes of good, local wine are set up on one trestle table along with cola and water. Plastic cups, plates and napkins appear and the smell of grilling bacon brings more hungry souls out to investigate.

Thick chunks of local bread are cut and piled onto plastic plates. The area in front of the trestles starts to fill as the first of the bacon, a little crisp if I am lucky enough to find a bit left slightly too long on the grill, is plonked onto the table. A mad rush ensues with seemingly ancient and doddery old folk suddenly plunging into the fray, emerging, triumphant with their hands full of dripping bacon, juggling the red hot rashers, burning their fingers as the fat drips from their chins.

JUNE

A momentary respite as more bacon is piled onto the barbecue then back once more into the fray dear friends for a second, third or fourth round of hot, salty bacon.

Another brief hiatus. Then the moment everyone has been saving their appetite for – the sardines. Huge, glistening, fat things looking almost alive still in the misty lamplight, are laid on their bed of coals. Grilled beautifully, the fat from the bacon mingles with the crisp fish skin to produce an explosion of flavours in the mouth

. Once one gets used to trying to rip the fish off the bone, leaving behind the entrails (which are never removed for some reason) whilst juggling plastic plate and wine cup and sucking on burnt fingers laced with lingering bits of sardine skin and simultaneously trying not to let the fish juice drip onto one's clean, white... why white for goodness sake? T-shirt, it's heaven.

Back and forward we go, devouring all the sardines in the land. The bucket is empty. The sardines are gone. Is it over? No! More bacon goes on the barbecue. A sort of sardine sandwich with the bacon as the ends. More bread is cut, more wine is poured and the bonfires are lit.

Flames shoot into the air from one of the piles of old pallets, sticks and broom cuttings but the other is tardy to get going. A little petrol helps and our resident fireman watches, carefully wiping his chin of fish guts, ready in case of an emergency (like the wind blowing the wrong way and a nearby tree going up in flames).

It never ceases to amaze me how many Galician festivals include fire or fireworks, or both, at the height of a hot summer when the ground is tinder dry and just waiting for a spark to fall. Still, the *bombeiro* does an excellent job as always, and the bonfires burn merrily, lighting up a few glowing faces.

A cry of *bizcocho* goes up as great platters of egg-yolk yellow, lemony sponge cake arrive on the tables. Another dive for the edge of a plate and I emerge with a nice pyramid of cake squares for our party. My prize is soon devoured.

The *queimada* is nearing completion and I must return to win a few cups of this glistening liquid delight. Many *Galegos* make their own *augardente*, a type of moonshine made by distilling grape juice. Usually clear and potent, it can be used to make a liqueur flavoured with coffee, herbs or fruits or, it can be turned into *queimada*. *Augardente* is added to a huge earthen pot along with sugar, coffee beans and lemon rind and set alight. Bright blue flames leap skyward. The officer in charge of the *queimada* continues to stir and lift the flaming brew until most of the alcohol (but by no means all... do not try and drive after a *queimada*) is burnt away and the flames have died down enough to pour the hot liquid into the waiting cups of the participants.

Once, at a fiesta we had been invited to, an Englishman, unused to the flaming brew, poured the *queimada* into a plastic cup without first cooling it slightly and blowing out the flames which still raced around the ladle. Needless to say the cup began to melt and shrink, the hot liquid pooling around his embarrassed feet.

Galegos of course, are born knowing how to make *queimada*, which doesn't, sadly, stop a few being seriously injured every year from burning liquid. Or from the following activity...

The bonfires are now a glowing pile of dull red. Innocent in the dark but still scorchingly hot when you walk near or jump them. Jump a red hot coals? It is said to be lucky (unless, of course one falls in, when the ever vigilant *bombeiro* comes to life and to the rescue). Fuelled with *augardente* and wine, accidents do happen but most people in our

JUNE

gathering are the top end of seventy and decide their jumping days are over.

A friend gives a hoot and runs full tilt at the coals. Taking off just in front of the glowing edges, he launches himself in the air and runs very quickly through the ashes where he landed, only a metre short of the far side. A little hopping to put out his slightly scorched trainers and he returns triumphant and lucky to a round of applause from us more cowardly folk.

As midnight leaves and the day of St. John begins people start to drift away, sated and happy. The council workers, who organise, prepare and cook this extravaganza each year clear away the plastic remains of the feast and the town dogs enjoy a few scraps of leftover sardines. Soon, the square will be back to normal, all traces of the fiesta gone. Until the next one that is...

Diary Tuesday 24th June Humid am. Hot pm
Bacon butties for breakfast courtesy of last night's leftovers. What a feast! Today is San Juan Bautista (St. John the Baptist) and last night was the traditional sardiñada... I have yet to discover the relationship between the two but who's complaining.
Lunch: Frittata with our peas, asparagus and leek. Parsley, walnut, tomato and green bean salad.

The *sardiñada* is a traditional feast in many places around Galicia on the eve of *San Juan Bautista*. I still cannot find a reference to the significance of sardines to St. John the Baptist. There are frequent, massive sardine runs at this time of year and sardines are supposed to be at their tastiest in June. Or maybe it is an obscure link to Jesus being a fisher of men. Whatever the reason, in our local town it is a great big fishy food fest.

PLUM, COURGETTE & GREEN BEAN TART

Saint John the Baptist was, according to the angel Gabriel (Luke 1:36), to be born exactly six months before his cousin Jesus, on midsummer's day.

The longest day of the year is also of supreme importance to non-Christian religions. Rather than simply banning existing pagan festivals, the early Christian church chose to superimpose their own special days upon them. Thus, Christ's birthday falls on December 25th, the birthday of Mithras, a Persian/Roman deity, and close to the pagan midwinter feast of Yule. Easter, the celebration of Christ's resurrection, is at the time of the pagan/Anglo-Saxon spring festival of the goddess Eostre, which celebrates the resurrection of life following the barren winter months. And San Juan coincides with the pagan festival celebrating the summer solstice.

If midsummer's eve is an important pagan festival the eve of San Juan is an important Galician one. In many places it is celebrated in a decidedly pagan manner with flowers, feasting, drinking and fire.

Traditionally the women collect special medicinal herbs, among them rosemary, St. John's wort, and rue (the latter to ward off evil spirits). The herbs are steeped in pure water from a number of springs before being left outdoors to catch the early morning dew. The face is washed with the water in the morning to ensure health and beauty over the coming year. Our neighbours still collect these herbs and wash in the pure water. They have excellent skin.

The brewing and drinking of the *queimada,* whilst chanting a special invocation to ward off the *meiga* or evil spirits, is also a rather pagan ritual for this Catholic country in which we live.

Fire is another element which can purify and banish evil spirits. At San Juan, bonfires are lit throughout Galicia and if one jumps the dying embers nine times it is said to bring luck and ward off evil. I feel once is more than enough personally!

Then of course there is the feasting and dancing. This is something all *Galegos* enjoy no matter the reason.

Diary Wednesday 25th June Hot
Carmen arrived this am with a rabbit! A huge fat California White... also looking very pregnant. She must've spotted Brown Bunny arriving. Of course she wouldn't take any money for it. Put White Bunny in the ark with Brown Bunny. They scrapped incessantly and didn't eat any grass. Decided we had better rehouse them so spent the afternoon moving the chariot, old bedheads and other junk so we could fit the new cage into the long barn where they can't kill each other.
Mixed grill for lunch with pig kidney, liver, chops and egg plus green beans and mushrooms.

Diary Thursday 26th June Hot again but clouding over late pm
Drove to Carballiño to look for the plasterboard place. Eventually found it hidden on the industrial estate (polígono) out of town. Friendly chap (Juan) showed us all around the place – they make plaster mouldings as well as plasterboard and of course all the gubbings to go with it. S decided what sizes and thicknesses he wanted. Will deliver for free if we don't mind waiting until he is next passing. No problemo, thank you very much.
Cuppa in Carballiño next to a little park/zoo with a large cage with birds and turtles in it. Peaceful spot.
Had lunch at the restaurant on the corner in Taboada, Casa Descalzo. Lovely little place run by two sisters (I'm guessing) who must both be in their seventies. I didn't even know it was a

PLUM, COURGETTE & GREEN BEAN TART

restaurant. You walk in their front door, past the staircase, then turn left through the kitchen saying 'hola' to sister who does the cooking (on a wood burning 'cocina' I notice) and into their dining room. A tiny place with probably 16 covers. The second sister is waitress and does the washing up too. The menú isn't long but the food is excellent. Sopa de fideos (noodle soup in a chicken broth... carried rather precariously in wide, flat bowls by our waitress) followed by liver and chips, beautifully tender. Homemade flan for pudding is soft and juicy, the caramel just bitter enough to offset the pudding's sweetness.
Home to put Brown Bunny out in the ark then polish up some of the ceiling in Bed 1.

Diary Saturday 28th June Cloud early then very hot and sunny
Watered strawberries and hazel tree. Strimmed west 'lawn' and orchard. Grass is still growing despite the dry! Stood staring across at the trees and the valley where they are going to build that damned great motorway. Our valley is so beautiful as it is. At least no more has been said or done so far.

Monday 30th June. Hot. 27' on terrace
Dear Mum

Where is my vino guzzling mother when I need her? Carmen stopped us on the way out this morning to ask, 'would we be in later for wine?' 'Er, yes?'

Had a wander round town and bought some more rabbit food. Saw Anne & Simon, she was very pleased with the bun tin you got her as she can now make Yorkshire puddings again (she lost the last one in the *move somewhere). Anyway, I was beavering away sanding the bedroom floor later when Carmen arrived bearing another bushel (read entire garden of) spinach, and carrots. Very nice though the freezer is getting full up - I do keep saying we are only two people but... Behind her was hubby Daniel bearing a 15L box of Mencia wine. He refused payment of course so, back to my first question... where are you?*

Expecting our new plasterboard this week. The very nice man from Carballiño, who said he would deliver when he was in the area, rang today very excited to say he was going to be in Portomarin on Thursday and would call. So, in a week or two the bedroom should be done. I have polished all the ceiling which looks really nice and we are just sanding the floor. We have decided to varnish it the same as the bathroom. I liked the idea of polished boards but, as S pointed out they need a lot of maintenance and would get damaged easier. The bathroom floor <u>does</u> look good too. Once I've tiled in the bathroom (S has put battens up on the wall for me, just need my edge tiles and I can start) and we have the plasterboard ceiling and wall up we can fit the loo and bath and put a light up and... it's all go here!

It has been sooo hot with only 2 rainy days in June and none in the last 3 weeks so we decided to treat the car to a garage! S cut

PLUM, COURGETTE & GREEN BEAN TART

the wooden slats out of a section of the long barn to make a doorway and we cleared out a mountain of junk and restacked the firewood to make room for the car to be backed in. For such a long barn we are running out of space in there what with the bunnies one end, the firewood in the middle and now the car at the other end! It is so much cooler now when you get in the car though so well worth it.

S has also been busy waterproofing the chimney as it still dripped in the kitchen in a heavy downpour. The red waterproof stuff around the bottom looked so nice he decided to paint the rest of the chimney bright white to Eusebio's delight (He had told us to paint it last summer... these English are a bit slow to catch on but they get there in the end). S then got creative and cut out a big red newt from the leftover red waterproof stuff and stuck it on the chimney. It makes us stand out, though what the neighbours think of that one I don't know!

The produce is still growing despite the dry, though we are watering the strawberries daily (hoping once the bathroom is functioning there will be enough grey water runoff from the leaky pipe into the leach field to water them). The veggies are off and away now, especially the beans and the courgettes. We had chicken and chorizo casserole and rice plus green beans for

JUNE

lunch... they are compulsory now at every meal haha. Also had apple meringue pie with our apples from last year (frozen rather than fresh but pretty good).

The bunnies seem okay. We put them in the ark on alternate days as they fight. They don't do much. Spend most of the time lying down. I think it's too hot even in the shade. Found White Bunny sitting with her paws in the water dish to cool off (instead of moving into the shady side). Think they are as clever as the hens!
Love you tons and tons
xxx

In between breaks for *fiestas* and Spanish bureaucracy we were making progress on the house.

We had decided to renovate the two western rooms first for a number of reasons...

Firstly, the roof was waterproof on that side. Well, more or less, except for the ridge tiles which had to be cemented on as the final job.

Secondly they were to be a bedroom and bathroom so we would be able to move into that end of the house before starting on the next bit. And thirdly, that section of the house was easy to seal off and keep clean and dry.

Once the two rooms were ready to move into S could get started cutting out the openings for the new windows in our current bedroom, the sunroom-to-be. And, providing the new windows arrived in time, mum could have our existing bedroom/sunroom, with the 'en-suite' loo in the living room, when she visited at Christmas.

That was the plan!

PLUM, COURGETTE & GREEN BEAN TART

In the meantime, the garden and our menagerie of animals were flourishing. My first crops of vegetables had arrived and the fruit trees looked ready for another good season. I was looking forward to getting stuck into preserving our crop – *fiestas* notwithstanding.

JULY
Courgettes and plums

If I inherited my love of gardening from my father, then any skill I have in the kitchen most assuredly came from my mother. Dad could not be trusted to watch the toast without letting it burn. "Watching is watching, not interfering," he would say. No, all the lovingly prepared home-cooked meals I ate as a child were thanks to mum.

I apparently started off as a very poor eater, living, I am told, on milk and bread (preferably stale or at least dry). My grandfather clapped the first time I ate all my dinner. Not that I was given an alternative if I didn't eat what was on the table. No crisps or cola or Big Macs in those days. You ate what had been prepared or nothing. I survived, and luckily grew out of it. Other than an experiment with veganism in my thirties I now eat pretty much anything (except tripe).

Mum was, and still is, a good home cook. With her weekly 'allowance' she managed to provide tasty and nourishing food every single day. We usually had a roast on Sunday. With a bit of prudence, this did Monday (bubble and squeak and cold meat), Tuesday (rissoles) and maybe even 'tater and meat pie on Wednesday. She also experimented with more 'exotic' meals. We had cannelloni before I had ever seen it on a café menu and she was a home tester for the Pillsbury

PLUM, COURGETTE & GREEN BEAN TART

Company. A lady would come round monthly (or so it seemed to my young mind) with new products for mum to bake and the family to rate.

In winter mum went 'tater picking with a group of local women to one of the farms nearby. One year I joined in as I had 'lost' my expensive duffle coat and had to earn some money to buy a new one. It was hard work in the cold and damp of an October morning, trying to collect potatoes from the frozen churned up earth. I got 50p for my efforts (I think the 'adults' got £1.50). Luckily for me I found the coat so got to keep my earnings. Oddly, I quite enjoyed the experience.

In summer we would all go to the local farm for 'pick your own' strawberries. Mum diligently filled her basket. Me, dad and Aunty Jean diligently filled our faces. Autumn meant blackberrying. We would all troop down the lanes near to our house with wicker baskets and walking sticks to hook the just-out-of-reach brambles down. The very best, juiciest blackberries were always at the top of the bush, always just out of reach, and always over a nettle filled ditch. I remember my father losing his entire basket of fruit one year because he wanted that one blackberry! This was also the time for preserving the feasts we had obtained.

Here in Galicia, the plums had already started to drop from the trees in July, the vegetables were thriving and the summer sun was blisteringly hot.

Diary Tuesday 1st July Hot
Watered the allotment. S watered the strawberries and hazel tree. All looking a bit sick in the heat. Hoed the artichokes, which seem happy, and picked some plums. Are they early this year?
To the market in Monterroso. Bought honey from the nice old chap. He wanted to know how mum was and how we were enjoying Galicia and if we liked the honey. I tried to explain the difficulty of

getting good local honey in the UK but not sure I got my point across... never mind. Bought some cheese, avoiding the scary little lady, and bought some veg from the stalls along Rua Nova. The size of the cabbages was ridiculous, would have fed us for a month.
Lunch in town with A&S who then came back to look at our bunnies. They want some of the babies when we get them. Anne announced that both does are pregnant and white bunny will give birth this week (It won't dare not to now!). They finally left around 6pm in time for us to water and weed and for S to strim the 'backfront' lawn. S laid pallets out for the plasterboard as Juan rang again to say he was coming tomorrow.

Diary Wednesday 2nd July Hot and windy
Watered tomatoes and peppers. Plasterboard arrived 10.30am. Juan, same chap as in the factory. Very friendly but he couldn't help move them as he has a bad back. He put them all onto the pallets on the grass using a little forklift then us two manhandled them all between us into the house. Only broke one in the process. S said it didn't matter.

The cherries were also ripening. Concha's daughter Sonia came over to me on the allotment one day to point at the loaded yellow cherry tree.

"*Son cerezas.*" She said.

Cherries, yes I know.

"*Se puede comer.*" She continued kindly, pointing at her mouth and making eating motions.

This type of encounter was a regular occurrence. Many rural *Galegos* know only the capital of England, which some unfortunate relative probably visited in 1981 and hated. All English must be from London and therefore have never seen a fruit tree before. It is not worth trying to explain I grew up in the country nor that there are plenty of fruit trees in London. I did what I always do, I smiled and thanked her.

At least we managed to collect some of the yellow cherries. The red ones were disappearing quicker than they could ripen. I would watch the blackbirds and jays coming in for their feast from the bathroom window. They would settle on the tallest tree, jostling for position and snatching at a pair of cherries. One cherry would disappear down a bird's gullet leaving the other to fall to the grassy floor, then they would snatch at the next pair. Carmen was away over the weekend and told me her tree was stripped bare by the time she returned. I'm sure she thought someone had been in scrumping.

I was also watering constantly. Carrying buckets of water across the sunken track to the allotment twice a day was becoming wearing and time consuming. As was all the hoeing and path clearing (also using a hoe as there was no power to use our electric strimmer, the only grass cutter we had). But I had no regrets. I was getting fresh air and exercise and the promise of many home grown meals to come. This was *la vida dulce* that I longed for.

Diary Sunday 6th July 3 drops of rain?!
Up late. Scrummy boiled eggs. Watered cabbages (will they ever grow as big as the ones on the market?) Hoed corn and paths again!
White bunny gave birth overnight! We are parents! Score one to Anne. (I did say it wouldn't dare not!).
Lunch: Our gammon and chips. Rice pud with fig conserve from last year (keeping well) Delicious!

Monday 7th July. Still no rain
Dear Mum
I know it sounds like bragging but we have

JULY

now had no useful rain (i.e. more than 5 minutes of drizzle) since the beginning of June and the allotment looks like a desert scene: One good gust of wind and it would all blow away.

Apparently it is damp and misty on the coast, according to Cris & Steve who have now moved in (I guess that is payback for them having warmer weather over winter). They say the locals become worried there if they have 3 _days_ without rain!

We have arranged to go up to theirs on Friday for the Ortigueira Celtic folk festival and to stay Saturday night too. That way we get 2 evening sessions in at the festival. Of course, being Spain the first act isn't on until 10pm (or so). It will be a long night!

The chickens seem to know we are going away. They are not at all keen on the automatic feeder we bought (a big upside down funnel) - one gave it a vicious kick today when she couldn't get any food out of it. The rabbits are much less trouble as they tend to just sit and nibble. We think White Bunny has at least 4 babies but I keep losing count and we are trying not to disturb her although she never seems to be in the nest box with them! Brown Bunny is getting very fat so either Anne is right about her being pregnant too or she is just eating too much.

We have to be back by lunchtime on Sunday as the Anglo-Galician Association are coming our way for the meeting for a change so we can't not show a local presence. Anne & Simon are coming and bringing us a huge water tank on their trailer. The idea is to put it on the allotment to catch water when it rains then use it to get water to the plants when it's dry! Such a busy life!

CJ came over today with his buddy Carlos. They have not a word in common but a joint love of football seems to see them through! Carlos brought his trailer to collect the old metal plough out of the barn which we had offered CJ. (He's going to put it on his garden wall). Being Spanish, Carlos took the opportunity to have a good look round, to give plenty of advice about re-roofing and vine management and to tell us how much our hórreo is worth. He then proceeded to narrowly avoid demolishing the chicken pen and my washing whilst turning the trailer round!

Both CJ & Gala and Jayne & Richard are hoping to make it to the lunch on Sunday too so we should have a good 'Lugonian' contingent there. We were just saying tonight how strange that we know so many like-minded people here already. Of course most of us are in the same (somewhat ruinous) boat but nevertheless interesting.

We have invited CJ & Gala over tomorrow to help us put a dent in the wine box. We have so far had 3 glasses each so about 14.25 litres to go.

JULY

Now, I need advice here: something is still eating my leeks one by one. Everytime I go over to the allotment another one seems to have vanished. One looked sick today and when I pulled it, there were no roots at all and a definite chewed end. Anne reckons mole crickets (huge things with big spade-like front legs); someone else said water voles although they wouldn't generally travel this far from the river bank and anyway leave quite distinct feeding evidence. We have moles but they are insectivores. According to my book mole rats eat underground stems but they (apparently) don't exist in Galicia so I'm stuck. Whatever it is I'm rapidly running out of leeks.

I know it isn't cows although the beep beeps have eaten the sweet williams I put in the trough on the west side. I was furious but Concha didn't seem at all bothered. I suppose to her, cows are important but flowers aren't. Just hope they aren't poisonous! I've told S I want a proper fence - when he's finished the bedroom, bathroom and roof that is!

He has put wooden battens in the stone exterior wall in the bedroom ready to plasterboard it and nearly wrecked his drill - it smells like burning when I go in - the granite is so tough, almost impossible to drill into. We have decided to board out the exterior walls as Jeni's plasterer never came back to us (and brother never took me up on my offer either!) This way we can insulate behind it too.

I have been cleaning up the old sleigh bed from the bathroom (bedroom as was). It looks really smart and has some initials on the back. Thought it was the joiner who made it but Carmen says it was Pepe's great-grandfather (who was probably the joiner too) so an interesting bit of history with it. S will make me a slatted base and a back so we can use it as a day bed or chaise longue. Or as a spare bed when we have special visitors for Christmas!

Carmen also told me a bit about the village. She says that when she was a child (around 50 years ago) there were over 80 people in our little aldea. There were 11 in our house apparently. Imagine! There are only 11 of us in the village now! Our wig maker apparently worked from the middle bedroom.

Tuesday 10.50pm. Very warm. CJ & Gala just left having put a <u>very</u> small dent in the vino. Gala had half a glass mixed with water (not up to your standard at all) and CJ was driving, so 14L to go! We sat on the terrace and chatted. Very pleasant. Sorry, I'm bragging again, but it is supposed to rain at the weekend… just in time for us to be standing in a field!

S is cracking on with plasterboarding the wall in the bedroom. He has had to chisel away a few bits of protruding granite to get his battens flush and the drill is only just about holding out. It has had a fair bit of use this last year!

He has also put the hot and cold water tanks that Richard brought back from the UK up into the loft space. The Spanish don't seem to do hot water cylinders like he wanted. This one has an electric immersion heater attached but also two separate heat exchange coils inside. The idea is that in winter we will get hot water from the stove (which will be in the Big Barn eventually... when we get to that bit) via a back boiler. He is planning to fit up a solar heating system for summer which will attach to the second coil. It all sounds very clever though I admit that at the moment I'd be happy just with running water... even cold running water haha.

Wednesday am. Still hot. Thought I'd better pop this in the post. Plums are dropping off all over the place. Better get preserving! Need courgette recipes too... can't believe how quickly they are growing now!
Love you tons and tons
Xxx
PS love to Aunty Jean xx

I love both the idea of preserving things, and the actual process of turning my hard-grown produce into something to savour throughout the next twelve months. I also love seeing the shelves in my pantry fill up as the season progresses.

PLUM, COURGETTE & GREEN BEAN TART

In the days before freezers all produce had to be eaten fresh or preserved in some way. I have dozens of cook books (S would say hundreds, but that is a (slight) exaggeration) but one of my very favourites is a slim volume from 1975 called *Making your own preserves* by Robin Howe. As well as being a mine of information about jams and jellies, marmalades, pickles and chutneys, the author writes it all with a wonderful sense of humour. Of bottling fruit in alcohol he says (I am assuming the author is a he as Robin was not, in those days, a common female name but offer apologies if I am wrong) '*It is an expensive method of preserving but quite delightful. I do it only for certain fruits and only in moments of extravagance.*'

Now I have the chance to put Mr Howe's recipes to the test on a regular basis. That summer I bottled beans in brine, made endless jams of various coloured plums and tried a rumtopf (a layered concoction of fruits as they come into season, each layer covered by a layer of sugar and the whole topped up with brandy or other distilled alcohol – here in Galicia the *augardente* is perfect for this treatment). I made chutney and bottled courgettes in oil (that one didn't work, they fermented dreadfully). I made cakes with courgettes and courgette quiche or tart. I spent many happy hours in the kitchen experimenting with the best way to preserve my produce.

Diary Wednesday 9th July Hot and very dry
Watered beans and cabbages. Not sure why I bother as they are dry again an hour later! I've decided the cabbages are definitely not going to outgrow Carmen's this year at least! Dug a second trench, moved rest of old muck to fill it and sowed more peas. S dug out for new compost heap. Sowed spring cabbage and 'All the Year Round' lettuce.

*Lunch: Baked pasta with veg and cheese sauce.
2 eggs, one in bushes near the red plum!
Finished 10pm*

*Diary Friday 11*th *July Sunny
S finished plasterboarding the walls in Bed 1 then cleaned it all ready for varnishing the floor after the weekend.
Made cheese muffins to take to Ortigueira with us (plus the rest of the vino).
Lunch: Salmon new potatoes, courgettes and peas
Had showers, fed menagerie.
Ready to leave at 8pm when vigas (beams) arrived for the roofing. Finally left 8.45pm.*

*Tuesday 15*th *July. HAPPY DAY AFTER BIRTHDAY!!
Still very very hot and v.v.v dry
Dear Mum,*

I have been out earning tonight! Maria rang to say she had a job application to complete in English and could I help. Took us 1½ hours hard work as I'm not really sure what she does! Admin of some kind to do with tourism and new business grants.

We almost didn't get to Ortigueira for our weekend away. On Weds eve José arrived with a huge sack of sand and was just backing into the gate to drop it on the drive when we heard him. No way we could have moved it and the car was in the garage. Then the next day the man came with our firewood and was just about to empty <u>that</u> on the driveway when we saw him. As the car was <u>still</u> in the garage and we have only just finished stacking the wood we

PLUM, COURGETTE & GREEN BEAN TART

would have had to walk to Ortigueira. Then, Friday night about 5 mins after we had planned to set off the man arrived with the roof beams which he dumped on the grass so S had to put his overalls back on and move them all into the barn as we feared rain (haha) over the weekend. He needed another shower by the time he had sweated through shifting them all.

Funny thing is... all of those people have our 'phone number and not one of them rang us before turning up!! (At least they turned up though!!)

We had a good run to Ortigueira and were made very welcome. The house has been done lovely. Totally gutted with new beams and everything. Very modern inside with a huge living-dining room and 3 bedrooms upstairs, one en-suite. They have some snagging left for the builders: like the bath doesn't empty and the lovely oak flooring on the stairs has warped and lifted but I am slightly jealous that they have running water, bedrooms and <u>two</u> bathrooms!

We sat and chatted on the Friday night with Cris & Steve until 2am and didn't end up going to the festival! We went into Ortigueira on the Saturday afternoon though and then again in the evening. I enjoyed the afternoon session best, we lay on the grass listening to the bands and had to fill in a form to vote for the best. We had a beer and got free beanie hats each from the brewery (Estrella Galicia). In the evening it rained so we had to stand up and it was very crowded. In fact it poured Friday night, Saturday morning and Saturday evening - And here? NOTHING; NIL; ZILCH; NADA. Desert!

We managed to get back in time for lunch on Sunday. Anne & Simon were waiting for us with 2 Wwoofers (willing workers on organic farms) and a huge 1000L water tub for us. (To put on the allotment for rainwater). One of their helpers wanted the loo so I directed her 'up the stairs, turn left and it's there'. Next minute she was trying to get out of the door back onto the terrace where we were having a cuppa. 'NO, turn round' I shouted and heard an 'OOO'. I guess most people don't have a loo in their sitting room hiding behind the sofa. We like to confound and confuse haha.

The Anglo-Galician Association meal was very enjoyable. There were about 15 of us in total but only one poor girl serving. The main course was huge platters of churrasco (mixed grill). At first some people were worried there wouldn't be enough and Colin (our secretary/leader!) asked if we could have more chips as they were a little sparse. Turned out the kitchen was struggling too as just after that the food started coming... and coming and coming... until we had to shout 'stop!'

We plan to move in to the guest bedroom

PLUM, COURGETTE & GREEN BEAN TART

this week so S can start cutting the wall in our bedroom (the sunroom to be) for the new supporting pillars. If you remember, we found that instead of being a single beam supporting the roof, there are two which meet somewhere above where he needs to cut the new window apertures.

The floor is all varnished in the guest room and I am painting the new plasterboard walls. They have promised us the windows will be here by the end of July so we need to get a wriggle on. He will cut the actual openings once they confirm the windows are on the way… I did ask for a week's notice haha. Will be incredible to have a view from that room after so long with opaque plastic at the windows.

In the meantime I have the animals to feed - Scruff will be off soon as he is crowing properly now and we don't need two cockerels; the White Bunny babies are all fluffy and look like exact copies of mum, They are all wriggling about, 8 in total. Brown Bunny has not yet popped. I reckon this weekend - and watering to do. I watered the courgettes last night (why did I sow 7 plants again?!!) and got bitten by midges for my trouble. This evening they were really floppy again. I must devise a better method. The green beans are running (haha) away with themselves. I thought they weren't setting at first but the book said to spray the flowers to help

JULY

pollination and that seems to have worked well.
Love you tons
Xxx

My vegetables really were romping away, bad puns notwithstanding. I think the piles of old goat, cow and/or rabbit muck I'd heaped onto the newly dug beds back in winter had given everything a racing start. The wet weather in April and May had helped them to grow strong and the sunshine since June was encouraging them to fruit madly.

Our daily morning tea and cake break became an experimental ground for cakes of all kinds: cherry was a firm favourite whilst tangy plum and ginger was a close contender. Anything with fruit and chocolate seemed to work and courgette cake, using a carrot cake recipe, was delicious and pretty, speckled as it was with tiny green flecks. Green bean cake was... no, that was a cake too far even for me, but you get the idea.

Then one evening, we had another surprise visit.

Diary Tuesday 15th July Very hot and dry
Electricians arrived late eve with their bill! (from last August wow!) Must've added on interest as it was a bit steep. I think they had forgotten what they had done to be honest. One bit read 'tornillos, tacas etc. 35€'. For a few screws and clips? Mmm. Also 30€ for plugs. If I remember correctly they put one on the blender and one on the breadmaker and both were quite clearly second hand plugs. I will check my notes I think.

Diary Wednesday 16th July Hot and dry
To Lugo. Looked for border tiles for the bathroom wall in Roca but nothing I fancy. S treated himself to an angle grinder at Bricoking. Priced up some

PLUM, COURGETTE & GREEN BEAN TART

of the items the electricians have charged us for. Don't know what 'zocalos' are as I thought they were the kick boards on kitchen units – will ask about that one as he has charged 89€ for them, but plugs are only 2€ a piece new and the switches ('interruptores 30€') 2.50€ each. He put in two of those. Is this a normal mark up for Galicia? Am I being paranoid thinking it is because we are foreigners? Who knows?

Brown bunny had had her babies when we got back. Double parents!!

Only 1 egg.

Diary Thursday 17th July Cloud am then hot and dry

S started playing with his new angle grinder cutting a slit in the sunroom wall and making a lovely dust (but much quicker than with the chisel which he had to use for the chimney).

Lunch: pasta with meatballs (albóndigas) and spinach. Plum tart.

We now have a long thin hole in the wall in sunroom for the new pillars. Great views, if a little narrow. It's like looking through a medieval arrow slit. Can't wait to be able to sit in there and enjoy the scenery! S cemented in the first concrete block for the first pillar then both had hosepipe showers.

Watered everything and fed everyone. Only 2 eggs, someone is hiding them...

Diary Friday 18th July Hot and dry. 29°c early am

S into town for bits and pieces from Xesteira (I don't ask – it's his birthday treat!) while I made special lunch.

Lunch: Fillet pork in paper with all our own veg (spuds, carrots, onion, courgette and French beans). Plus excellent chocolate soufflé pudding! (AGREED (S)!)

JULY

S put all the remaining blocks up to the first opening in the sunroom wall and cemented them. (16 loads of cement, until 7.45pm).

To swimming baths. Bought some skirting boards for the bedroom on the way and paid the electricians' bill. Tried to ask my list of questions but either my Spanish is getting worse or José didn't want to understand as he did his own version of our 'no entiendo' trick. Still not sure if this is 'normal' practice but Carmen called round earlier to chat about some tiles she liked for her new room. Later she told me the builders already had some tiles of their own which they were fitting instead of the ones she wanted so maybe it's not just us!

Tuesday 22nd July. So unbelievably hot and dry. 10pm

Dear Mum,

Do you remember the film 'The day the earth caught fire?' Earth had been knocked out of orbit and was heading toward the sun and it was getting hotter and hotter. It registered 30° on the terrace today - bearing in mind it is always in the shade where the thermometer is. The kitchen is my favourite spot so long as I don't put the oven on at all, as I had to today, making cakes for our visitors. Les and family are holidaying in Galicia and staying in that hotel we found in Monterroso for a few days. They are coming over tomorrow to view the estate!

I made 2 cakes, and a plum tart for lunch tomorrow, then 6 pots of plum jam and 2 bottles of plum sauce, which is like tomato

PLUM, COURGETTE & GREEN BEAN TART

ketchup but richer and sort of sweet and sour. Very good on bacon butties!

I do hope you are having a bit of our weather on your hols - though not quite as hot as I can't cross the lawn without putting a sunhat on (and Concha accosts me and makes me put one on if I do happen to forget). At least I am finding out which veg and flowers like the heat (French beans, courgettes and tomatoes so long as I water them copiously and California poppies) and which don't (lettuce, leeks, most rockery plants and grass - we have none left)

Had a hosepipe shower today and burnt me. Would think after a year we could have figured a cold tap!

S has now put 2 new pillars up in the sunroom to support the roof beams (which we found didn't span the whole of the wall) so he can then cut out the openings for the new (big) windows. I have knocked the plaster off the back wall of that room (the only stone wall in there as it was the original outside wall before they covered in the terrace and made a room). It needs cleaning up and repointing properly but looks like it will be a pretty one. I do love the old granite walls. Makes me wonder just how they lifted some of the stones up to first floor level pre-tractor and crane! Of course we created loads of dust between us so S spent the afternoon clearing up while I slaved over a hot stove.

JULY

We have moved into the end bedroom. It is very nice and quiet in there and is great looking up at the polished wooden ceiling, like an old manor house. May have to claim that room for ourselves! (Only joking, it will be yours once we have the other bedroom done). Dad's liquid polish recipe is fantastic for cleaning up and feeding the old wood. I can almost hear it sighing in pleasure! S even made a wooden fascia board for above the window where the plasterboard meets the ceiling boards. It looks amazing, as if it has always been there. Clever chappie!

Have put an old door curtain up at that end of the house to keep the 'clean' part (relatively) dust free! Nanna's old oak wardrobe and chest of drawers look perfect in the bedroom. Just the bathroom to tile and fixtures to plumb in and the roof to finish and stage one is complete. Easy.

We are doing well on the self-sufficiency front. Poor Scruff was very tasty on Sunday (and stewed Monday). We gave him a good send off with a totally home grown dinner. Potatoes, onions, carrots and green beans. Plum crumble and custard. The yellow plums (Mirabellas) are dropping off the tree for fun, they are very tasty in your loaf cake recipe. They stay juicy as the cake cooks. Our little white Wyandotte also started laying on Sunday. Such a kerfuffle. The cockerel was standing guard and puffing his chest out. He only needed a rifle to complete the

PLUM, COURGETTE & GREEN BEAN TART

picture! She was on the nest for ages with the 3 browns all giving big sisterly advice. And afterwards the noise, everyone clucking and congratulating her. It was one and a quarter ounce… like a banty egg! We are going to call her Sarah Bernhardt as she is such an actress!!

Love you lots
Xxxxxxxxx

Diary Wednesday 23rd July.
Actually drizzled this am… probably because visitors are due. I think the weather just knows! Even had thunder too but the rain didn't wet the ground. Fine again by the time Les, Judith and the girls arrived. Gave them breakfast (eggs done various ways according to preference) then a grand tour of the premises, with S and Les chatting about roofing and other burning building issues. Made lunch while everyone picked the green beans. Les and S got the long, old pine trestle table out of the barn. I found a couple of tablecloths and we ate on the terrace. Very pleasant.
Lunch: Chinese style fish with stirfry veg (courgette, beans, onions) and Chinese plum sauce. Plum tart and ice cream. Lashings of homemade ginger beer (and local vino).
All went for a walk pm then back for tea and drinks in town.

Diary Friday 25th July Drizzly
But actual rain yesterday (because we went into Lugo with our visitors of course). The girls were happy to wander around the shops (can't say I was but hey ho… I know women are supposed to enjoy shopping but I'd rather be roofing personally!!). Had lunch at Café Recatelo outside

JULY

the walls. Good meal. The pescatarians had sole, the rest of us chicken breast or bacon and eggs! He seemed pleased we had taken visitors.
Had 4 baby eggs (Sarah's) this morning, fried on toast for breakfast. Yum! Played on the allotment (rain hasn't soaked in at all). S finished putting the skirting boards on (he wasn't allowed to get dirty as we were going out for lunch!) Booked hotel room for Belle next month then met our visitors for lunch in the Anduriña restaurant. Forgot it was Santiago day so special higher price! Should have realised as all the shops were shut. Will learn all these saint's days eventually. Only ourselves and Santiago the electrician in the restaurant.
Took our visitors up to the windmills and petroglyphs (getting a lot of attention suddenly these old carvings!!) All out for drinks in Monterroso in the evening. Promised to meet up in Santiago before they fly home.
Back 9.30pm to feed animals.

Diary Sunday 27th July Back to very hot
Hope Les is having it this good at the coast.
Picked thousands! of plums. Cut some to dry. Strung onions to store in the barn. Reminds me of doing the same with dad. Think he would be proud of our progress this year.
Lunch: Pork belly roasted with courgettes and carrots. Spuds and beans. Crêpes with walnuts and plums.
Made a jar of plum and marrow (read big courgette that I missed) chutney.

One of the preserving methods I had not tried previously was drying. In the north of England the weather doesn't really co-operate for drying produce in the sun. Here though, the possibilities are endless. I found plums worked really well, cut

PLUM, COURGETTE & GREEN BEAN TART

in half, stoned and placed cut side up on a table outside. Once I had figured a way to keep the flies off (mesh cake cover) and the ants from crawling up the table legs (talc) they usually dried to prunes within three days if it was hot and sunny and not too humid. Apricots also dried well this way. Leaving them until they have no moisture in means they can be put into sterile jars and kept for at least a year. The apricots are better still if I cut them thinly. Cherry tomatoes, halved, salted and laid cut side up also dry to a leathery toughness (and being salty avoid the worst of the ant attacks). When it wasn't so hot the old Escort made a surprisingly good dryer. I ran it out of the garage, tilted the sunroof to allow air circulation, and placed the trays of plums on the front dashboard.

Diary Wednesday July 30th Hot
Good for drying the plums anyway! Made a loaf and 2 cakes. Cooked plums for plum ripple ice cream. Strained the cooked plums, added sugar syrup then rippled it through nearly set ice cream.
I started cleaning ceiling in sunroom. Amazing wide wooden planks, sweet chestnut like Bed 1. Did about half and got thoroughly filthy with soapy water dripping on my head... nice! Had quick shower. CJ and Gala came over 6pm for tea and cakes and brought some courgettes with them (!!) Gala promised us some courgette pancakes for Friday supper after swimming.
Brown Bunny has 5 babies definite.
Plum and egg hunt. Number 3 is hiding hers under the brambles.

Gala's pancakes turned out to be a revelation, sweet and delicious. And I definitely needed all the courgette, and plum recipes I could find!

JULY

In addition to drying, jams, and jellies I made plum wine which reminded me of my years of home brewing when I lived in London. I made some good stuff there. I called it Grand Union after the canal which ran alongside the house I lived in. One chap in the housing department at Hammersmith Council was a real 'professional' home wine maker. He would occasionally bring in a few bottles as a treat to one of our staff meetings. His parsnip wine was delicious. Note that this was in the 80s, I'm sure wine tasting during office hours would be frowned upon nowadays! Actually, I remember one of our senior social workers bringing poteen back from his trips home to Ireland too. We would enjoy P&Ts in his office. Staff meetings were more fun in those days!

That first summer at *A Casa do Campo,* I made plum vinegar, and the Chinese plum sauce we had with our fish. I dry-salted beans and bottled peppers. I made endless cakes and desserts. I hung onions, walnuts and apples in the cool barn below the house. I spent half my day preserving, half watering and half helping renovate our wreck. My pile of preserves grew and I continued to think up yet more recipes to use and preserve our vast haul for the winter months ahead. I was in my element.

AUGUST
Plum, courgette & green bean tart

August had arrived, hot and sultry. Our promised windows had not. The brand new supporting pillars were in and ready. S was raring to go cutting out the new huge openings in the wall but we had heard nothing at all from our window man, Paulino. In the absence of anything to be done in the sunroom, S decided to go back onto the roof in the summer heat. Since February we had been busy with other renovations but now he was at a standstill indoors. The idea was to get the roof completely renovated before the autumn rains but first he was planning to finally fit that skylight in the barn.

In the meantime, I still had mountains of produce to do something with, animals to feed and of course watering to do.

Diary Saturday 2nd August Hot from 11.30am
Up early to water courgettes etc. I've found early morning before the sun gets round to the allotment and late evening after it has gone down is best. The big pine tree provides welcome shade when there's no early morning mist. Weeded beans and peas. Even corn is floppy now. Must come up with a better system for watering and mulching beds for next year. S continued on the roof.

AUGUST

Made a jar of courgette sauce plus extra for lunch with pasta and veg. Quite tasty. Tried the plum ripple ice cream for afters. Delicious, another big tick for plum use.
More watering. Done 10pm.

Diary Sunday 3rd August V hot after mist cleared at 11am
Boiled eggs for breakfast on the terrace. S onto the roof before the sun gets to him! Collected veg from allotment and made another 5lb of plum jam. Good job S has a sweet tooth!
Lunch: Chops, glazed shallot, carrot, courgette. Spuds. Crema catalana
S still on roof. V v hot up there. Number two (fatty) not well. Tried to have a look at her but can't see anything obvious. Maybe sunstroke? Can chickens get sunstroke? Put her in the cool anyway as she doesn't have the sense to do it herself. I trust S will have the sense to come down before he gets sunstroke!

Diary Monday 4th August Hot after mist cleared 10.30am
Washed down the exposed stone wall in sunroom with hose. Washed down me too. Got most of the loose stuff off, mainly transferring it to myself! Good enough to see where to start pointing up and where I've missed removing the old mortar.

Tuesday 5th August. 9.30pm and hot (for a change. Haha).
Dear Mum,
  We had an escapee this evening. I was watering the allotment and heard a fluttering and lo! A chicken on the track. She had jumped off the high stone wall (which of course we hadn't fenced as who

PLUM, COURGETTE & GREEN BEAN TART

would be daft enough to jump 6ft onto a stone track?... a chicken obviously!). She thought it was great fun and didn't want to be caught at all. I just hope her usual poor memory prevents her from having another go. S has more fencing to put up I guess! Daft thing is that she was quite poorly the day before with, I think, sunstroke! She has obviously recovered!

Well, our weather continues scorching. Within 10 minutes of the sun coming out (at least we are having mist until about 10.30am) everything is flopping including the chickens and us! My French beans obviously love the sun, as do the courgettes and tomatoes but most other things are suffering. I shall have to rethink for next year. The leeks need to go in much earlier so they have a bit of a chance to grow before the heat (and before the beast eats them. CJ came over with a sort of mini land mine the other day to try. The idea is that you bury it, then the beast, whatever it is, comes along and boom... no more beast. Needless to say it hasn't worked either, though something had dug very carefully all the way around it and missed oblivion by centimetres!). I will need to mulch more too and we are thinking about raised beds to level the ground as with everything being on a slope any watering we do ends up back down in the river.

S is finally back on the roof... now it's nice

and hot up there. He is doing the skylight in the big barn at last. Makes it much brighter. You can see all the cobwebs! The bats don't like it so much and have moved downstairs to the other barns. That room will be wonderful with the mezzanine, the snug below with a big wood burner and the full height dining room with skylight and big glass doors... well, I can dream!

We are nicely settled in 'your' bedroom though still not sure which way round to have it. Had the bed looking down the room toward my beautifully repointed stone wall but then the wardrobe would have to go in front of the beautifully repointed stone wall so may turn the bed to face the window so we can see the mill (if we stood up on the bed that is!).

Still no windows but I am busy cleaning up the stone wall in the sunroom. I cleaned the chestnut ceiling and that is in pretty good condition with fewer gaps than in the bedroom one as it is tongue and groove boarding. The wall will look good too. Had fun today removing the old pointing and fitting small stones in the gaps ready for mortaring it all.

At least I have the cooler jobs, other than having jam and chutneys on the hob and cakes in the oven. Have lots of new experimental recipes for courgettes! Made some courgette and chickpea burgers yesterday, then there's courgette soup (with

PLUM, COURGETTE & GREEN BEAN TART

mint), and a pasta sauce using courgettes. Not tried courgette ice-cream yet but made a yummy plum ripple ice cream. The chutney combines two of my over producers; plums and courgettes and Aunty Jean's piccalilli combines courgettes and beans, the other mad producer this year. I swapped some of the plums for a load of much needed 1lb jars from Anne & Simon. They came over last night with their latest helpers. Anne loves the bunnies. Chose her three! All the white bunnies are running about annoying mum now. They like nibbling onion tops and cabbage and don't mind being handled. They are exact copies of mum whereas Brown Bunny seems to have one brown baby and 4 white and black ones. They grow so quickly! Anne also said there is a craft fair at Agolada next week so we may pop along there and have a look and chase the windows again while we are at it!

Off to Santiago tomorrow (if the windows don't arrive... haha) to meet up with Les and family before they fly home. They have had a week on the coast. We will call at the big DIY store again whilst we are over that way. All our tools are dying one by one. First his drill went then the jigsaw. The big torch has had it too. I guess they have worked harder this last year than for a while, and as CJ says it's all in a good cause! We are back to Santiago to collect Belle for her visit

AUGUST

the next day (poor timing on our part, never mind). We booked her room at the hotel in town and the lady asked me three times if I wanted a single room. Don't know what she thinks the poor girl will get up to!

Local fiesta this weekend and parish one next. Coo! Think of us all partying haha.
Love you tons and tons
Xxxxxxxx
Don't forget you and Aunty Jean are still welcome in September.
Love you xxx OO you got 2 lots!!

Diary Wednesday 6th August Cloud am then sun
Up early! No windows, unsurprisingly. Fed all and off to Santiago. Brief return to cover the roof as it started to rain 5km along the road. Not a drop back at home! Covered the roof anyway. Bought wall edging tiles from Leroy Merlin in Santiago. Little starfish and shells. Cute! Wandered round looking at other bits and day dreaming about bathrooms. Bought a 50m hosepipe for the allotment. We can hook it up to the stand pipe in the garden and drag it across the track.
Met up with Les and family, they have had a good time at the coast near O Grove. Somewhere else to add to places to visit list. Wandered round Santiago and said farewell. Home via Agolada to check where the windows are (it's now August and he definitely said July). 'Factory very busy,' says José...Who knows then!!! Bought drill in ferreteria on way back. Home. Fed and watered all. Done 9.30pm

The windows seemed as elusive as ever. Why I expected them to turn up in July as promised after our experiences with the first lot I have no idea. Put it down to misguided optimism! Of course now it was the August shutdown so nothing was going to happen before September. I just needed them to be in before Christmas when mum had promised to visit and stay at the house. S wanted them before though, so he could strip the roof above our current sitting room, an impossibility with us in it.

§

We had no sooner said farewell to Les and family, than it was time to return to Santiago to collect my niece. This was Belle's third visit to Galicia and we had more work lined up for her!

It was an evening flight and we arrived at the airport early for a change so I sat chatting to Colin Davies from the Anglo-Galician Association whilst we waited for the passengers to disembark. At one point I glanced up as a flash of red caught my eye. It looked remarkably like a cardigan that mum owned. When I looked again it had gone but the passengers were starting to come through and Belle would only have hand luggage.

As I turned to say goodbye to Colin that flash caught my eye again. This time she wasn't quick enough to duck back inside the sliding doors. It *was* mum.

"What the…?"

"I bet that's a surprise," said mum, laughing at the amazement on my face.

"I just said a rude word in front of Colin. I hope he didn't think I meant him," I replied, stunned. I couldn't believe mum had managed to keep her visit a secret. She is hopeless at secrets. Belle, I knew, can't lie to save her life so how they had cooked up this little surprise I'll never understand.

"You sneaky pair," I continued, laughing too. "Why were you hiding anyway Mum, I spotted you peeking out."

"My bag was taking ages," she replied. "I couldn't wait. And I wanted to see you. And Christmas is too far away," she added.

"Well, it's brilliant." I had a sudden thought. "But the hotel room might be a single!"

On the way home we found a *fiesta* just starting. It seemed an appropriate way to begin their holiday so we sat at a café-bar on the square sipping vinos and chatting. By the time we got to the hotel it was too late to change the room.

I took the key I had collected from reception earlier that day.

"Fingers crossed."

No such luck. One, smallish double bed almost filled the room. Oh well, the lady *did* ask if we wanted a single! Mum didn't care at all. She was here, and that was all that mattered.

Diary Friday 8th August Hot
Collected mum and Belle. Explained to hotel that we had an extra surprise guest and could they swap to a twin room. Lady seemed a bit bemused like 'why didn't you say so when you booked?' Oops.
Back home to have a tour of the house, pick veg for lunch and chat.
Lunch: Stuffed marrow with goat's cheese and walnuts. Plum fool.
Went a walk and showed our guests the two water mills. Lovely circular walk round. Surprisingly cool down by the river. Back into town in the evening. Wandered round the feira. No music until after midnight so had a few vinos before dropping guests off to their nice new twin room.

Diary Saturday 9th August Hotter
Mum and Belle walked from town. Mum helped water and picked white beans for me. Belle and I helped S put the bathroom ceiling on. Heavy that

plasterboard, even on such a low ceiling and using his clever tall 'T' shaped wooden bars to push it up and jam it in place (pushers as S calls them). Very glad of the help. Belle is much stronger than me (and more patient). She is stoic too, even when I threatened to tickle her… though she did give me a 'look' so I'd didn't dare carry through my threat!
Lunch: Stirfry veg. Trout in Chinese plum sauce. Custard tart and fig sauce.
Drinks in town in evening. Stayed for bit of fiesta.

Diary Monday 11th August Hot. One Year at A Casa do Campo!
Celebratory lunch at Caracacho restaurant in Monterroso then down to the river to sunbathe and read. Walked along the riverbank. Lots of damoiselles darting about and a couple of tiny frogs hopping along the track. Tea at home then sneaked a quick shower at hotel before drinks in town. Didn't water as it rained in the evening. Would look silly watering wearing a mac even if I do have a hosepipe long enough to reach over the wall to the allotment (and which isn't connected yet!)

Diary Tuesday 12th August Hot
Off to Agolada market/craft fair. Held in the old medieval market place in the centre of town. When we visited before it looked forlorn and abandoned. Today it was alive and heaving. The streets are old, well-worn stone flags. The stalls are all made of low granite blocks with slate tops under a very low tiled roof. Definitely made for a shorter generation. Nevertheless with all the artisan produce on display, it was like going back in time. A talented blacksmith was getting the kids to make proper nails (like the ones in the house). Now I know how they are made. Back

AUGUST

home in time for late lunch: Roast Pork. Veg from the allotment (broccoli, runner beans, kohl rabi). Blackberry and apple pie and plum ripple ice cream. Bottle of albariño.
Had a walk up the track from the house. Mum wanted to show Belle her 'plot' where she says she wants a log cabin. If only she was serious we would do something about getting it for her! Maybe one day.
All to Santiago airport to drop off our guests via The Caracacho to collect mum's new espadrilles which she left on the chair on Monday. Had a great weekend.

Diary Thursday 14th August Sun and cloud. No proper rain
Into town for stamps. New guy on. Couldn't work the machine. Couldn't add up 10 x 60 cents. And couldn't understand why I wanted 10 stamps for one letter! Popped into health centre to turn S back into a man. He was somehow called up for a mammogram! Apparently, due to a typo his health card has a '0' on it which is the code for female instead of '1' which is male. Home via village square to see what was happening. Nothing it seems.
Omelette with mushrooms, courgette and onion
Fried and froze some courgettes. S Put new hose together for me and attached it to the well. Bit awkward to carry across the lane, and we have to watch for the tractor wanting to pass by, but much easier than buckets!
Dark at 9.30pm. Nights are drawing in!

Monday 18th August 4.30pm Drizzle, cool
Dear mum,
 Enclosed is your mobile. Earned a very nice smile from the little man in the bar when

PLUM, COURGETTE & GREEN BEAN TART

we collected it. Think he was waiting for us!

Of course now I have my long hosepipe finally connected to the well it has started to rain. Typical! Think the tomatoes and courgettes have taken advantage of the bit of wet to put a spurt on. My book says 16 courgettes per plant is normal, think we have had double that and they are turning into marrows quicker than I can use them! I really don't think I needed 7 plants! Read something the other day, it said plant 3 courgettes and hope 2 die haha.

I had a day in the kitchen on Wednesday after you left using the plum and marrow glut (can't call them courgettes any longer, found one I'd missed today. It was 4.2kg (about 9lb) and as thick as your arm!) Made some marrow and ginger jam and more chutney, this one with green plums (and marrow of course). My little cubby hole is getting rather crowded. Also have some plum wine on the go and some plum cordial... oh and a bit more jam!!

Tell Belle we had a bunny breakout last night. S had cleaned out the nest box but couldn't have put it back in properly so when a bunny hopped in, it dropped through onto the floor below. He heard a snuffling in the dark and between us at around midnight we rounded up the entire litter. They all seemed quite unperturbed by their ordeal and mummy rabbit hadn't moved an inch the whole time!

AUGUST

In between chasing rabbits, S is busy finishing the roof over the big barn. The skylight window is in and is lovely. Will be very bright once we get the new doors too. The plasterboard is done in the bathroom and I have started to tile in there. The picture tiles are all on. I have done a line of them at waist height. They break up the white tiles and look really pretty.

Otherwise not much of note since you left. Have been picking blackberries and 100s of French beans. If I didn't know better I wouldn't think you had picked any at all.

Wednesday 20th. Feels quite cool today although the sun shone earlier. Even thinking about lighting a fire although it doesn't help that there are long slits in the wall in the adjoining room. The moths keep flying in to see us. S says they are heading for the moon but it looks like a light bulb to me! He says that moths have smaller brains than chickens but I can't believe that either.

We have finished tiling in the bathroom. Looks very smart. S has been plastering the screw holes in the plasterboard so I can paint it all. Then just the loo, bath, sink and bidet to fit and 'ya está' (done). He also wants to do the roof over the sunroom while it is empty so you don't get rained on at Christmas. Then we will temporarily move into there (once the windows appear) while he does over the living room part and that will be the roof nearly done. I've finished

PLUM, COURGETTE & GREEN BEAN TART

polishing the ceiling in the sunroom and pointing the wall. Just needs cleaning up after the windows are in!

My tomatoes are succumbing to blight! All started going brown and yucky a few days ago. I am trying to rescue what I can. Very sad to have to throw so many away but a good lesson to learn now. My book says Copper sulphate and quicklime prevents blight. Sounds rather lethal. I'll plant further apart and not let them sprawl next year I think. Didn't realise how humid it is here throughout the summer. Live and learn eh?

Some of the dried plums have gone mouldy. Maybe I didn't leave them long enough or had damp jars, another lesson! The cabbages are enjoying the bit of rain. I have 6 big white ones (though not as big as the market) plus a brussel plant I somehow interplanted oops!

Talking of veg, if you see any sweet potatoes for seed anywhere. The bought ones don't seem to grow (have probably been sprayed) but I think they would do well here - sandy soil, hot. Also if Wilkos have an end of season sell off, think of me. Especially a pea variety which likes the heat haha and some more parsnip seeds - they apparently are not much good a second year. Will try and let some go to seed.
Love you tons
Xxxxxxxxx

AUGUST

Missing you both. S got two lovely scratches off White Bunny yesterday when he went to put her out and the washing up is filling the sink haha.
Hurry back
Love you (again)
Xxx
And no, we certainly didn't mind you turning up unannounced!!

Diary Thursday 21st August Cool
Had a fun night. Just asleep when we felt a whooshing sound. Turned on the light and there was a bat sitting on the new piece of wood above the window. S opened the window to shoo it out and it bared its teeth... really! Not a pipistrelle, far bigger. Maybe a horseshoe? Anyway, to see S running around the bedroom in his altogether flapping his T shirt and trying to encourage it outside was wonderful!
Finished grouting tiles. S filled rest of gaps in plasterboard and tidied up bathroom then set out the loo etc to check the fitting.
Lunch: Apricot and walnut pilaf with caramelised ginger, onion and green beans. Pancakes with fig jam.
No eggs to be found again.

Diary Friday 22nd August Mist and cloud. Hot pm
S up onto roof over sunroom to strip the tiles since no windows have appeared. I spent all morning painting the bathroom walls and ceiling.
Lunch: Stuffed marrow with goat's cheese. Golden syrup cake with nectarine puree and chocolate sauce.
Did second coat on bathroom. Looks very white and surprisingly large.
Roast tomato soup for tea with dumplings.

PLUM, COURGETTE & GREEN BEAN TART

Diary Tuesday 26th August Mist to 1030 then hot
Hoed on the allotment until driven off by flies. Pulled some of the blighted tomatoes up to bag and throw. Sad! Dug carrots and picked beans for lunch. Then started sanding sunroom floor ready to varnish. S received another letter calling him for a mammogram as he hadn't attended the first. Think we have a communication issue. Suggested he attends. There's a free bus from the town centre!
Lunch: Stirfry pork with peppers, courgette, runner beans, carrot and sweetcorn.
Helped S get a couple of uralitas across the roof. Long way to carry them now and a bit dodgy if it's windy! They make a good sail. S finished putting all the uralitas over the sunroom. Covered gap to next section over the living room.
Tried to chase up windows but no reply. Great! Now what do we do?

Wednesday 27th August Hot
Sitting in the bathroom listening to music!
Dear mum

I'd better explain - you know how for months we have had (part of) a bathroom in the living room? Well, now we have a (temporary) living room in the bathroom!

Still no news on the windows and S wants to get on and finish the roof over the living room and terrace before the weather changes. The idea was to get the windows in then move into the completed and re-roofed sunroom while he did the last bit but no windows and we didn't fancy stripping that part of the roof whilst we were living below as it would be sure to rain then. So, I had a

AUGUST

bright idea. We had a clean, painted and tiled bathroom, as yet free of bathroom equipment and really quite large. This pm we moved the sofa, TV and stereo and here we are. The acoustics are really quite good though I think he made a mistake not putting in the loo first... I mean, what sort of a lounge is it without a loo?

So, other than living in a bathroom, S has, as I said, put the roof on over the sunroom and I have sanded the floors. If the windows don't come this week (and I'm not hopeful) I shall varnish the floor. It will then be ready for our Xmas visitor. These windows had better turn up! I shall then sand and varnish the ex-living room whilst it is empty. Hopefully that bit of the roof won't take long if the weather stays kind!

Friday. Tea and cake break. Made a lovely honey cake yesterday but the silly thing sagged in the middle so I have had to put jam all over it. Have been trying to think up more ideas for using our glut up. So far I have made plum jam, plum syrup, plum vinegar, dried plums, plum flan, plum sauce; courgette soup, courgette fritters, courgette cake and courgette quiche; bottled green beans, salted green beans and eaten mountains of green beans. Maybe I'll just combine all three over producers... plum, courgette and green bean tart. Do you think it will be a hit?

The hens have a new game to play...

cricket! We stand outside the run and try to direct a cricket towards the wire and they have to catch it before it leaps away again. Fatty wins most of the time or the cricket just jumps off as they all run around chasing thin air. It's good exercise for them anyway!

Back up to 4 eggs after our blip. No. 3 laid her first for ages just after you left... 2.5oz. It was huge. I took a photo next to Sarah's little banty egg.

As expected, now we have committed ourselves to living in the bathroom (and having no roof over the ex-living room) we awoke to clouds and then rain! S is manfully on the roof between showers.

Off into town to get essentials (bread, rabbit food, nails) so will post this. Sun out now so fingers crossed.
Love you tons and tons
Xxxxxxxxxxxxxx
PS Hope your chest is getting better now you are on antibiotics (yes, you spelt it right). Thank you for being good for once and seeing the GP. 'Planes are horrid for germs, we will just have to get that log cabin built so you can move over and we can keep an eye on you (and I get an egg collector and washer-upper!).
Love you tons and tons
Xxxxxxx

The year, and our produce, had come full circle. We had lived in Galicia for 12 months, four seasons, an entire year to write home about.

AUGUST

We had a functioning WC (albeit having to use a bucket to flush) – in the living room – and a temporary living room in the bathroom-to-be. There was running water in the kitchen but nowhere else in the house. There was no hot water at all except from the kettle or, on a sunny day, from the outside hosepipe shower. But *A Casa do Campo* felt like home.

We still had holes in the floors in the second bedroom and hallway, which were next year's project, and bats occasionally flying around the completed bedroom. That bedroom was however, cosy, warm and well-insulated.

There were newly cut holes in the walls of the sunroom-to-be due to a complete lack of windows (again) which did not arrive in July as promised, nor in August, nor September, but that's another story...

People in town greeted us when we passed. It had taken one elderly lady almost the whole year to acknowledge us despite our repeated '*holas*' each time we saw her. But, when she did finally realise, I think, that we were staying, she became almost loquacious overnight. The bar owners had our *vinos* lined up when we entered and we even got to pay for our own drinks on occasions. People still asked if we were staying, but with less frequency than before. We had participated in *fiestas* from pigs to sardines to cheese and had even been spotted dancing. And, Galicia felt like home.

We had an almost completely reconditioned roof, despite the fact that the permissions had still to arrive from the council offices three kilometres away. There was a cosy stove in the (temporarily ex) living room and a mouse free, old range in the kitchen. Once I had learnt to cook on it, I had fallen head over heels in love with my rusty stove. I could cook our meals, heat our washing water and preserve our produce – after my exceptionally clever fella had done what no expert could and fixed it of course.

Although we were nowhere near self-sufficient, and maybe never would be, the allotment was producing enough vegetables for us to eat throughout the summer months with plenty over to preserve for winter. The orchard provided more than enough fruit and nuts to eat and to store. We hadn't bought any eggs for four months nor any meat since the *matanza* back in January. We had chickens and rabbits that seemed to be thriving. The freezer was full and my shelves heavy with preserves.

The year had been a steep learning curve in pretty much everything we had tried. With the possible exception of Galician red tape and Spanish *mañana* time keeping, we had mastered most things to an acceptable standard. S had been roofer, plumber, electrician and master builder. I had learnt to point stone walls, to tile walls and to tile roofs. We had grown our own food in sometimes interesting weather conditions and had plenty of ideas for reducing our ridiculously time-consuming weeding, hoeing and watering regime.

We still had mountains to climb but the view was pretty good from where we were sitting. We knew we were home.

The story continues in...

Tomato, Fig & Pumpkin Jelly - A year to write home about too

"D'you think we should just get married then?" asked S, apropos of nothing, over the breakfast table one morning.

"That's romantic darling," I replied, peering over the top of my eggy soldiers. "I thought you were going to adopt me."

"I don't think adopting a 44 year old would work."

I pondered this news for a couple of seconds. Neither of us had considered matrimony before. Then I had a brainwave...

"Do you think we could do it here, in Galicia?" I asked, warming to my theme. "We could have a party in Taboada, invite everyone." I was suddenly enthused. Marriage may be an institution, but a party - now there's a thing!

Tomato, Fig & Pumpkin Jelly - A year to write home about too

For two people struggling to understand a foreign language in a remote part of Northwest Spain Lisa and her partner, the enigmatic S, were not making life easy for themselves.

With a partly renovated but still mainly derelict house, an allotment which was proving too big to handle and some *very bad* experiences with Spanish paperwork to look back on the last thing they needed was to try and negotiate their way around a Spanish wedding - wasn't it?

Coming soon............

PLUM, COURGETTE & GREEN BEAN TART

For updates and free offers follow me at:

http://www.facebook.com/lisarosewright.author
http://www.lisarosewright.wixsite.com/author

If you enjoyed this book, please consider leaving me a review on Amazon or Goodreads. Reader support is important to indie authors and I really appreciate your feedback.

https://www.goodreads.com/book/show/54150601-plum-courgette-green-bean-tart
https://www.amazon.co.uk/dp/B08B6CXX8H

To download your free photo album which accompanies the stories in this book month by month go to:

https://www.flipsnack.com/65E9E6B9E8C/plum-courgette-green-bean-tart.html

Plum, Courgette & Green Bean Tart - The recipes:

Winter in Galicia: *Salpicón de marisco*

We never have found that seafood restaurant Mark took us to straight from the 'plane but this recipe for the seafood salad we ate there is pretty good nevertheless. Raw seafood has to cleaned and cooked properly. If you are in doubt check a good book, or use ready prepared seafood for a quick and easy salad.

This serves 6 people as a starter or light lunch:

For the salad
250g langoustines or large prawns (cooked, shelled and cooled)
250g octopus (cooked, cut into bite sized pieces and cooled)
100g tiger mussels (cooked, shelled and cooled)
8 crab sticks (or 1 monk fish tail cooked and cooled)
1 red pepper (cut into bite sized pieces)
1 green pepper (cut into bite sized pieces)
100g black olives
Arrange the salad ingredients on a platter and add the dressing (below)
For the dressing
1 clove of Garlic minced
2tbsp white wine or cider vinegar
4tbsp olive oil
A pinch of salt, black pepper and sugar
Put the dressing ingredients into a screw top jar and shake vigorously until well blended. Pour over the salad and leave for 30 minutes in a cool place for the flavours to develop before serving

PLUM, COURGETTE & GREEN BEAN TART

August: Butter biscuits

These are a re-imagined take on the biscuits my neighbour plied me with and which cheered me up after a frustrating week!

8oz self-raising flour
¼tsp salt
½ level tsp baking powder
4oz unsalted butter
4oz sugar
1 egg
2tbsp milk

Sift the flour, salt and baking powder. Rub in the butter until it resembles breadcrumbs then stir in the sugar. Add the egg and enough milk to form a soft dough.
Roll the dough out as thinly as possible and cut out 2 inch rounds. (My neighbour has a special press, adorned with designs on both sides for this purpose. I really covet one!) Place on a baking tray well-spaced and bake at 190°c for 15 minutes or until just golden.
Cool and eat!

The recipes:

September: *Tarta de Santiago*

This gluten-free and diary-free Galician cake is a moist almond sponge with a soft texture and a divine taste. Worthy of the apostle St. James himself.
This makes an 8"/20cm flat cake. Simply double the mixture for a larger cake.

3 eggs
6oz/150g caster sugar
6oz/150g ground almonds
Zest of a small orange and a lemon
2 drops almond extract (optional)

Whisk the sugar, almond extract and the eggs until thick, pale and mousse-like. As this cake has no raising agent, the whisking of the eggs creates the light texture so don't be tempted to skip the beating! Carefully fold in the orange and lemon zests and the ground almonds. Spoon into a round shallow cake tin and bake in a moderate oven, 170°c, for approximately 40 minutes or until just set. Allow to cool and dust with icing sugar.
Traditionally these cakes have the cross of St. James on them. If you wish, find a picture online of the cross, print it off and cut out. Dust icing sugar around the cross leaving a clear bit in the shape of the cross in the centre of the cake.

PLUM, COURGETTE & GREEN BEAN TART

October: *Torta de aceite a la Galega*

The recipe for this moist lemony cake, which uses olive oil instead of butter, was given to me by a very good friend living in Galicia and is delicious with a very English cuppa!

4oz/100g plain flour
1tsp baking powder
4oz/100g sugar
5tbsps mild olive oil or walnut oil
3tbsps milk
2 medium eggs, separated
Grated rind and juice of 1 lemon

Sift the flour and baking powder into a bowl, stir in the sugar and make a well in the centre. Pour in the oil, milk, egg yolks, lemon juice and rind. Mix well.
Whisk the egg whites until stiff then fold into the mixture above.
Pour into an 8"/ 20cm round cake tin and bake at 180°c for 45 minutes or until well risen and lightly browned.

The recipes:

November: *Castañas en leche*

We had this delicious dessert at *Dezaseis* in Santiago at our farewell CELTA course meal. It is traditional in the Lugo area around sweet chestnut time. It is also very simple to make.

1kg fresh sweet chestnuts (see note below)
Salted water
1L milk
1 cinnamon stick
Sugar to taste
Anis, grated chocolate to serve (optional)

Cook the chestnuts in salted water until just tender. Cool, remove the brown outer shell and the soft brown inner husk keeping the chestnuts whole. Note: fresh chestnuts are incredibly fiddly to shell so it is perfectly acceptable to use whole canned ones (unsweetened) or have a family peeling day. Fresh peeled chestnuts freeze well. Of course precooked chestnuts will need much less cooking subsequently.
Boil the milk with the cinnamon stick then add the peeled chestnuts and sugar to taste. Cook until the chestnuts are very soft but not broken up. Remove the cinnamon stick and serve. If liked add a few drops of anis and sprinkle with grated chocolate.

PLUM, COURGETTE & GREEN BEAN TART

December: *Caldo Galego*

This warming Galego broth is on pretty much any *menú del dia* in the winter time. As with most Galego soups, it is simplicity to make but relies on a long cooking time for its depth of flavour. *Grelos* is a very special Galician green. It has a denomination of origin label and is one of those things Galegos can't do without. The best approximation in English are bitter greens. It is likened to turnip tops but is really something else entirely. Spinach will do as a substitute or Brussels sprouts tops or endive – anything with a bitter taste. Note tinned beans don't work as well in this recipe as they don't have time to soak up the flavours during cooking. The *unto* is another Galician ingredient. It is the fat from around the intestines of the pig which Luisa salted and rolled to form a white dome. This is kept throughout the year in a cool place and pieces are often cut off to add flavour to soups and stews. The word means 'grease'. You can use a good beef dripping as a substitute.

For 10 people:
250g dried white beans, soaked overnight
350g salt bacon cut into bite sized pieces
250g pork meat or a mixture of pork and chorizo or pork and beef (chopped)
One beef bone
4litres of water
50g *Unto*
1kg *Grelos* or bitter winter greens
600g floury potatoes.

Put the water, beans, bacon, beef bone and meats into a large cooking pot. Add the *unto* or dripping and cook for at least an hour. Remove the bone. Add the greens, sliced, and the potatoes cut into

The recipes:

bite sized chunks. Check the seasoning adding salt if necessary. Boil for a further 15-20 minutes until the potatoes and beans are soft and begin to break up but before they turn to mush.

Caldo should be served hot with good crusty bread. It has plenty of substance with lots of vegetables for the amount of liquid. It is even better if left overnight for the flavours to further develop then reheated and served the following day.

PLUM, COURGETTE & GREEN BEAN TART

January: *Chorizos*

Our friend Luisa always makes *chorizos* with her pig. She was kind enough to give us a whole bunch that first year. And her recipe of course! This recipe makes around five kilos of *chorizos*.

3.5kg lean pork from the shoulder or ham (70%)
1.5kg pork fat from the belly (30%)
50g salt
150ml red wine
125g sweet paprika
50g hot paprika (optional)

Cleaned pigs' intestines or commercial sausage skins

Coarse grind the meat and fat or chop very small by hand. It doesn't want to be a homologous 'paste'. Add salt to taste in the quantity of around 10g per kilo of meat mix. Add a glass of red wine plus the sweet paprika. If wanted add hot paprika to taste.
Knead well until the mixture becomes sticky and starts to bind together. Leave overnight in a cool place covered with a cloth for the flavours to develop.
The next day take a small amount of this '*zorza*' and fry. Taste and adjust the seasonings as necessary.
Take a length of small intestine or sausage skins and stuff with the mixture. A proper sausage stuffer is wonderful but we have found it is feasible to use the (clean) rose end of a watering can as a makeshift funnel or you could try a piping bag with a large nozzle.
Tie the *chorizos* at around 5"/150cm intervals with string.

The recipes:

If you wish to eat the chorizos raw they need to be cured by hanging from a pole above a smoky but cool fire for 10 days. Chorizos for cooking (*criollos*) do not need smoking, simply hang until dry then grill.

PLUM, COURGETTE & GREEN BEAN TART

February: *Orejas dulces*

Carmen brought these delicious crispy sweet treats over for us to try along with the recipe. I have to say that they taste so much better than genuine ears!

150g/6oz butter
1tsp salt
1kg flour
1 small glass of water
1tsp dried yeast
8 eggs
250g/10oz sugar
1 small glass of anis or other sweet liqueur

Melt the butter in the water with the salt. Bring to the boil and leave to cool.
Place the flour in a large bowl. Make a well in the centre then add the yeast, eggs, sugar, the cooled butter mixture and the anis. Mix thoroughly. Tip onto a worktop and knead the dough to a smooth mass. Leave in a warm place for 2-3 hours.
Roll out the mixture to a rectangle 5mm thick. Cut into 15mm/6" squares then halve these to form triangles. Squeeze together two points of each triangle to make the 'ear' shape.
Deep fry until golden. Sprinkle with sugar and serve whilst warm.

The recipes:

March: *Tortilla de patatas*

There are as many ways of making *tortilla* as there are cooks making it. One of my favourite *tortillas* is a tapa in one of the bars in Lugo, *El Galeón*. I call it a breakfast *tortilla* – two layers of potato omelette sandwiched together with ham and melted cheese. Delicious but not exactly traditional. This recipe is from a dear *Galego* friend. The onions are meltingly sweet from long slow cooking, the potatoes tender and the eggs soft and fresh. What's not to like! This recipe makes a 6"/15cm round

4 large potatoes
1 large onion
100ml (4floz) olive oil
Salt
6 eggs

Peel the potatoes and cut into thin rounds. Halve the onion and slice thinly. Heat the olive oil in a 6"/15cm non-stick frying pan. Add the potato and onion rounds in layers, lightly salting as you go. Fry very slowly on the lowest heat (I move the pan to the far end of the *cocina* (range cooker) until the potatoes are tender and the onions soft and just coloured. Cool. (Note: this part can be done in advance and the *tortilla* finished off later)
Beat the eggs in a large bowl then add the cooked potato mixture and mix gently. You want all the vegetables coated in egg but not to end up with a mush.
Reheat the pan with a tablespoon of reserved oil, pour in the egg mixture and cook until there is no visible liquid egg left. At this point you can be clever and flip the *tortilla* over using a plate to help or, if your pan is oven proof, do what my neighbour suggested and pop it under the grill until the top is nicely brown.

PLUM, COURGETTE & GREEN BEAN TART

April: *Flan*

Flan (or crème caramel in English!), is one of the most ubiquitous of *Galego* desserts, which is not to say it isn't still delicious. It is popular for good reason. This is a simple recipe given to me by a Canadian friend who is married to a *Galego* and has lived here for 30 years. I consider her a local!

For the *flan*
1 large can (1kg) condensed milk
2 eggs
1 condensed milk can full of regular milk

For the caramel sauce
4oz/100g sugar
2-3tbsp water or fruit juice.

Make the sauce by dissolving the sugar in the water then boiling rapidly until it turns a nice caramel brown. A darker colour means a more bitter caramel sauce which offsets the sweetness of the pudding.
Pour the caramel sauce into the bottom of a 1 pint/1/2 litre pudding basin and allow to cool.
Mix the ingredients for the flan together and pour over the cooled caramel sauce.
Place in a roasting tin, half full of hot water and cook in low oven (160°c) for 1 hour or until just set. Invert onto a large dish to serve.

The recipes:

May: *Sopa de fideos*

This chicken noodle soup is served as a starter in virtually every restaurant in Galicia. The ingredients are very simple. The trick lies in the stock, homemade if possible, which adds the depth of flavour. It is worth freezing bones from a chicken carcass to make your own stock, it tastes great and reduces waste. In this recipe a whole chicken is used to make the stock. Some of the meat is added to the *sopa* the rest can be saved for another use.

Chicken stock:
Place a roasting chicken in 3litres of water together with a quartered onion, 2 quartered carrots, 2 bay leaves and 2 celery stalks. Season with pepper. Simmer for 3-4 hours, until the bird is tender, or place in a very low oven for up to 6 hours (I leave it in the range cooker overnight. A slow cooker also works very well for making stock)
Once the chicken is tender, remove the meat from the bones and set aside. Strain the vegetables out then leave the stock to cool. Skim off any fat, which will rise to the top as the stock cools.
The stock can be made in advance and frozen.

Sopa:
Reheat a litre of chicken stock slowly (this prevents the stock becoming cloudy). Shred the meat from the chicken breast (the rest of the chicken may be saved for other meals). Once the stock is simmering add 50g (2oz) vermicelli pasta, broken into short lengths, a good pinch of salt and the chicken pieces. Continue to simmer for 5-10 minutes until the pasta is tender.
Serve immediately in flat soup bowls.

PLUM, COURGETTE & GREEN BEAN TART

June: *Queimada*

Queimada is very important to Galician culture. If prepared correctly it is said to protect people from evil spirits or the *meiga.* There is even an incantation which should be said over the *queimada* as the flaming liquid is lifted from the brew, over and over. *Queimada* is traditionally made in a clay pot but one of the tastiest I've ever had was cooked in a huge pumpkin shell which imparted its earthy flavour to the brew.

One bottle of *augardente* or clear distilled alcohol
Sugar to taste, in the region of 4oz/100g to a bottle of alcohol.
The peeled rind of a lemon and a hand full of coffee beans (or try orange rind with a 'pumpkin' *queimada).*

Put all the ingredients into a heat proof pot or casserole. Lift a ladle of the mixture out of the pot, warm it over a flame (being very careful) and set it alight. Carefully lower the burning ladle back into the *queimada* pot and stir slowly, raising the ladle in and out of the brew whilst doing so.
Continue until the flames start to die a little, the sugar has dissolved, and the flavours are fully mingled. Cover the pot or casserole to put out the flames.
Take a ladleful of *queimada,* blowing out any remaining flames and pour carefully into a heat proof glass or cup.
If you wish to do a *queimada* properly. The invocation, to be read out whilst stirring the brew, can be found online.

The recipes:

July: Plum wine

No, plum wine isn't a particularly Galician recipe but I needed something to do with all those plums. And it was pretty good! This is enough for a standard UK one gallon (8 pint) demijohn. Spanish ones are larger!

3-4lb very ripe plums. (I found purple ones gave the best colour and the right amount of acidity to the wine.)
8 pints of boiling water
4lb granulated sugar
1 sachet of easy bake yeast or ¼oz brewer's yeast

Wash or wipe the plums (especially if they are windfalls in a chicken run!) Stone them and crack or crush half the stones. Wrap the stones in a piece of muslin and tie it to make a bag. Put the plums and the stones into a clean 2 gallon lidded bucket. Pour over the boiling water. Mash the plums using a wooden spoon.
Cover and leave for 10 days. By this time there will be a mould growing on the top. Remove this carefully but don't panic it is the natural yeasts working on the fruit.
Strain the liquid into a one gallon/eight pint saucepan. Add the sugar and heat gently, stirring, until the sugar dissolves. Cool to 21°c then strain into a sterilised demijohn. Sprinkle on the yeast and fit an airlock. Leave in a warm place (below my *cocina* is pretty good) until fermentation stops. Rack (syphon off the clear liquid from the sediment) the wine at least twice. This helps any remaining yeast to continue working and ensures there is no taint from the sediment which accumulates at the bottom of the demijohn. Once all fermentation has ceased, bottle the wine and store for at least 6 months.

PLUM, COURGETTE & GREEN BEAN TART

August: Plum, courgette & green bean tart

I couldn't let this book end without the cover recipe! Although this was merely intended as a joke when I originally wrote to mum, certain friends were very persuasive that I should actually make the tart so here it is! It is basically a quiche and was surprisingly tasty even if I do say so myself! This makes four individual tarts.

4 individual (4") savoury pastry cases, homemade or bought
4 eggs
400ml single cream
A pinch of salt
12 fresh plums, halved and dried in a low oven until plump or 12 ready to eat dried plums.
1 small courgette cut into thin rounds
A handful of French beans, blanched and refreshed under cold water.

Bake the tart cases blind then brush with egg white (from one of the 4 eggs) and return to the oven briefly to set. Place the cases onto an oven tray.
Fry the courgette rounds in a little oil until nicely brown. Leave to cool.
Beat the remaining eggs with the cream and salt until amalgamated.
Place 3 dried half plums in the base of each tart case. Add the courgette rings and add a small bunch of French beans to one side. If you leave these slightly protruding they look pretty!
Pour the filling into the individual cases leaving a slight gap at the top for the mixture to rise.
Gently put the tray into the oven and cook at a moderate heat (180°c) for 40 minutes or until risen and browned.
Enjoy eating the book!

The recipes:

I hope you enjoy these recipes. There are more on my website for you to try and I always love to receive more recipes from around the world. Please do contact me.

http://www.lisarosewright.wixsite.com/author

Thank you
Lisa

ACKNOWLEDGEMENTS

An Indie author can never succeed alone so here's my chance to say a great big thank you to all those wonderful people who have helped this book come to fruition.

To my beta readers, Mervyn Kaufmann, Norman and Wendy Fry, Noel Boonzaaier, Shirley Fedorak, and the Writers' group of Galicia. Thank you for daring to read the first draft and for all your helpful comments. I hope this final version meets all your approvals!

To Maayan Atias for her wonderful cover artwork, for understanding not only what I wanted for the cover but what would actually work better than I did.

To Craig Briggs for taking time out from writing book seven in his best seller series to help me with formatting and other wondrous computer related issues. You can check out Craig's books here:
http://www.journeytoadream.co.uk

To Dawn Hawkins for checking out my recipes. Any recipes that don't work now are purely my fault.

And to S, my blue-eyed prince, for alpha, beta and omega reading, for your patience and for being you

ABOUT THE AUTHOR

In 2007 Lisa left a promising career as an ecologist catching protected reptiles and amphibians, and kissing frogs, to move to beautiful green Galicia with her blue-eyed prince (who has since become her blue-eyed husband but that's another story).

She divides her time equally between growing her own food, helping to renovate a semi-derelict house (or actually two... but that's also another story) and getting out and about to discover more of the stunningly beautiful area she calls home.

Lisa is happiest outside in her *huerta* weeding; watching the antics of her chickens; or in her kitchen cooking interesting recipes on her wood burning range.

Plum, Courgette & Green Bean Tart is the first book in the *Writing Home* trilogy. The series is available in paperback, eBook and free with Kindle Unlimited at Amazon stores worldwide.

For more details about Lisa, her life in Galicia, and her writing, go to her website at
http://www.lisarosewright.wixsite.com/author
or follow her on
Facebook
http://www.facebook.com/lisarosewright.author
Twitter
http://www.twitter.com/lisarosewright.author

Printed in Great Britain
by Amazon